William Brown's autobiography is a unique historical document, since he is the only memoirist to have come to light from the ranks of the 45th (1st Nottinghamshire) Regiment of Foot for the period of the Peninsula War – a regiment that was one of Wellington's longest-serving and most valiant in that turbulent era, a proud member of Sir Thomas Picton's 'Fighting' Third Division.

William was born in Kilmarnock in 1788, the son of a poor cobbler, but seems to have been given a good education since the narrative is clear and lively, with many learned literary references. Like many young men, William Brown originally volunteered into the militia, Britain's second-line army intended for home defence only. And like a goodly percentage of these young men, he found that the life more-or-less agreed with him, and willingly took the bounty on offer to volunteer into the regular army a few weeks after Wellington's victory at Talavera.

In the next five years he served at Busaco, Ciudad Rodrigo, Badajoz, Salamanca, Madrid, Vittoria, Orthez, and Toulouse, and his descriptions of these actions provide worthy additions to our knowledge of these great battles.

William seems to have been generally a reliable soldier, often 'on command' doing ancillary regimental service involving a degree of trust, including service as an officer's batman. His outrage at the antics of his fellow-soldiers in the sack of Ciudad Rodrigo and Badajoz is palpable. Nonetheless, he occasionally seems to have slipped into questionable behaviour and comes across in the text as a bit of a likeable rogue. His romantic pursuits also get plenty of coverage in the text.

William's pen-portraits of commanders such as Picton, Kempt, Pakenham, and Brisbane are revealing, and he was not slow in criticising his senior battalion officers or their actions; nor indeed is the Duke of Wellington above William's barbed criticism.

Maps are provided to allow the reader to understand the route travelled within Portugal and Spain by William and the 45th Regiment in those turbulent years, and the whole text is annotated by historian Steve Brown, an expert on the 45th and its deeds in the Napoleonic era

I0892890

William Brown served in 45th Regiment of Foot from 1809 until 1816, including most of the Peninsula War 1809-1814; he was last recorded as a pauper living in Kilmarnock, Scotland. He is the only known memoirist from within the 45th Foot, one of a handful of regiments to have served for the entire duration of the Peninsula War.

Steve Brown is the author of *Wellington's Redjackets, the History of the 45th Regiment of Foot 1807-1815*. He also a frequent contributor to, and book reviewer for, the Napoleon Series website. His forthcoming works include a history of Sir Charles Grey's West Indies Campaign of 1794 to be published by Helion as *By Fire and Bayonet*. He is not related to William Brown.

The Autobiography, or Narrative of a Soldier

The Peninsular War Memoirs of William Brown of the 45th Foot

William Brown, with New Introduction, Notes, and Commentary by Steve Brown

Helion & Company Limited

Helion & Company Limited
26 Willow Road
Solihull
West Midlands
B91 1UE
England
Tel. 0121 705 3393
Fax 0121 711 4075
Email: info@helion.co.uk
Website: www.helion.co.uk
Twitter: @helionbooks
Visit our blog at http://blog.helion.co.uk/

Published by Helion & Company 2017
Designed and typeset by Mach 3 Solutions Ltd (www.mach3solutions.co.uk)
Cover designed by Paul Hewitt, Battlefield Design (www.battlefield-design.co.uk)
Printed by Lightning Source Ltd, Milton Keynes, Buckinghamshire

Text from the 1829 edition published by J. Paterson, J. Robertson and Co.
Introduction, notes, and commentary © Steve Brown 2017
Maps © Steve Brown 2017
Cover: The Battle of Bussaco from 'A View of the Sierra de Busaco at St. Antonio de Cantaro' by Thomas Staunton St. Clair. © Anne S.K. Brown Collection.

Every reasonable effort has been made to trace copyright holders and to obtain their permission for the use of copyright material. The author and publisher apologise for any errors or omissions in this work, and would be grateful if notified of any corrections that should be incorporated in future reprints or editions of this book.

ISBN 978-1-911512-94-3

British Library Cataloguing-in-Publication Data.

A catalogue record for this book is available from the British Library.
All rights reserved. No part of this publication may be reproduced, stored in a retrieval system, or transmitted, in any form, or by any means, electronic, mechanical, photocopying, recording or otherwise, without the express written consent of Helion & Company Limited.
For details of other military history titles published by Helion & Company Limited, contact the above address, or visit our website: http://www.helion.co.uk
We always welcome receiving book proposals from prospective authors.

Contents

List of Plates

List of Maps

New Introduction

By Steve Brown

The Man

For the avoidance of doubt, lest some think that this autobiography is a worshipful eulogy of a distant ancestor, I am in fact no relation to William Brown. His background was Ayrshire; my ancestors were coal-miners from Nottinghamshire, which is what drew me to the project in the first instance, following on from the publication of my history of the 45th (1st Nottinghamshire) Regiment of Foot in the Peninsular War, *Wellingtons Redjackets*. William Brown's autobiography was one of my major sources for that work, he being (so far as I am aware) the only Peninsula War memoirist from the ranks in that illustrious regiment for the period 1809-1814.

William Brown was 5 foot 6 inches tall, with blue eyes, a brown complexion, and brown hair; at least this was as Army muster rolls described him in 1815. The 'brown complexion' no doubt came from six years under the Iberian sun, but otherwise he sounds physically unremarkable; his height was more-or-less the average height for a Briton of that era. Like many young men, he volunteered into the militia, Britain's second-line army (equivalent perhaps to the Army Reserve today, previously known as the Territorials) intended for home defence only. And like a goodly percentage of these young men, he found that the martial life agreed with him and willingly took the bounty on offer to volunteer into the regular army. But why the 45th from Nottinghamshire? The answer lies in the fact that county titles of regiments were, at the time, mostly window-dressing and it was not unusual for a Scotsman to enlist in an English midlands county regiment.

Certain elements of William's background remain opaque. A search through Scottish Old Parish Registers for Kilmarnock has not produced a William Brown born or baptised in that town during his reputed month of birth, and nor has a death record been found. Further searching has located three William Browns born in Scotland in July 1788, one of whom was the son of a weaver from Greenock, Renfrewshire, some forty miles north-west of Kilmarnock; this might be him, but we may never know for sure. There was a pauper named William Brown living in Kilmarnock in the 1841 census who looks very much like our man, but again the fact cannot be confirmed. He claimed to be the son of poor folks, 'an unlettered mechanic... a rough untutored soldier', yet much of his tale does not read so. His home town of Kilmarnock was said to '...possess[es] an excellent academy, in which various branches of education are taught by able masters; there are, besides, several private seminaries of a high character, and many schools that impart instruction to children of the poorer classes'. It seems highly likely one of these was responsible for his learning. But did he get help in the writing? On the surface this might seem unlikely, for at the time of writing in 1829 he described himself as a pauper, and presumably unable to pay for any professional assistance; unless of course the help came gratis from a brother soldier or officer. A reference to the 'Grand Architect' in his narrative strongly suggests he was a Freemason, so it is possible that literary assistance came from this quarter.

His narrative was written in 1829, some twenty years after his volunteering into a party of replacements bound for the Peninsular War, which begs the question how much is pure recollection, against the re-writing of a diary (of which no mention is made)? Many of his descriptions and references clearly owe a debt to Sir William Napier's *History of the War in the Peninsula and in the South of France*, the first volume of which was published the year before his narrative; elsewhere I have determined through research that he has misplaced certain events in time, and misplaced or composited certain individuals. Luckily these instances are few and explained in the footnotes, but the errors strongly suggest a narrative written from memory rather than by reference to a journal.

As a soldier, the evidence indicates he was a trusted individual. Some of the lengthy absences described in the text can be attributed to services 'On Command', a catch-all term to describe any detached service authorised by officers and serjeants – which might include duties such as guarding the officer's baggage or escorting the regimental pay-chest. He also served as an officer's servant for several periods – hardly the sort of job that would have been given to a scoundrel. Yet, he was clearly no angel and at times indulged in activities that must have come perilously close to his finding himself before a court-martial. So for his good qualities, he was never offered a promotion, something that (on the surface) should seem to naturally flow to an educated, steady soldier. One is left with the impression that his behaviour was rather uneven, good and bad, which denied him advancement beyond private soldier. He was also somewhat of a hopeless romantic, and one absence caused by an affair of the heart almost saw him feeling the ends of the lash.

The Regiment

The first battalion of the 45th (or the 1st Nottinghamshire) Regiment of Foot was one of the hardest-fighting and longest-serving units in Wellington's Peninsula army, being one of the few units to serve continuously from the fresh-faced landing at Mondego Bay in August 1808 until the war-soiled remnants sailed home from

Bordeaux in July 1814. The 45th fought at nearly every major engagement in the Peninsula War, and formed one-third of a famous brigade in Lieutenant General Thomas Picton's Fighting Third Division, alongside its old friends the wild Irishmen of the 88th Foot, the Connaught Rangers; and the temperate Scotsmen of the 74th Foot.

Like all British regiments at the time, the 45th Regiment of Foot was an organisational entity; the sub-division of the regiment was the battalion, of which the 45th had two (after 1804). The intent behind the creation of second battalions was that they would stay at home and act as a trainer of new recruits and feeder of said recruits to the first battalion on service. In reality, shortages of troops meant that many second battalions went on service themselves, although the second battalion of the 45th (or 2/45th in shorthand) stayed at home for its entire existence, and it was in this battalion that William started his army career after volunteering into the regular army from the militia in 1809. After basic training in Nottinghamshire, he volunteered into the first battalion, and was thus shipped to Portugal to start his adventures.

The sub-division of a battalion was the company, of which every British battalion had ten. Companies were numbered, although in the field these were generally referred to by the commander's name (i.e. Captain Cole's Company) and assumed seniority within the battalion by the relative seniority of the company commander. Throughout his service, William seems to have served in No. 4 Company, under a variety of company officers.

The officers of the 45th led from the front. Of the six lieutenant colonels who commanded the battalion in the Peninsula, two were killed in action, one died from his wounds, a fourth was wounded and captured, while the last battalion commander, Lieutenant Colonel Leonard Greenwell, had been wounded five times prior to assuming command in May 1814. Twenty-five of the 123 officers who served with the first battalion in the Peninsula were killed in action or died from their wounds, while another 37 were wounded, many multiple times. During the siege of Badajoz in April 1812, out of 35 infantry officers present, the battalion had three officers killed, three who died of their wounds, and another nine wounded – a 40 per cent casualty rate for one battle. The 45th was not a regiment for shirkers.

After the war ended, the Duke of Wellington made his final inspection of the 3rd Division in France in June 1814. 'Observe this regiment – how well they look!' the great man whispered to a fellow general officer as he rode within ear-shot of the 45th. 'They have been with me the whole time. They have gone through everything – what fine fellows!'[1] Indeed, they had gone through everything. The 1/45th was just one of three British battalions to have served in the Iberian Peninsula

1 As quoted in H. C. Wylly, *History of the 1st and 2nd Battalions the Sherwood Foresters (Nottinghamshire and Derbyshire Regiment)* (Two volumes. London: Privately Published for the Regiment, 1929), p.281.

continuously from the landing in Portugal on 1 August 1808 until departure home in July 1814.

The 45th landed at Monkstown, Ireland on 23 and 24 July 1814. Anyone familiar with the regiment in 1808 would have struggled to identify any of the officers at all, and in any event only four returning officers had embarked with the battalion six years earlier. Three of the drummers – John Murdagh, John Mahoney and Michael Carthy – were teenagers who had seen six year's foreign military service and therefore could probably barely remember home. Behind followed a column of impossibly tattered, lean nut-brown men, many with long hair and beards, with white Bourbon cockades on their battered shakoes, tossing about foreign words at random, some of which we still use in English today. They must have looked as hard as nails; many were scarcely recognisable even to loved ones. These were the veterans who had formed the backbone of Wellington's 'most perfect machine of its kind' to be found in Europe.[2]

The Military General Service Medal was belatedly awarded in 1847 to the survivors of campaigns between 1793 and 1814. Any surviving soldier who fought in any of the twenty-eight battles covered by the award was eligible to receive it. For many, William included, the medal came too late. Of the twenty-eight battles named in the award, twenty were fought in the Peninsula between 1808 and 1814. A veteran could receive a clasp on the medal with the name of each battle for which the War Office could verify his participation. Over 26,000 medals were awarded, 278 of them going to the 45th Regiment of Foot. The 45th's long years of service meant that there were many veterans who could claim a very large number of clasps. Only two soldiers – the most decorated British soldiers of the era – earned fifteen clasps, meaning that they had fought in fifteen of the twenty major battles of the Peninsular War; and one of the recipients was Private James Talbot from the 45th Foot. Thirteen veterans received the medal with fourteen clasps, of whom five were from the 45th. Eleven of the forty soldiers who were awarded the medal with thirteen clasps, served in the 45th, while twelve veterans of the 45th were among the seventy-seven soldiers who earned twelve clasps. The 45th represented something like twenty percent of the longest-serving soldiers in the Peninsular War, and William Brown was indeed one of them. Had he lived to collect a medal in 1847, he might have been eligible for ten or eleven clasps.

The Book

Brown's Narrative was first published in 1829 by J. Paterson, J. Robertson and Co. in Edinburgh, Robertson and Atkinson in Glasgow, and J. Dick, M'Cormick and Carnie in Ayr. The first edition had a 'contemporary half calf, gilt banded

2 Quoted in James Edward Alexander, *Life of the Duke of Wellington* (London: Henry Colburne, 1840), Vol. II, p.252.

spine, dark red morocco label, marbled sides, [and] red speckled edges'. It was adorned with the armorial bookplate of Alexander Gordon of Auchlunies, uncle to Sir Alexander Gordon, Wellington's chief ADC who was mortally wounded at Waterloo. It was not a cheap tuppenny throwaway, but a serious publication designed to satisfy the public's appetite for tales of the wars even then fading into distant memory. It seems to have had a brief burst of popularity in the pre-Victorian years before dimming into obscurity. From that day down to this, it has been a hard volume to find. Hopefully this re-issue allows William's vivid tales to reach a wider audience.

I have left the text as continuous and uncluttered as the author intended, relegating all comments and explanations to footnotes, rather than trying to bracket each chapter with context, which I felt would interrupt the overall flow. The only imposition I have made is to generally correct certain oddities of grammar and spelling which in my opinion disrupted the readability of the narrative, none of which have in any way altered the detail or interpretation of the story; that said, in some instances I have left an oddity in the original text in play where it provides some 'historical colour'. Place-names I have left as William wrote them (as the spelling may well have been different at the time) but provided modern equivalents in the footnotes. William generally only referred to officers by the first letter of their surname, in such cases I have completed the name and shown the additional letters within square brackets, viz. Captain S[mith]. The maps are provided to allow the reader to understand the route travelled by William and the 45th Regiment of Foot in those turbulent years.

Enjoy then what I believe is one of the most vivid and entertaining memoirs to come from the pen of a 'ranker' who served in the famous Peninsular War of 1808-1814.

Steve Brown
Melbourne, Australia
August 2017

Preface

By William Brown

As a book without a Preface has been deemed by some like a body without a head, the Author feels constrained to say something concerning the following pages.

In works of fiction especially, some authors are very ingenious, and in a tale of much mystery inform us how they became possessed of the original MS. In some instances, such papers are represented as having been handed down from generation to generation – in others, that they have been found in an old oaken chest, or on some deceased antiquarian's shelf. Some, too, have been discovered in cloistered cells, being in the hand writing of an unknown holy monk, who flourished anterior to the days of John Knox. Other authors, again, introduce their publication with much seeming diffidence, by intimating that the work they have presumed to lay before the public, was originally not intended for the press, but composed solely for the amusement of a few friends, by whose earnest solicitations they have been prevailed upon to publish, although conscious of its numerous defects.

But the writer of this autobiography has no such plea to make. Instead of a reverend prelate, he is an unlettered mechanic, and was for a series of years a rough untutored soldier; and in lieu of a cloistered cell, the apartment he occupies is an attic fourteen feet by twelve, in which he has been for several years cooped up with a wife and four children, in the midst of whose crying and clamour he has, without the solicitations or importunities of friends, and often in the absence of health, without means, money, or credit, persevered, and got up the following Narrative.

Notwithstanding, the writer lays no claim to merit for his production, it is simply a connected chain of facts and incidents, which he has seen and felt. But he wishes it to be understood, that, in attempting to give general descriptions of engagements, he has been materially indebted to M'Queen's History of the War;[1] for it

1 MacQueen was at the time the editor of the *Glasgow Courier*. His history, whilst popular in Scotland at the time, is almost unobtainable and nearly forgotten now.

must be known to every person, that no individual soldier could do it from actual observation – such information being generally gleaned from official documents.

The inauspicious circumstances of the author being thus made known, it is hoped the reader will judge tenderly of his work, and forgive the presumption he has evinced in publishing a book so faulty, which forbearance will be gratefully recognized by

The Author
October 26, 1829.

Chapter 1

The Author's Birth – Education – Trade – Preamble

Oh! enviable, early days,
When dancing thoughtless Pleasure's Maze;
To care, to guilt, unknown!
How ill exchanged for riper times,
To feel the follies or the crimes,
Of others, or my own!
Ye tiny elves that guiltless sport,
Like linnets in the bush,
Ye little know the ills ye court
When manhood is your wish.

BURNS

It was early one morning in July, 1788, I first beheld the light. Trifling as this event may appear to many, it was, nevertheless, the cause of much bustle, hope, fear, and joy, in my father's family. When my mother's accouchement drew near, an old matron, said to be deeply versed in the obstetric art, commonly yclept a midwife, was sent for. This old lady no sooner entered the house than she pronounced her patient in a very dangerous state; but, whether it was to show my contempt of the midwife's evil prognostics, or from impatience to see what was doing around me, (be that as it may) I soon made my appearance, to the great satisfaction of my father, while my mother's heart beat with joy, that a man-child was born. This, and a deal more, I have been informed of since; but as I do not wish to fill a volume concerning the circumstances attending my birth, as the worthy Mr Tristram Shandy has done,[1] I will be brief, and proceed with my narrative.

At six years of age I was put to school. The teacher of the seminary had a peculiar mode, as I thought at least, of instilling the rudiments of learning into his pupils,

1 *The Life and Opinions of Tristram Shandy, Gentleman* was a humorous novel by Lawrence Sterne, published in nine parts between 1759 and 1767. It was adapted into a film in 2005.

for he generally bestowed more pains in imprinting the lash of his birch on their posteriors, than in teaching them the alphabet.[2] But everything has an end, and so had this; for as soon as I could read tolerably, and draw pot-hooks with the pen, it was thought by my parents, who were poor, that I might be sent to work, and become a little help to the family; which at that time consisted of one son and two daughters older, and two sons younger than myself. The youngest died when three years of age; whose fate, in being thus early taken from a world of sorrow and care, his surviving brethren may envy; for we all entered the army, to serve hard and thankless masters. My elder brother, after fighting bravely at Martinique, and other islands in the West Indies, fell a victim to the climate. Poor Thomas! Thou died in the land of strangers, un-pitied and unknown; perhaps without a friend to soothe thee in thy last moments – without one to close thine eyes in death; may thy shade rest in peace until that blessed period arrives, when all will be united to part no more. My younger brother, after serving in foreign climes, was sent home discharged, with a shattered constitution, to drag out the remainder of his days in poverty and disease. While I, poor I – but I will not anticipate.

According to the wish of my parents, I was put to work at a woollen mill, where the wages I received was 1s.6d per week, a poor mite indeed at that time, when meal was rating as high as 3s.6d. to 4s. and even 5s. per peck; and other provisions in proportion. After being three years in the mill, I was put to the weaving, which was a good business at that time, but as it has since turned out, t'would have been more to my honour and profit had I been made a chimney sweep.

Notwithstanding the flagellations I had undergone at school, of itself enough to have destroyed the most ardent taste for reading, by the time I was twelve years of age I had read a great deal, considering my youth. I seldom joined in the pastimes of my compeers. The whole of my felicity existed in poring over books, especially those of chivalry and romance. By them I often found myself carried beyond the eye of human ken – launched into a boundless region of fancy. There I revelled in ecstasy, and sipped the ambrosial draught with gods and goddesses. In imagination I followed and fought, and often overcame the greatest of heroes. My heroines, when unprotected, were guarded by me with unwearied vigilance and the most devoted fidelity: never was knight more true in practice than I was in theory. But voyages and travels were still, if possible, my greatest hobby. With them I was truly delighted, and fondly anticipated that the time would yet come, when, instead of reading of foreign countries, I would myself see the various empires, kingdoms and states of which the world is composed, with the diversity of men and manners

2 An 1837 directory for Kilmarnock notes that 'Kilmarnock possesses an excellent academy, in which various branches of education are taught by able masters; there are, besides, several private seminaries of a high character, and many schools that impart instruction to children of the poorer classes.' It seems that William was fortunate to be given a good education, care of this enlightened system.

in each. Thus were false and fatal ideas instilled into my mind, the consequence of which was discontentment, and a violent desire for traveling.

Notwithstanding all this I believe I would have served out my apprenticeship, for I had a kind and indulgent master; but an event took place, when I had just eight months to serve, which determined me at once to leave Kilmarnock, and all my friends. The affair in itself was trifling, but produced serious consequences. Having gone one day with cloth to the warehouse, the agent, J--n M-ff-t, found fault with the work, and told me that heavy stoppages would be the consequence. I knew J--n to be a man of his word in these kind of things, and might be depended on; no one being better known for integrity and fair dealing in trade than J---; his generous and humane bearing towards the poor, in the ward in which he was overseer, is quite proverbial. I therefore resolved to leave the affair in the hands of so very respectable a person, and, as the modern slang has it, cut my stick. Not that I cared a single straw for the righteous warden, or his stoppages, but from a false sense of *honour.* If that term be thought improper for a weaver, I shall leave it for nobler tongues to mouth, and say, I had imbibed certain notions, that when my work was quarrelled, I could not look my master in the face.

Without letting anyone know my intentions, I set out next morning with a heavy heart, for I really was sorry at leaving home. As soon as I got to the end of the town, I commenced running as fast as I could, looking behind now and then, to see if anyone was following me. As Paisley was then, as it is yet, the grand emporium of weaving, I bent my steps for that town. I had proceeded about five miles on the road, when I overtook a man and boy, who, I soon understood, were weavers, residing near Paisley, and were master and apprentice. The boy had run away, and the master was now taking him home again. For this information, I was asked where I belonged to, where I was going, and what was my trade? To all which I answered by telling the cause of my leaving home. The weaver advised me to return to my friends and work, but the recollection of J--n M-ff-t and his stoppages, aided by a still more powerful motive, that of seeing the world a little, induced me to reject the wholesome advice.

When we arrived at the house of my fellow travellers, I was invited in to rest myself, and partake of a comfortable dish of tea. During the repast, the mistress, who was a good-looking woman, informed the master, that during his absence the other apprentice had run away. It was therefore settled that I should have his loom, and get my bed and board in the house.

After resting two hours, being impatient to see Paisley, from which I was now but a mile distant, I set out, accompanied by the boy who had been brought home by his master. As we entered the town I greatly admired the order in which the streets were built, being generally laid out on a regular plan; but what attracted my attention most, was the remains of the Abbey Church.[3] This relic of the olden time

3 Built in 1163. It was rebuilt from 1858 onwards.

was the first good specimen of gothic architecture I had ever seen, and I gazed on it with rapture. The magnificent and venerable appearance of the ancient pile had a great effect upon my romantic and heated imagination – it mustered up an association of ideas I had never been master of before. I was now upon the sacred ground, where holy monks and mitred priests had lived, and even got fat, under their vows of abstinence and poverty. Even royalty itself once lived here in kingly pomp; and now lay interred under my feet. I got admittance to a small chapel adjoining the church, generally termed the Sounding Isle, on account of its wonderful echo. 'In this chapel is the monument of Marjery Bruce, daughter of King Robert Bruce, and wife of Walter, Great Steward of Scotland, from whom descended the regal line of Stewart. Near her monument are the graves of Elizabeth Muir, and Euphemia Ross, both consorts to Robert the second. The Abbey of Paisley, of which the Abbey Church and the Isle are the only remains, was founded in 1160, by Walter, Great Steward of Scotland, for the monks of the order of Clugni.'[4]

When I had been nine months in Paisley, two of my old comrades came from Kilmarnock – I was very glad to see them. They remained one day with me, and then went to Glasgow, to which city I accompanied them. After strolling about the streets a few hours, my companions suddenly resolved upon going home that night. Being unwilling to part, I consented to go also to Kilmarnock, where we arrived late at night, with weary limbs and empty stomachs. I intended to return to Paisley next day, but my parents entreated me to remain at home, to which I consented. So ended my first ramble, and with it I will close the first chapter.

4 Quoted from *The Gazetteer of Scotland*, published by W. Chalmers in Dundee in 1803.

Chapter 2

Juvenile Inconsistencies – Enlists – a March

Self-flattered inexperienced, high in hope,
When young, with sanguine cheer, and streamers gay,
We cut our cable, launch into the world,
And fondly dream each wind and star our friend.
YOUNG

I come now to a period of my life over which I wish a veil were drawn, or that it might be left a blank in my memory. Not that I wish to hide or palliate my faults or follies, for I intend to let all the truth be known, and nothing but the truth; but as I consider the foolishness of this period the foundation of my future woes, I remember it with regret. I had not been long at home before I became acquainted with some young lads about my own age, whose taste and pursuits were similar with my own – that is, they were determined to do anything but that they ought to do. We were resolved to see the world, and push our fortunes in another sphere than a weaver's shop. Accordingly, we wrought little, but planned, debated, and visited from time to time all the seaports on the west coast, in order to find berths amongst the shipping. We were always unsuccessful, as the masters generally conceived us to be runaway apprentices. At one time a companion and I agreed upon an expedition to Greenock, having heard that several vessels were bound from that port to the West Indies. Accordingly, at the appointed hour, which was early in the morning, we set out under a heavy fall of rain, which continued the whole day without intermission, and by the time we reached Lochwinnoch[1] it was quite dark. We there called at the house of a friend of mine, who kindly gave us supper and bed; and when he understood our intentions, advised us not to go to Greenock, nor think of the sea, but to go home; or if we did not choose that, we might get work in Lochwinnoch. Being pretty well cooled by the day's rain we were

1 About fifteen miles south-east of Greenock.

easily advised, and went out next morning to look for work. Soon after, however, changing our minds, we set off for Paisley, and arrived there in the afternoon.

Next morning, being on the street, we saw two stage coaches at an inn, which we learned were to start for Greenock as soon as the horses were changed. We immediately bargained with the driver, and had seated ourselves on the top, when looking round to the other coach, we perceived a Kilmarnock man upon it, who no sooner saw us than he exclaimed 'Oh! Good morning, gentlemen, I am happy I have found you.' He immediately alighted, desiring us to do the same and informed us he had been sent by my companion's father in order to bring us home. We yielded to his authority, and next day got ensconced in a caravan, arriving the same evening in safe moorings at the Turf Inn, which I daresay was better than any station the Windward or Leeward Islands could afford.

A short time after this, some of my comrades enlisted, and of course I did the same; but upon inspection at the district office in Glasgow I was rejected, owing to a blotch on my ankle, caused by a cut I had received some time before, in falling from the top of a wall. This was a sad rebuff. To be called the King's refuse I could not brook. Instead, therefore, of going home, I once more took the road for Paisley.

The person I was employed by at this period was a townsman of my own, but had resided many years in Paisley, and married a woman belonging to that place. He was a sober, industrious, and good natured man, but the woman was a devil. Being a warm devotee of Bacchus, she frequently paid her devoir at the shrine of the jolly god, and as often turned everything in the house upside down. As I lodged in the house, and not being accustomed to such revelry, I felt very uncomfortable; for of all the evils under the sun, I counted this the worst. A man given to liquor is a beast, but a drunken woman is a demon. I, however, remained six months, and then returned to Kilmarnock.

Being still as restless in mind as ever, and wishing to see more about me, I again soon left home, and went to Maybole. My shop-mates there, were all natives of the Emerald Isle, and spoke so highly of that blessed country, that at the end of three months I was determined to see Ireland. I accordingly set out on my way solus,[2] passed the long town of Girvan, climbed the braes of Glennap, winded my way along the shores of Loch Ryan, until I came to the ancient royal burgh of Stranraer, which is a handsome little place; and on the afternoon of the second day, found myself on the pier point of Portpatrick. While standing there, admiring the broad expanse of water before me, and each succeeding wave lashing against the cliffy shore, which rises with peculiar abruptness, a sail hove in sight, and soon came to anchor in the little harbor. A number of passengers immediately landed from the vessel, which proved to be a packet from Donaghadee. They were chiefly Irish, come to push their fortune in Scotland. I got into conversation with two of them, both young lads about my own age. They gave me so very bad account of Ireland

2 Solus – alone or unaccompanied; a term typically encountered as a stage direction.

in general, and of Belfast in particular, the place I intended to go to, that I resolved upon retracing my steps to Maybole, which I did in company with the two Irish lads, where we all got work. I soon grew intimate with my fellow travellers, whom I found honest and simple. They were impatient to get to the 'head' as they termed Glasgow; for when coming to this country Irishmen look upon that city as the fountain of wealth.[3]

After remaining two months in Maybole, we all three left it, on a fine summer afternoon, and slept that night in Ayr. Next morning, we took the road very early, and passed through Kilmarnock before many people were up. I even passed the door of my parents without heaving a sigh. O how often has this ungrateful action corroded my heart! To pass the door of the authors of my being, who reared me tenderly in infancy, and whose hearts still yearned for me, although a wayward and undutiful son! But I had afterwards ample time allowed me to think of it, and think of it I did. When buffeted by the stormy ocean, when the foaming deep yawned as it were to receive me, when on the ensanguined plain, and in the deadly breach, I thought of it to madness. Ten long years elapsed before I was allowed to see that door again!

On the day we left Ayr we arrived in Glasgow, where my two companions soon got work. But the shops had such a dismal appearance, being more like cells allotted to criminals than anything else, I resolved to go to my old favourite ground Paisley. When I reached that place it happened to be a fast day, which I considered a serious misfortune, as in general I endeavoured to make sure of work before looking for lodgings. Having no acquaintances in the place, for, strange as it may appear, it is true, though I had been long and often in Paisley, there was not an individual in it I could say good day to – I spoke to no one, nor scarcely ever looked a person in the face, excepting when they addressed me – never speaking first myself. This did not proceed from any kind of misanthropic disposition; on the contrary I was fond of company and conversation, but from a degree of false modesty or diffidence, which continued to hang about me for a long time. Being at a stand, and not knowing well what to do, I at length though of visiting Lawrence Crawford, the person I worked and lodged with, when I first left home. I was kindly received, and chided for not paying them a visit sooner, for they understood I had been working in the town since I left their house. At the same time they let me know there was an empty loom in the shop, which I might have if I chose – of course I readily accepted the offer.

When I had been nearly six months here, Lawrence, on coming home from the town one day, said there were great bounties giving for the militia; I carelessly asked how much was going – thirty, forty, and even fifty guineas was the reply. Well, said I, if they give me forty guineas I am their man, and will go, when and

3 Glasgow started its transformation into one of the foremost industrial centres in Britain at the start of the nineteenth century. Much of the workforce came from Ireland.

wherever they please to take me. Lawrence laughed, and said it was a good price for anyone who wished to sell himself to the devil; but for his own part, he would not enlist for his weight in gold. I still persisted in declaring I would run all chances. Lawrence and his wife seriously advised me not to think of it, stating how much their son, who was in the Militia, disliked the army. They gave me a few of his letters to peruse, which indeed was enough to make one's hair stand on end – such hardships he had undergone, and was still undergoing, at Stilton Barracks; the duty there, over the French prisoners, being so great, human nature could not stand it long![4] I was thrown into a still further perspiration on looking over one of the epistles, in which this beloved son informed his parents, that during the three first days the regiment was in camp they had no victuals, save bread and cheese and porter, and no bedding but straw! Independent of all this I was determined to serve the King.

At last Lawrence consented, and said he would go to the town to see me get fair play. We accordingly soon found a rendezvous, where two highlanders wanted four substitutes for the Argyleshire Militia.[5] They offered thirty guineas of bounty; but I would not accept of less than forty, which they agreed to give. I was then taken to a surgeon, and, upon inspection, found sound in wind and limb. Next morning, before a magistrate, I declared upon oath, to serve his Majesty King George the Third, his heirs and successors, &c. &c.[6] The next day I left Paisley, in company with the two highlanders and three recruits. That night we rested in Greenock, next morning crossed the Clyde at Gourock, and after traveling the whole day over a rough uncultivated country, got to a ferry-house on Loch Fine. At this highland inn, all that could be procured for supper was potatoes and herring, for which we paid one shilling each. We crossed the Loch next morning, and same evening reached Inveraray. There I had to go through another ordeal with a surgeon, whose opinion, in regard to the soundness of my wind and limbs, exactly coincided with my first inspectors; but when my height came to be ascertained, I was found half-an-inch below the standard. This seemed a death-blow to my prospects. A remedy, however, was found, by putting some pasteboard betwixt my feet and stockings, which made me just the thing.

When I received my bounty I sincerely intended sending home twenty pounds; but I delayed from time to time, until it was too late. O Procrastination! Much evil haste thou done.

At the end of six weeks, the party, which consisted of sixty recruits, under the command of a subaltern, and two non-commissioned officers, left Inveraray, for

4 This in fact refers to Normancross Barracks, about one mile north of Stilton; the principal gaol for French prisoners-of-war throughout the Napoleonic era.

5 Service in the militia was determined by ballot, with a set quota per parish. Any man wishing to avoid militia service could do so by furnishing a substitute, or in this case, two substitutes.

6 Based on the time-line described later in the text, this must have been in August 1807, when William had just turned 19.

the purpose of joining the regiment at Aberdeen. On our route we passed several poor-looking highland villages, amongst which were Comrie and Crieff. I recollect little about them, farther than in both the whisky was good; and that the latter village stands upon a rising ground near the foot of the Grampian mountains.

The party rested one day in Perth, which is a large and populous town, situated on the banks of the Tay, over which is an elegant stone bridge of ten arches. Prior to the reformation there were many religious establishments in Perth, but the disciples of John Knox took his advice, so down came the nests, and the rooks flew away.

Leaving Perth, and passing over twelve miles of fine country, we reached Coupar Angus, a considerable town in the valley of Strathmore. Forfar was our next day's stage, a place honoured with the title of Royal Burgh; but whatever benefits its inhabitants may derive from their political privileges, little can be expected from their streets, which are narrowly built, in a zigzag manner. Next day we came to Brechin, seated on the side of a hill, and consisting of a handsome street, with by-lanes. In former times Brechin was an Episcopal See, a rich bishopric, founded in the year 1110, by David the First. Passing Lawrence Kirk and Stonehaven, which are both inconsiderable, we arrived in Aberdeen on the eleventh day's march from Inveraray.

Chapter 3

Aberdeen – Meets with an old Companion – Fort George – Earl of Kintore – a Voyage – Arrived at Newcastle

> Now a soldier bold and free,
> Now a soldier's life for me.
> ANONYMOUS

The party having arrived at the barracks, was taken to the orderly room, where we underwent a kind of inspection, and were attached to our respective companies; after which we were ordered to our several rooms. I was put into one along with two other recruits, where, before we had rightly seated ourselves, our entry money was requested. One fellow in particular came forward, and in set speech informed us of our duty in that respect. Prior to his entering the militia, this man had served some two or three years in a Fencible regiment of cavalry;[1] and above all, had been in England nine months with them, which he considered the 'ne plus ultra' of the service. Having seen, and done so much for his King and country, he seemed to think he had a license to be arrogant and overbearing, especially where he thought he could be so with safety. This person is a native of Paisley, and is well known in that town by the appellation of Granny Park. He addressed us as follows: – 'Well, my lads, I suppose you are all well aware, that it is customary for recruits, on joining their regiments, to pay garnish to the room they are put into; and as you have got great bounties we expect you will bleed freely.' When the orator had finished, no one seemed inclined to answer him. Silence pervaded the room for a few seconds. For my own part, I was willing to give them a moderate treat, and intended so before I entered the room, knowing it would be my interest, but had no idea of its being so abruptly asked. Therefore, being willing to see how far they would carry the subject, I kept quiet with the others. Seeing us make no answer, this Cicero

1 Fencibles were temporary volunteer regiments raised in times of national crisis, commanded by regular army officers, intended to serve at home only.

addressed us again, but in a more humble and entreating tune – 'Whatever you give us, if it be anything at all, you will never regret it; we will do all that is in our power for you. We will clean your accoutrements and arms; tie your hair; nay, even brush your shoes; so the more you give the better for yourselves.' It being impossible to withstand this, James Bryson, one of the recruits, laid a pound note on the table, which I covered with another; but all persuasion, even Park's eloquence, had no effect on the third recruit, who would give nothing. They seemed, however, well pleased with what they had got; and the question now was, what should be had with the two pounds? Some proposed part in beer, and part in whisky; but Park swore it should be all 'blue', having drank enough of good water boiled to death in England. This was overruled and to the great mortification of our hero, beer and whisky were sent for, along with some biscuit. The exhilarating glass circulated freely, and soon produced a deal of noise. At last, Park, having still a grudge in his mind on account of the beer, dashed a full can of it in the face of a comrade, which, being returned by a blow, produced instant hostility. How long, or how bloody this fray might have been, I know not, for a sergeant and file of the guard entered, and took the combatants to the guardhouse. At the same time the lights were ordered to be put out, which left us in total darkness. This, however, did not deter them from issuing the liquor; and as they could not see to pour it into glasses, put the bottle to their head, and drank, as they termed it, by word of mouth.

Early next morning the drum beat for the recruits to turn out to drill. As this was my first appearance in a military character, I felt very diffident; besides, I had heard enough of the gentle bearing and tender mercies of drill-sergeants, to cause certain palpitations and misgivings at heart. The sergeant I was under, however, might be considered a very civil person, in his line; for, excepting the danger our eyes were in, from the several oaths levelled at them, we got over our morning's work pretty smoothly.

A short time after joining the regiment, I was one day standing in front of the barracks, when a party of recruits marched into the square. I walked towards them, in the hopes of finding some old acquaintance, and soon recognized a comrade from Kilmarnock. 'Well, Jack, how are you?' said I. 'Hush,' said he, in an undertone, 'my name is now Tom.' While expressing my surprise at the changing of his name, he was called into the orderly room, and from that time I have never seen him. That night he volunteered into a regiment of the line, and, as I heard, deserted on the road to Edinburgh. He was again taken, and sent to the Isle of Wight, from thence to be transported to a banished regiment; but previously made his escape from that place also. Poor Jack! (for I must still call him so, notwithstanding the intimation given) was a lively and spirited boy; and I doubt not would have made a good soldier, had he remained in the army. The leaving of which, I daresay, he must have often regretted. Desertion is the greatest folly a soldier can be guilty of.[2]

2 Deserters were usually flogged. Serial deserters were often transported for seven years.

When about sixteen months in the service, I was ordered, as one of an escort, with a deserter to Fort George. The prisoner was a sergeant in the 74th; but having embezzled some money belonging to the company of which he was pay-sergeant, thought proper to leave his colours. He fled to Aberdeen, being a native of that place, but soon after was apprehended. As we proceeded on our march, each of the party in turn had to sleep hand-cuffed with the prisoner at night. This unpleasant mode of rest was indispensably necessary, as there were no proper jails by the way. Passing through Huntly, Elgin of Murray, and several other considerable towns, we arrived at our destination on the day's march.

Owing to the length of time I had been in Aberdeen, to me the place had lost all its novelty. I therefore determined upon extending my service to the line, if the regiment did not change quarters previous to a volunteer offer being given. This resolution did not proceed from any dislike to the Corps I was in; on the contrary, I was well aware I could not change for the better, but solely because I could not think of remaining so long in one place as militia regiments generally were kept.[3] Being thus resolved, Fort George was an object of great interest. I thought that perhaps ere long I might be called upon to attack or defend some place similar.

When on our return to Aberdeen we met a coach-and-four, in which were two young ladies and an elderly gentleman. On coming alongside, the coach stopped, and after asking several questions respecting our route and destination, the gentleman handed out a crown, desiring us to drink the Earl of Kintore's health with it. Rejoicing at our good fortune, we proceeded until we came to a house on the roadside, over the door of which was placed a board, daubed with certain hieroglyphics, seemingly to intimate that entertainment for man and beast might be had inside. It was not long before we were seated in a snug little parlour, with a comfortable peat fire, and a drop of good mountain dew at our elbow, in the quaffing of which we gave all due honour to the good Earl of Kintore.[4]

At last, after being twenty months in the militia, an order was read one morning on parade, intimating that all those who wished to extend their service, had now an opportunity of gratifying their honourable intentions, as a number of volunteers were wanted for the regular army; that now the road to preferment was open to all young men, ambitious of serving their King and country in a just and necessary war; that a broad field displayed itself, in which enterprising youth might achieve those valorous deeds so characteristic of Britons. Also, that the honest and generous inhabitants of Holland were ready to receive with open arms the promised aid from England, to assist them in hurling from the throne the all-grasping usurper and tyrant; that the Spaniards, then engaged in the sacred and patriotic

3 Militia regiments were not required to serve outside the United Kingdom, so usually spent their days on garrison duty, thus freeing up regular regiments for overseas service.

4 William Keith-Falconer, 6th Earl of Kintore (1766-1812) was an Aberdeenshire peer. Perhaps he was the 'elderly gentleman' in the coach.

cause of liberty, would, upon our landing in the Peninsula, hail us as the deliverers of their country, and of mankind; that the whole of Europe was in arms, and it was expected we would step forward promptly, and signalize ourselves in the glorious cause of freedom.

Although I had no thought of, or even a wish for preferment; nor yet believed all that was said about the intentions of the Dutch, and the patriotic flame of the Spaniards, I had, as already hinted, been long resolved upon leaving the militia. I therefore volunteered into the 45th regiment, then serving in Spain, but which had a second battalion recruiting in England.[5] My comrade, James Bryson, who joined the militia with me, also took the bounty for the same regiment. He was a warm-hearted and true companion.[6]

After volunteering, I remained a month in Aberdeen, and then embarked with ten more recruits, on board a small vessel which was to land us at Newcastle, and from thence were to proceed to our respective regiments, six being for the 10th, then quartered in Gainsborough, and the other four for Nottingham, where the second battalion of the 45th were lying. Soon after getting on board, we perceived that, in the person of the captain, we had one of the rudest of the rough sons of Neptune to deal with. Nature had not been overly lavish in the formation of this man's mind and body. The latter was short, broad, brawny, and muscular, but out of all proportion; his legs being very short, while his finger-ends nearly reached his knee, when standing upright. His physiognomy bespoke him as one fitted for deeds of darkness; and if taken for the index of his mind, told of sad things that rankled in his bosom. The crew consisted of two men and two boys, over whom he exercised the most wanton tyranny, which he endeavoured to extend to us, by imposing certain oppressive and useless restrictions, such as obliging our party to keep on the fore part of the vessel, not suffering one to pass the mainmast; a restraint I never saw imposed on any but prisoners.

This man, in the plenitude of his malice, was imbued with all the senseless antipathies that exist between the sons of Neptune and the followers of Mars – the whole of which originate in ignorance, and are fostered by folly. He heaped upon us every indignity in his power, and even attempted to wrong us of part of our allowance; but this we would not stand. When remonstrated with he called us a parcel of low minded, red coated b----rs. This was a favourite and frequent expression of his. The sergeant, however, told him, that he who would not fight for his belly would not fight for his king; and insisted that we should have our rights, and

5 The 45th (or 1st Nottinghamshire) Regiment of Foot. Proof that the country titles held by regiments at the time were largely arbitrary; most took recruits wherever they could get them – Highland and Irish regiments were perhaps the only exceptions. According to records, William volunteered on 7 April 1809 for seven years' service.

6 James Bryson was born in Glasgow in 1791 and was thus three years younger than William. He survived the war.

be treated as we ought, else he would report him to his superiors when he got on shore.

On the fifth day of our voyage, which was a tedious one, we passed Berwick so near that we counted the arches of the bridge; and in running between Holy Isle and the coast of Northumberland, a pilot came on board to take us up the Tyne. At this time the weather was particularly pleasant. The sun shone in all the effulgence of a Mayday; while the green fields of England, with their scattered copses of oak, elm, and other trees, with the distant village tower, or steeple, peeping through between, appeared to my imagination as the region of romance, or fabled fairy-land. The pilot, however, had not been long on board, when suddenly a thick fog came on, which so much increased, that, in a short time, any object a few yards distant could not be seen. As there was but little wind, we sailed at a slow rate, expecting every minute to make the mouth of the river, when all of a sudden the bow of the vessel grated upon a rock, which, however, she cleared; but in a few seconds after came in contact with another, and stuck fast. The master, ascribing the whole misfortune to the negligence or ignorance of the pilot, a warm altercation commenced; and at last, seizing a marling spike, would, in all probability have ended the dispute in no very amicable manner, had the pilot not leaped overboard into his boat, leaving us to our meditations, which were of no very pleasant nature. It was about 2 o'clock, p.m., when the misfortune happened; but as the sea was calm, and the vessel sailing slow, she had received little or no damage in sitting down. There was, therefore, no immediate danger to be apprehended; but, as it was not in our power to bring her off, the affair might become serious, if aid was not speedily procured. Having no firearms on board, we had recourse to a tin horn, which we in turn sounded the whole night, in the hopes of being heard by the people on shore. In this we were not deceived, for at day-break a boat came along side, with two men, who assured the master they would bring off the vessel at high water.

As our party did not wish to remain longer on board than it was possible to get on shore, we engaged the boatmen, who, for sixpence each, landed us on the beach near North Shields, from which, after partaking of some refreshment, we proceeded on our road to Newcastle.

Chapter 4

Kind Hostess – Joins the Regiment – Birds-eye view of the Commanders – a Tragedy – a Defeat – a Fight – Leaves Nottingham for Portsmouth

> Well, Mr Stockwell, for the first time in my life here am I in England; at the fountain-head of pleasure, in the land of beauty, of arts, and elegancies.[1]

When the party arrived at Newcastle, each man received a billet for himself. I was quartered at the Black Bull, a small public house, the people of which were the most kind and affectionate I ever met in England. I was no sooner arrived than the landlady presented me with a pint of strong beer, saying I would be the better of a draught of ale after the fatigue of the march; at the same time, she apologized about a dinner for me, saying that as the family had dined, and nothing being ready, she did not know rightly what to give me. I told her not to be uneasy on my account, nor put herself to trouble, as I would be satisfied with anything she had. In a short time I was desired to go into a parlour, where I was surprised to find a table covered in such a manner as I had never dined at before. I thought to myself I should like to see an English dinner, since this, which required such an apology, would be counted a new year's days' feast in my country. When I had finished my meal, the landlady desired me to shift my trousers, which were in a bad state with pitch and tar, and promised to have them washed and dried in the morning.

Towards evening I called at the sergeant's quarters, situated on the quay, where the party met to receive their pay. While we were sitting over a pot of beer, and looking at the shipping in front of the window, the vessel in which we had our passage came up the river, and cast anchor directly opposite the house we were in. One of our party went out and brought up a boy belonging to the vessel, intending to treat him to a drink of beer, for some good office he had done us while on board.

1 Extracted from the comedy *The West Indian* by Richard Cumberland, first performed in 1771.

He was scarcely seated ere his master entered the room, foaming with rage, and without the least ceremony seized the boy by the collar. He proceeded to abuse him in the most brutal manner, but was in turn laid hold of by some of our party, who gave him a hearty drubbing, and kicked him downstairs.

Next morning, being about to take the road, I asked my kind hostess how much I owed her. 'My dear young lad,' she replied, 'you owe me nothing. I have a son in the army, whom I have not seen or heard of these many years. In whose hands he may be in at this time I know not; but for his sake you owe me nothing, and have his mother's blessing. But oh! Thou art going an awful road; thou art going, to the great slaughter-house, where many a mother is made childless! You tell me thou haste a mother – may God bless and support her in this trial; and may he bless and preserve you son. Farewell! Poor youth, farewell!' By the time this good and feeling woman had done speaking, she was diffused in tears. Sympathy is a thing so seldom experienced by the poor soldier, that when he does meet with it, he hardly knows how to behave. For my own part I was so overpowered by this woman's kindness, that I could scarcely bid her adieu, and left the house with a brimful eye.

Leaving Newcastle, we proceeded on our way to the ancient city of Durham, which is justly celebrated for the magnificent ruins of its cathedral and the picturesque scenery in the neighbourhood. Passing Darlington, and other towns, we reached York, which may well be termed the Northern metropolis of England. This is a large and beautiful city, seated on the Ouse, which river divides it into two parts, and is navigable for vessels of seventy-ton burden, although sixty miles from the sea. York contains many public buildings, but the Minster is what principally attracts the attention of strangers. On entering this superb pile, I was struck with astonishment and awe at the vastness of its dimensions, and the grandeur of its architecture; while the painted windows, the first I had seen of the kind, by their brilliancy and masterly design, absolutely filled me with delight. After passing Beverly and Hull, we crossed the Humber into Lincolnshire; and in three days entered Nottingham, being the thirteenth day of our march from North Shields.

The regiment I had now joined, was composed of a heterogeneous mass of old men and boys, all either English or Irish, with the exception of one man, who was a countryman of my own. Being generally illiterate, and consequently ignorant, I found little pleasure in their company. Their whole conversation was on eating and drinking, and their amours, which were mostly carried on with profligate and abandoned women. I therefore associated little with them, but generally spent what leisure time I had from duty in the vicinity of the town, which afforded many pleasant walks; or else in reading books from the circulating libraries in town.

The colonel, being a member of the legislative assembly of the empire, was often absent; and, no doubt, in his senatorial capacity, deeply engaged in business of vastly more importance than drilling a few boys. The command devolved upon

Major D[rew],[2] under whose fostering care, I am sorry to say, the battalion did not seem to make much improvement. The Major, I believe, had seen a deal of service, but, strange to tell, had yet much to learn. Early every morning he had us all out to drill, making no distinction – the man who had served twenty years, and the boy of twelve years old. Then, he seldom or never knew when a manoeuvre was done right; but by instinct, for I hardly think it was by acquired knowledge, always found out when it was wrong. Thus were a body of men teased and tormented by the ignorance or bad management of an individual: but cases of this sort are so numerous, that they have long ago ceased to create surprise.

The Major was a man pretty far advanced in years.[3] He might have been an efficient officer in his day, but was at the period I am speaking of, in no way calculated to command a regiment. In his person he was long and lank, and had such a portion of anxiety depicted in his face, that I never beheld him without remembering the 'Knight of the Rueful Countenance;' or when mounted on his light grey mare, he never failed to conjure up the vision of the 'Pale Horse and his Rider.'

Some may be inclined to think, that this is too much to say of an officer who had grown grey in the service; that it bespeaks ill-nature, or perhaps malice. To such I answer, that, as I do not write a romance, in which characters may be moulded according to fancy, but an impartial narrative, in which I mean to hold as it were 'the truth to natures mirror;' for as our immortal bard hath sung,

> Facts are chiels that winna ding,
> and downa be disputed.[4]

And in reference to the charge of ill-nature, I deny it. If the Major was so old, why not retire? there being ample allowance provided for such an event; with which he might, in some calm retreat, far from the fatigue and turmoil of war, pass the evening of his days in comparative peace and comfort:

> And husband out life's taper to the close;
> And keep it from wasting by repose.[5]

What a contrast this, to the fate of many a poor soldier, who, with all the ardour of youth, has often faced the foe; and by whose courage and vigour of arm the enemy have been often repulsed, and repeatedly defeated; who, after having been marched

2 Major George Purdon Drew, who exercised effective command of the second battalion of the 45th whilst in barracks.

3 Major Drew was in fact about 37 years old at the time. He had seen 17 years' service with the 45th, much of it in the West Indies.

4 From Burns' poem, *A Dream* dated 1786. The English translation is 'But facts are fellows that will not be overturned, / and cannot be disputed'.

5 Quote from Irish novelist Oliver Goldsmith (1728-1774).

here, and countermarched there, while suffering under the privations of hunger and thirst, and undergoing unheard of hardships, is at last turned adrift, with health destroyed, his body shattered and unhinged, and in many cases 'doomed to beg bitter bread through realms his valour saved, and bear the contumely of those he shed his blood for!'

I have little doubt that some will think this an over-charged picture, and say, surely men who have served in the army are provided for according to their service, and the rank they held while serving. This I acknowledge to be so far true. But if such doubters choose to use their visual organs, they may have an ocular demonstration of the fact I advance, every hour of the day, in every town in Great Britain.

I had been but a short time with the regiment when the colonel, the Honourable T.M.,[6] assumed the command, under whose administration I found things no better; indeed, it was like getting out of the frying pan into the fire: for, while the same course of discipline was carried on as before, the disposition of our commander seemed to be tinged with a sanguinary hue, being nowise loath to distribute a few hundred lashes among the boys, in a morning, by way of letting them know that they were free-born Britons, and in the service of Old England. But though the servants of his Majesty were obliged to submit to this degrading system, the people of England did not seem to relish it, and embraced every opportunity of showing their disapprobation, an instance of which I shall here relate:

Being obliged to move our quarters, on account of an election taking place at Nottingham, the regiment removed to Mansfield; in which town we had been only a few days, when our commander thought proper to punish some of the men. The place chosen for this tragical business was Sherwood Forest, two miles out of town, where a number of the inhabitants assembled to witness the tyrannical and degrading scene. They, however, did not interfere; but when entering the town, we perceived a number of women upon an out-stair, to the bannister of which was fastened the effigy of a man, who, in derision of the feat that had been transacted in the forest, was receiving an unmerciful flogging, while the crowd in the street levelled volleys of stones and other missiles at our doughty commander, who clapped spurs to his horse, and galloped off as fast as his steed could carry him, leaving the field undisputed to the victors.

The regiment left Mansfield, in which place it had remained only eight days, and returned to Nottingham; there it was intimated to us, by an order read on parade, that a draught of an hundred men was wanted for the first battalion, then in Portugal, and that if they wished to go, they might step out in front. A number turned out, among whom I was one, and the next day left Nottingham for

6 T.M. is almost certainly a transcription error of J.M. – Lieutenant Colonel the Honourable John Meade, a 34-year-old Irishman and nominal commander of the second battalion of the 45th, although he seems to have spent much of his time absent with leave.

Portsmouth, at which place we were to embark.[7] On our march we passed Leicester, Oxford, Winchester, and other large towns; but as my narrative is likely to exceed the bounds intended, I will not attempt a description of them. Let it therefore suffice that we reached Portsmouth in ten days, without any material occurrence.

British infantry on campaign c.1808. The red coats and white 'trowsers' wore out quickly and were patched by troops in the field, leading to the ragged appearance well-described by the author. (Anne S. K. Brown Collection)

7 According to regimental records this parade took place in mid-August 1809. The first battalion of the 45th had participated at the Battle of Talavera on 28 June 1809 and suffered 160 casualties. The men of William Brown's draft were, to use the modern parlance, 'replacements'.

Chapter 5

Embarks for Portugal – Reflections – Lands at Lisbon – Belem – a March – an Assault – a Chapel – Estremoz – Elvas

Now to the Spanish coast we are bound, brave boys,
We'll still our right maintain;
Come bear a hand, be steady, boys,
Soon we'll see old England once again.

OLD SONG

The party, when arrived at Portsmouth, was not permitted to halt, but marched down to Point Street, where boats were in readiness to receive us, into which we immediately embarked, and in a few minutes pushed off, with loud shouts and huzzas. Surely, thought I, there is little occasion for such noise and boisterous mirth, by men leaving their native country, and about to engage in all the fatigue and horror of war on a hostile shore; but perhaps it is customary, and if so, who dare challenge the propriety of it? Although I embarked with all the ardour and buoyancy of spirit peculiar to youth, (for I anticipated many strange adventures, and had in my mind's eye all the men and manners that were before me,) still I thought of home, my friends, and my country; and while I viewed the mirth and jollity of my companions, I could not help mentally exclaiming, poor fellows, you are now leaving the land, which perhaps, you will never be allowed to tread again! This was indeed sadly verified, for, out of the party, which consisted of one hundred men, only ten ever returned.[1] I was at length roused from reflection, by the boats coming alongside the transports at Spithead.[2]

1 The draft consisted of five officers and 97 other ranks (TNA, WO27/93). Based upon known mortality figures for the 45th, William's figure is almost certainly too pessimistic.

2 According to transportation records at the National Archives, these men embarked on 27 August 1809 aboard the vessel *Peace*.

We found a number of troops already embarked, which daily increased; and at the end of three weeks we finally left the shores of England, Major D[rew] having come on board the day before, and assumed the command. It was a charming afternoon in August on which we sailed; and the fleet, or rather combined fleet, for there was one for the Mediterranean and the other for Lisbon, made a grand and imposing spectacle. Several hundred vessels left port at one time, which covered the ocean as it were with Britain's glory; and I felt a rising pride within me, while reflecting that I was an individual of that nation which produced such potent fleets and armies, and was ever ready to assist friends and allies, or strike terror into their enemies.

On the eleventh day of our voyage we got in view of the highlands of Portugal, rearing their lofty summits to the clouds. while yet some miles from shore, a number of boats came alongside, laden with wine and fruit. We went up the Tagus by moonlight, and same evening came to anchor in front of Lisbon. At daybreak I was greatly delighted with the appearance of this city, rising from the water's edge, and stretching itself along the heights on the right bank of the river, while its palaces, monasteries, minarets and towers, crowding above one another, had an air of grandeur I never before witnessed. The same day the troops disembarked, being the 7th of September, 1809, and five months from the time I volunteered out of the militia.

After landing, we were marched to Belem barracks, where orders were given that none of us should leave the garrison; but James Bryson and I were so impatient to see the town, that we resolved upon running all hazards. Neither of us having any money, I packed up a few articles which I knew would be useless to me in this country, and proceeding to the gate, we dived among the crowd in the street, unperceived by the sentinel. I sold the articles I had to a Portugue,[3] and with the money regaled ourselves with wine, which we had at the rate of two-pence per bottle.[4]

We remained eight days in Belem, and then crossed the Tagus in Portuguese boats to a town opposite Lisbon, where we were to remain for the night. It being dark when we landed, and the inhabitants having shut their doors on our approach, we were ordered to make our quarters good where we might. I thought it a strange mode of receiving us with open arms, to have doors bolted, and the people hid in holes and corners; but I ascribe the whole to the customs and manners of the nation, for I could not believe they had shut their doors on the deliverers of their country, who were to emancipate them from thraldom and slavery; however, it was found necessary to apply the butt end of our muskets to get entrance, and then were heard battering rams in all directions at work. I went down the street

3 Portuguese person.

4 Privates earned one shilling per day, less stoppages. Hence the need to sell the surplus-to-requirement possessions.

a long way with another three, hoping the intelligence of our landing would not have reached so far, but every door was shut. At last seeing light through a window shutter, we knocked at the door, when a man inside called out, 'ce cares',[5] but this we did not understand. The door, however, was soon opened, and we entered the house, which we found to be a wine shop. The family, consisting of the landlord, his wife and daughter, were very civil, and treated us to a supper of shell-fish and roasted chestnuts, to which were added a plate of pickled olives and some wine. There being no bed but the one the family occupied, we spread our blankets, which had been furnished at Lisbon, on the floor, where we slept soundly until morning. We arose early and found the daughter busied in preparing breakfast for us, which was composed of materials similar to the supper, with the exception of a glass of brandy each, instead of wine.

At six o'clock the party assembled in the market place where, after waiting two hours, it was intimated that we would not march for some time, as the baggage mule belonging to the Major had got one of its legs broken, when disembarking the preceding evening; we therefore lay on the street until our commander was supplied with another animal, and then marched off – the whole sick and feverish from lying under a hot sun for six hours. As soon as we left the town we entered upon a flat sandy road, the heat of which was intolerable, from the reflection of the sun's rays, and soon produced a parching thirst in all of us. Not being inured to much of hardship at this time, and having been furnished with a heavy load of ammunition, and other articles, at Lisbon, a number of the men fell out of the ranks, and were left on the road. The Major, mounted on a good steed, seemed to feel no inconvenience from the heat, nor anything else, and never thought of halting until he had very few of the party with him. At last, when near sunset, we halted at a spring of water, and being completely overpowered with fatigue and thirst, I lay down on the ground, and drank a whole canteen full of it; but soon after was seized with a cold shivering, which I suspected to be the ague. We remained nearly an hour at this place, when most of the men came up, and once more took the road. Having entered a forest, through which the road penetrated, and the evening becoming cool from the absence of the sun, I began to endure the march with more relish. My imagination immediately set to work, and wanted nothing but the appearance of some ancient castle, about to be stormed by our party, to give the whole the semblance of a romantic adventure. When near midnight, we came to a solitary house on the edge of the forest, where we remained for the night.

Early next morning we resumed our march, over a level but barren country, seemingly uninhabited, for I do not recollect of seeing a house by the way until far advanced in the afternoon, when we came to a village, at the end of which the party were lodge in a house said to be a royal palace. Next morning, as the party were sitting on a bank in front of where they had lodged during the night,

5 Almost certainly misheard or misremembered, possibly esquecer (algo), 'leave'.

waiting the arrival of the officers from the village, in which they were quartered, a man and a woman were seen on the opposite side of the road, busy at an oven baking bread. A few of the men went over to purchase some, amongst whom was an Englishman of the name of Horsley. This man was by habit and repute, a thief, and had received three hundred lashes for stealing, a short time before he left England. On his arrival at the oven he instantly seized a loaf with each hand; which a number of the party perceiving, also leaped over the road and attacked the oven, some endeavouring to draw the bread in the usual manner, while others damaged the sides, and tore the roof down, in order to get at it from the top. In a few minutes the frail tenement was levelled with the ground, while the poor owner, made piteous lamentation, invoking the vengeance of 'Tudas los Santos'[6] on the depredators. The officers coming up, and seeing part of the fray, secured a few of the most active, amongst whom was Horsley, the first aggressor, who, on joining the regiment, received a sound flogging. The affair being adjusted, by the Major giving the Portuguese some remuneration for the loss he had sustained, we marched off, and, long after it was dark, came to a large town, where we were quartered in a convent, but obliged to remain in the passages, the rooms and apartments being occupied by the holy brotherhood. Next day being the first in the week, we rested from all our works, which gave me an opportunity of visiting the chapel belonging to the convent, which at first sight appeared rich and magnificent, but on closer inspection, was found decked with gaudy, if not tawdry ornaments. Above the altar was placed the Virgin Mary, or 'Madre de Dios', while on each side stood a number of wooden saints deeply gilt, to which a crowd of people were seemingly paying adoration. The officiating priest, while celebrating mass, had so much gesticulation and grimace, never uttering a syllable, that I could not help thinking it a pantomime I saw acted.

Leaving the monks to act as they pleased, we set out next morning, and arrived in the afternoon at Estremoz, a handsome town, and surrounded by a wall. The market, which is large and spacious, instead of merchant's shops, is surrounded with convents and monasteries; religion, or its mummeries, being the staple of this country. Next day we reached Elvas, a strong fortified town, seated on a hill, having a fort on each flank. At this place I was quartered in a wine shop; the people of which were very kind and civil. In their house I first witnessed the 'Balaro',[7] a dance, in which, from the lascivious attitudes assumed, I concluded all the women engaged must be of bad fame. This idea I changed, however, on becoming better acquainted with the manners and customs of the people. Leaving Elvas, we proceeded to Campo Mayor, where we found our regiment in cantonments.[8]

6 Todas los Santos, all the Saints.

7 Bolero.

8 The draft joined the 1/45th at Campo Mayor at the end of October 1809. The draft would have been distributed amongst the ten companies to even up company strengths.

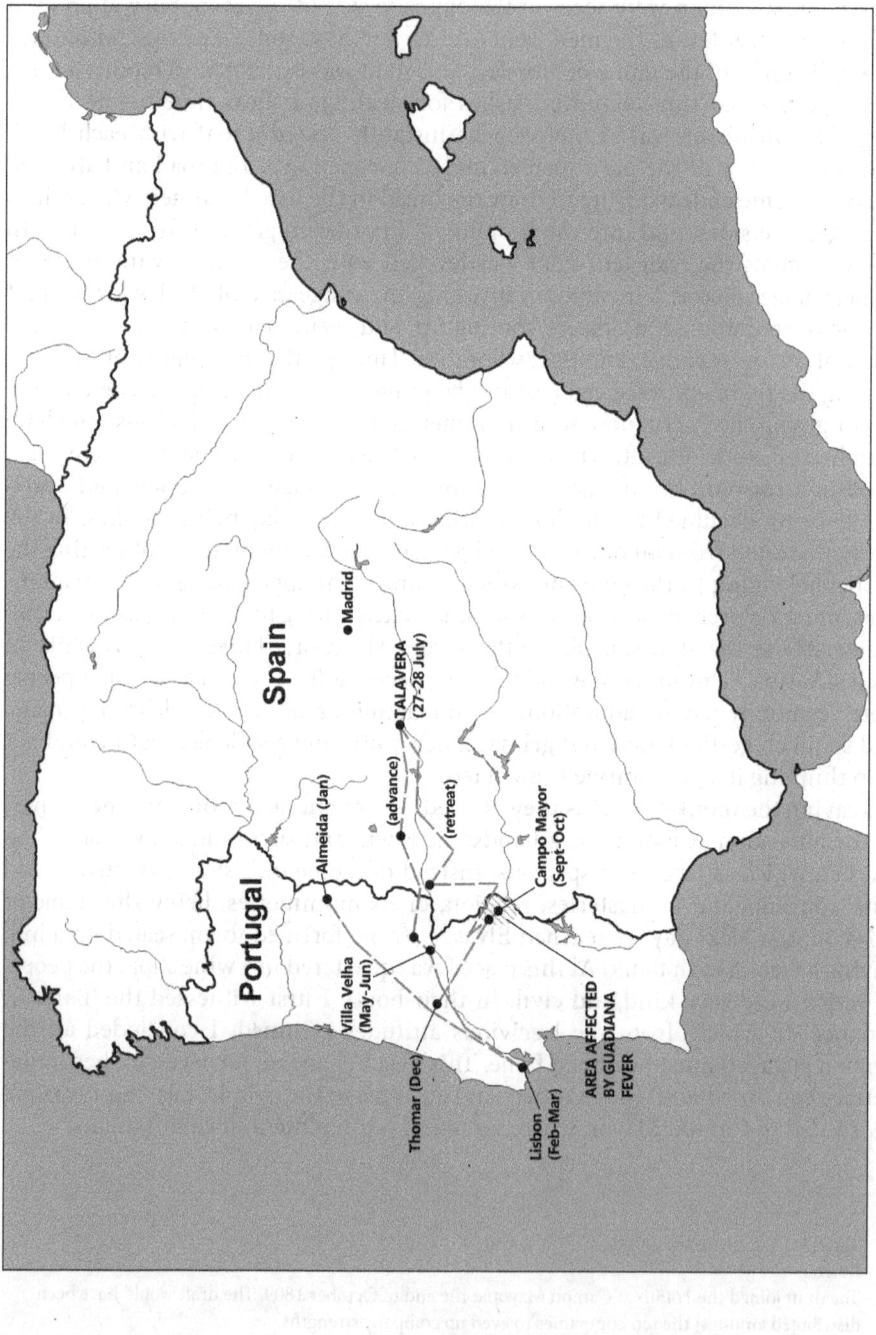

Map 1 Route of the 45th Foot in 1809.

Chapter 6

Campo Mayor – March for the Northern Frontiers – Falls Sick – Portuguese Cars – Staff Surgeon – Ward – Master – Reflection – a Storm – a Specific – Spirit Store – Coimbra

> Doctors I sincerely hate,
> Their nostrums I abhor.
> ANONYMOUS

Campo Mayor is a handsome town, surrounded by a wall, and situated near the frontier of Spain, within ten miles of Badajoz. When we had been about two months there, in consequence of some movements of the French Army, we left it in company of the division. Passing Portalegro and Nisa, we crossed the Tagus at Villa Valha, a romantic and picturesque spot, and same day reached Castel Branco,[1] where we were quartered in a convent. In the market place in this town honey sold at the rate of one half-penny per gill. From thence we proceeded by Penamacor, and after several days' marches arrived at Pinhel, a town in the province of Tras Los Montes. This was a long and fatiguing march, and being very warm when we got to our quarters, I stripped to my shirt and trousers, and having drank some water, sat down to rest myself. I was instantly seized with a fit of the ague, and after the cold shivering had left me, a fever ensued, under which I became delirious, and was carried to the hospital. After being a few days there, I was sent, in company with nearly three hundred more sick belonging to the division, to the general hospital at Coimbra – which march I will never forget.[2] Being unable to walk, or even sit on a mule, I was laid on a Portuguese car, drawn by a

1 Castelo Branco, an ancient town built on the ruins of a Roman fort in central Portugal, close to the Spanish border.

2 The mosquito-ridden valley of the Guadiana river caused hundreds of fever cases in Wellington's army in September and October 1809. At one point, nearly 30 per cent of the army men were on the sick-list. The final death toll was about 3,800 men, of which the 1/45th lost 121. Disease killed many more men than the French managed.

pair of bullocks. These cars are the most awkward and disagreeable vehicles that well can be imagined. The body is laid upon the axle-tree, which revolves with the wheels, and never being oiled or greased, produces the most loud and discordant noise, of itself enough to make a stout man sick. I once asked a car-man why he did not grease his wheels? To which he very seriously, and I believe sincerely, answered that it was to frighten the devil away! And I have no doubt it was a most efficient contrivance.

The wheels of the machine being far from circular, together with the roughness of the roads, caused such jolting, that I often anticipated being thrown off the car, which eventually did happen. In coming along the brow of a hill, where no attention had been paid in levelling the road, but which sloped in the same degree as the eminence, the car upset, when I, and another poor lad that was on it, were precipitated down the hill, the car and oxen rolling over us. We were more frightened than hurt, however, and both escaped without any material injury.

Having arrived at Coimbra, we were put into a convent, the order of St. Augustine, where a staff surgeon attended once a day. His visits, however, could have little influence on his patience, for in walking down the passage, on one side of which the sick were arranged like so many spectres, he seldom or never spoke, or even deigned to look at any of us, but passed on with as great majesty as if he had been a Turkish Bashaw.

The general doctor, who appeared to be a humane and feeling man, and seemed to have our welfare at heart, sometimes visited the hospital. On such occasions, our friend, the 'stucco-man', as the patients called the staff-surgeon, was servile, even to meanness, making good the old adage, that he who is haughty and supercilious to inferiors, will in the same ratio, be fawning sycophants to superiors.

There was another great annoyance to the inmates of this lazar-house,[3] which was the stupidity and carelessness of the superintendent or ward-master. This fellow was previously a corporal in the regiment which I belonged to, and had wormed himself into the situation he then held, by flattering the vanity of some of the surgeons. Not having capacity to rule a corporal's guard, a thing I had often seen him fail in, it was not likely things would do well where he was the conductor of business of a multifarious nature. The consequence was, little or nothing was done, and what he intended to do, the attendants or orderly men paid no attention to his orders, so that the sick were often left to shift for themselves. I have known it midnight before dinner was served; at which hour I have been aroused from sleep, to receive two ounces of meat, and a single potato, that had been left cooling five or six hours, while the attendants were regaling themselves over their cups. Upon the whole, the five weeks I passed in this place were the most tedious and irksome I ever spent in my life. Often while languishing under the enervating disease, with no one to assist and soothe me in my distress, but surrounded by a number of

3 An archaic term for a leper house.

beings as wretched and helpless as myself; while they whose duty it was to administer to our comfort, were as callous to our sufferings as if they had been enemies, I have almost been tempted to curse the hour of my birth, and wish it had been a blank in the ages of time:

> Man's inhumanity to man,
> Makes countless thousands mourn.[4]

The hospital being too full at Coimbra, it was proposed to send a number of the sick to Lisbon; accordingly, a selection was made of those who were not likely to recover, in which number I was included. On the afternoon of next day, four hundred were put on board of boats, in order to be sent to Figuera,[5] a seaport eight leagues off, where we were to be shipped for Lisbon; but after we were embarked, the boatmen, who were Portuguese, took the notion that the day was an unlucky one to sail, and left us in the boats on the river, to sink or swim, just as we could manage it. They were not long gone before the clouds began to lower and blacken, and soon after the rain fell in torrents, and continued to pour the whole night, while the vivid lightning blazed with little intermission, and the thunder formed one continued peal. Being under the influence of a fit of the ague, when I went on board, and a fever soon after succeeding, I became insensible to the war of elements, and the misery and distress that surrounded me; and lay drenched in the bottom of the boat, which they that were able kept baling, for fear of being filled with rain water. It was fondly hoped that we would be recalled to the hospital, to remain until morning, or to such time as the storm would subside. But no – the high mandate had gone forth from the mouth of a staff-surgeon, forsooth, who was here all-in-all; and whose word, like the laws of Medes and Persians, could not be altered. But the fact was, at least it appeared so, we were under the charge of those who did not care although we had been all dead by morning; indeed, several did die, and were afterwards buried on shore.

At daybreak the storm in a great measure subsided, and when the sun arose all was calm and serene. The boatmen having now come on board, we moved down the river, and same evening got on board a transport. Notwithstanding the inclemency of the weather, and the fatigue I had been exposed to, I rapidly recovered; and on the tenth day of being in the vessel, which had not then sailed, I was, to my great joy, put on shore. Not having received any medicine for some time, my rapid cure must of course be ascribed to the bargoo[6] and salt junk I got while on board – and excellent specific for the ague! Thirty more being put on shore at the same time,

4 From Robert Burns' *Man was made to mourn: A Dirge*, published in 1784.

5 Figueira da Foz, a sea town at the mouth of the Mondego River. It was the place where Wellesley disembarked his British expeditionary force (including the 45th) in August 1808.

6 William probably means burgoo, a thick soup or stew usually made by sailors.

we were quartered for the night in an old lumber garret, where, in turning over some empty casks that lay on the floor, a large hole was discovered, through which a wine and spirit store was seen underneath. This being a temptation we were neither able nor willing to resist, canteens, pack kettles &c. were immediately put in requisition, and one of the party descending, filled them all with good old rum, which soon made us forget the bad treatment we had experienced for some time past, even midnight dinners, staff-doctors – all were lost sight of.

Next morning, thinking it necessary to replenish our canteens for the march, another descent was made by one of the party, who was but a short time down when the door of the vault opened, and in walked a Portuguese. Our man with all possible speed, made for the aperture in the floor, and had so far gained his object, that some of us had hold of his arms. Ere we could get him up, however, the Portuguese laid hold of his legs, when such pulling and hauling commenced, and the poor fellow was in danger of being drawn and quartered. At last our party succeeded in rescuing the man from the grip of the Portuguese, who went away in high dudgeon, to report the affair to the commandant. On hearing this, the sergeant who had charge of us, thought proper to march the party off, which arrived at Coimbra the following day.

Coimbra is a large and populous city, seated on the Mondego, which is navigable, for boats, to Riva, four leagues above it. It is also the seat of a university, and is embellished with a great number of churches and convents, many of which are rich and elegant; but like the generality of towns in Portugal, the streets are narrow and crooked, and abominable with all kind of filth, for in no town in this country are the streets swept or cleaned. The vicinity is fertile, and produces a tolerable supply of wheat and maize, abundance of wine and oil, and fruits of the most delicious flavour may be had for little or nothing. In the market place I have seen a dozen oranges selling for five 'reis', being at the rate of four dozen for three halfpence, and a hatful of cherries might be had for the third of that sum.

I remained a month at the depot in Coimbra, and at the expiration of that period, was, in company with seven hundred more, sent to join the army, which we did in a few days, and found it nearly in the same position as when I left it. The 45th regiment, however, had moved from Pinhel, and lay detached in several villages in the neighbourhood. The company I belonged to was quartered, with two others, in the village of Managota,[7] under the command of Major Smith, an experienced and gallant officer.[8]

7 Manigoto, about five kilometres south of Pinhel.

8 Major William Smith. A man from Chirnside in the border regions of Berwickshire who had served as an 'exploring officer' (basically a uniformed spy) in Portugal the previous year due to his knowledge of the Spanish tongue.

Portrait of Major William Smith of the 45th Foot, killed in action at Busaco.
(Courtesy of Sherwood Foresters Regimental Annual)

Chapter 7

Managota – a Glutton – a Robbery – Fall of Ciudad Rodrigo – Capture of Almeida – Retreat of the British Army – an Out Post – Battle of Busaco – Reflections – a Pardon Lines of Torres Vedras

> Methinks I hear the drums tumultuous sound,
> The victors shout and groans confound;
> The dreadful burst of cannon rends the skies,
> And all the thunder of the battle rise.
>
> ADDISON

The village I was now in consisted of about a hundred and twenty houses, built in such an irregular manner as to form a kind of labyrinth, from which a stranger would have found some difficulty in extricating himself. The appearance it made was wretched in the extreme. The houses were all built of round stones gathered from the fields, and with clay instead of mortar, while the crookedness of the walls showed that neither line nor plummet had been used. The Padra Cura's mansion was an exception, being something superior to the others, and white-washed, a mark by which we always knew where these gentry resided. The circumstances of the people were analogous to the village they inhabited – they were poor, ignorant, and superstitious; yet kind and hospitable with the little they had. They were also innocent and harmless, unless when imposed on or irritated; and if wrongly dealt with, implacable and revengeful, being nothing loathe to use the 'catou,' or knife, under such circumstances. This character I think applicable to the Portuguese peasantry in general.

A green that skirted one side of the village, served at once for drill ground and a church. The Major being in the habit of reading prayers to us on Sunday, the detachment regularly turned out in full marching order. After divine service he generally put us through a smart field-day, and then piling arms, the whole had to strip, and plunge into the river, that winded past the green. There we remained till the bugle sounded; then emerging from the water, formed into line on its banks, where our commander made a strict inspection. Thus acting in the triple capacity of commander, doctor for the body, and physician for the soul.

In Manigota, and other villages in the neighbourhood, we passed the whole of the spring and part of the summer of 1810, in peace and plenty. In one of these villages I had an opportunity of witnessing a full display of the powers of a gormandizer, by a man of our own company. The fellow was a native of Nottinghamshire, a kind of half-wit, and greatly famed as a bolter,[1] even by his countrymen. One day, while sitting at the sunny end of a house with five or six others, amongst whom was this glutton, the quartermaster-sergeant joined us,[2] who, after some conversation, inquired at David, 'If ever he got a "blow-out" now?' 'Not so often as I would wish,' was the reply. 'Well David,' said the sergeant, pointing to a quantity of bread that lay on the floor of an old barn, which was used as a provision store, 'how many of these loaves could you eat if you had your will of them?' The loaves were three pounds' weight each, and David eyeing them very eagerly, said, 'it is not long since I got my breakfast, still I think I could yam a few of them.'[3] 'Well,' said the sergeant, 'I will give you a quart of wine to each loaf, to wash it down; so begin, and let us see what you can do.' Upon this David commenced the game, which proved dear to him, although most excellent sport to the bystanders. In rather more than an hour he finished four loaves, and swallowed as many quarts of wine, which, with his breakfast, amounted to thirteen pounds and a half of bread, four quarts of wine, and one of chocolate, all swallowed in the course of two hours. When he had done, he sat and stared as if his eyes would have started out of their sockets, and was totally unable to rise. The bread he had eaten being made of rye, and newly baked, swelled him to such a degree, that he was in great danger of bursting, and made him groan both long and loud. Some spoke of rolling him, which was immediately commenced on a green in front of the barn, but he roared so loud and hideously, calling upon God, and Pharaoh, King of Egypt, alternately, to assist and save him, that it was dropped. His belly was then rubbed with grease and oil, but not producing the desired effect; he was carried to the hospital, where he lay several days before recovering. For this the sergeant got a severe reprimand from the commanding officer.

About this time five men of our grenadier company were condemned to death for a highway robbery. They had attacked a Portuguese peasant and his wife, when on their way home from a fair that was held in a neighbouring village, and had taken what little money they had, and other articles. Horsley, the knight of the oven, already mentioned, was one of them, and was, even under the sentence of

1 Bolter: a glutton. The man in question was Private David Evans. He survived the war.
2 Quartermaster Sergeant Francis Tinkler.
3 Yam: a Nottinghamshire expression meaning 'eat'.

death, as incorrigible as ever.[4] The execution of the sentence being delayed from time to time, the prisoners were kept in charge by the Provost Marshal's guard, where Horsley had the address to rob a French officer, who was a prisoner, of his watch and money. When spoken to about it, he told the Provost, with the greatest nonchalance, that he did not care when he was executed, provided he was allowed a canteen of rum two hours previous to his exit.

But affairs of greater moment were soon to take place. The French, under General Massena, having laid siege to Ciudad Rodrigo, a Spanish frontier town, our army advanced in order to make a diversion in favour of the garrison, who were Spaniards, and who behaved well on this occasion, as they generally do when they have stone walls between them and their enemies.[5] Notwithstanding the bravery displayed by the garrison, however, the town fell into the hands of the French, although not until the fortress was no longer defensible.[6] This was the first time I had heard the sound of the enemy's cannon, which, with the fire from the besieged, had kept up a continued roll like thunder, for several days and nights successively. But alas! How unlike he of Sweden![7] For I must confess it had no charms for me; and instead of being like music in my ears, the bellowing sound seemed harsh, loud, and discordant. In fact, I almost wished I had remained at my loom, or even in the Militia, where there was little chance of having my head snapped off by a cannon ball, or my body shattered by the bursting of a shell. These thoughts, however, I concealed in my own breast; my disclosing them to my comrades would only have subjected me to the ridicule of those who, perhaps, participated in the same train of thinking, but, like myself, were afraid or ashamed to own it. I was but a young soldier, and had yet to learn to stand the smell of gunpowder, as our men termed the fire of the enemy. How I succeeded in this will be seen in the sequel.

On the capture of Ciudad Rodrigo, the French advanced upon Almeida, our army retiring before them, and our rear guard occasionally skirmishing with the advanced corps. This, however, did not much retard the progress of Massena, who opened his trenches before this fortress on the 19th of August, and on the morning of the 20th, eleven batteries mounted with sixty-five pieces of cannon opened their fire, keeping up a heavy cannonade the whole day and succeeding night.

The same day our division, commanded by General Picton,[8] re-crossed the Coa, and on the afternoon encamped on the left bank of that river, on a line with the

4 Only four men were condemned; Privates Thomas Horsley, Joseph Norman, Edward Perrot, and drummer Joseph Freeman.

5 The French laid siege to Ciudad Rodrigo with a 65,000-man army on 26 April 1810. Wellington sent the Light Division to the frontier but they did not come to the aid of Ciudad Rodrigo, as Wellington did not yet feel ready to meet the French in open battle.

6 Ciudad Rodrigo fell on 10 July 1810.

7 William is probably referring to King Charles XII (1682-1718), a notable Swedish commander and man of legendary reputation at the time, who had successfully besieged several fortresses.

8 Major General Thomas Picton, a sharp-tongued Welshman who commanded the Third Division.

Thomas Picton, the commander of Wellington's 'Fighting Third' Division, of which the 45th was a conspicuous part. (Anne S. K. Brown Collection)

road leading from Almeida to Cellerico.[9] When I say encamped, I do not mean that we had tents or splendid pavilions, such as we read of in romance, that served to screen the warriors of old from the scorching rays of the summer, or the withering and desolating blasts of winter. No, the bed of the soldier, for the first four years of the Peninsular war, was the bare, cold, and often wet ground, and nothing but the sky for his canopy. Our ground this day was a wet and marshy field, and the rain, which had commenced the preceding evening, poured down in torrents. Being for duty, I was sent with a sergeant and twelve men, to a considerable distance in front of the camp, and a little before dusk was posted on an eminence overhanging the river immediately in my front. On the opposite the ground formed a plain,

9 This is probably Celorico da Beira approximately 40 kilometres west of Almeida.

where stood the beleaguered city, which, by the incessant flashing of its guns on the ramparts, created a display of fireworks on an extensive scale, while the reports reverberating among the mountains, added solemnity to the whole – making the scene at once grand and terrific.

In the meantime, I continued to walk to-and-fro on my post, keeping a sharp look out to the river, as it was expected the enemy would endeavour to ford it at this place. The rain, which had partly subsided for some time, again fell in torrents, while the forked lightning formed one continued sheet of vivid fire, and the thunder rolled with a tremendous crash directly over my head. Having a stone wall immediately in the rear, against which I had been leaning for some time, viewing the war of elements and of men with a mixture of admiration and dread, I became fearful least the wall, which was composed of iron stone, might attract the subtle fluid. I therefore advanced a few yards in front, and had scarcely done so, when more than ten yards of it were levelled to the ground. What was the cause of this I know not; but felt very thankful I had removed in time, and was inclined to think that an over-ruling Providence had induced me to do so.

Owing to the rugged and broken nature of the ground, which was covered with bushes and bramble, together with the wetness of the night, and the darkness that intervened between the lightning, to relieve the outposts became a matter quite impracticable. Accordingly, I was obliged to remain on my post until morning; thus being nine hours exposed on a hill in the most dreadful night I ever witnessed. At daybreak the violence of the rain had abated, and the thunder entirely ceased. Being drenched with rain, I was walking smartly about, in order to keep myself warm, expecting every moment to be relieved, when my attention was attracted towards Almeida, by a tremendous explosion, the smoke of which darkened the whole atmosphere. This proceeded from the blowing up of a large magazine, by which more than one-half of the artillerymen, a great number of the garrison, and many of the inhabitants perished. The guns were dismounted, and their works being no longer defensible, an immediate surrender took place, and all the troops in the garrison became prisoners of war.[10]

In a few minutes after this misfortune, our outposts were withdrawn, and upon joining the division, which was under arms, we immediately marched off. Passing Cellorico, we that night encamped, and next day reached Mala, where we remained a few days. Leaving this village, we continued to retrograde until the 26th of September, when Lord Wellington took up a position on Busaco hill. This hill is part of a 'Sierra,' or chain of mountains, of considerable height, which extends from the Mondego, in a northerly direction, about eight miles. Our brigade

10 The explosion levelled Almeida at seven o'clock in the evening of 26 August 1810. A French shell had set fire to a trail of gun-powder that led through an open door to the garrison's magazine. The blast killed 600 defenders and wounded another 300. It was probably the largest single explosion of the Napoleonic Wars.

commanded by General M'Kinnon,[11] was stationed on one of the highest points of the ridge, while the rest of the army was posted to the right and left, with a strong corps of reserve in the rear. On the morning of the 27th a most desperate assault was made on our position. The whole of the French Army advanced in columns, and attacked our lines from right to left. Thrice the division under Marshall Ney ascended the hill on which General M'Kinnon's brigade was posted, but was as often repulsed at the point of the bayonet, with great slaughter. During the whole day the battle continued to rage with various success; and death, the king of terrors, stalked about in grim array, while his thousand doors stood open. At last, part of our reserve being brought up, the enemy retired, leaving two thousand dead on the field, an immense number of wounded, and about three hundred prisoners.

The loss of the British on this occasion was very considerable; and although the victory was claimed by us, we had not much to boast of. The regiment to which I belonged suffered severely. The brave Major Smith, while gallantly leading on the left wing to the charge, saw with sorrow and regret half of the regiment entirely cut off, while he was himself pierced with a number of the enemy's bayonets, and fell mortally wounded.[12] Major Gwyn, an intrepid officer belonging to the regiment, was severely wounded in the groin, and rendered unfit for active service, but was afterwards employed for a number of years as field officer of the recruiting district of Glasgow.[13] Three captains, with a number of subaltern officers, and about four hundred rank-and-file were lost to the regiment.[14] The total loss I never heard estimated; but as I traversed over the field next day, busily employed in burying the dead, I thought that all the Bourbons, with their thrones, crown and sceptres, would be but a poor equivalent for the blood that was shed, and the lives that were lost on this fated field. And although a victory was claimed, yet the loss sustained was more than ever Britain was likely to gain by the war.

When the melancholy task of interring the slain was performed, my mind felt deeply impressed with the contrast the scene then presented, with that exhibited the day before. The all was animation – now death-like silence pervaded the whole. But yesterday, the embattled line, the deep dense column, and the impenetrable phalanx, were drawn up in battle array, with their iron front to meet the impetuous shock, and repel the furious assault of the enemy. Then the trumpets shrill blast, the mellow notes of the bugle, the shouts of men, the roar of cannon, and

11 Henry MacKinnon, a 36-year-old guardsman who was at this time a substantive colonel. He had lived for a time in France as a boy, where he had been acquainted with the future Emperor Napoleon.

12 Major William Smith was cut off, pulled from his horse, and bayoneted to death by the French.

13 William Gwyn, a 35-year-old Londoner who had previously served three tours of duty in the West Indies. He died of complications due to his wound in Scotland in 1815.

14 The 45th was under-strength at Busaco; only four captains were present, so most of the companies were commanded by lieutenants. The actual loss to the 1/45th was 7 officers and 143 other ranks, out of five companies (roughly 260 men) principally involved. William's No. 4 company was with the right wing, so was not in the thick of the action, hence the lack of personal details in his account.

the clang of arms, served at once to animate the scene, and inspire the combatants with courage to meet the mortal strife. Now but a few individuals straggling from their parties were seen, while patches of newly-turned soil denoted where friend and foe, husbands, sons, and brothers, lay huddled in one promiscuous mass. In fancy I already heard the deep groan of the father, on receiving the intelligence of his son's death – the weeping mother, the widows wail, and the orphans cry. When about to depart for the camp, I turned to take a look and last farewell of this melancholy scene. The beautiful lines of Falconer,[15] on the loss of his companions, flashed upon my memory, which I could not refrain from repeating:

Ye lost companions of distress adieu!
Your toils, and pains, and dangers, are no more!
The tempest now may howl, unheard by you,
While ocean smites in vain the trembling shore.

On you the blast, surcharg'd with rain and snow,
In winters dismal nights no more shall beat;
Unfelt by you the vertic sun may glow,
And scorch the panting earth with baneful heat.

No more you feel contagious mortal's breath,
That taints the realms with misery severe;
No more behold pale famine scattering death,
With cruel ravage desolate the year.

The thundering drum, the trumpets swelling strain,
Unheard shall form the long embattled line;
Unheard, the deep foundations of the main,
Shall tremble when the hostile squadrons join.

What tho' no funeral pomp, no borrow'd tear,
Your hour of death to gazing crowds shall tell,
Nor weeping friends attend your sable bier,
Who sadly listen to the passing bell.

Yet shall remembrance from oblivion's veil,
Relieve your scene, and sigh with grief sincere;
And soft compassion at your tragic tale,
In silent tribute pay her kindred tear.[16]

15 The Scots sailor and epic poet William Falconer (1732-1769).
16 Extracts from the poem *The Shipwreck* by William Falconer, published in 1762.

The execution of Horsley and his companions having been still delayed, they, during the engagement, broke from the guard that had them in charge, and joining their regiment, behaved so well during the action, that Lord Wellington was graciously pleased to grant them a pardon. One of them lost an arm in the battle, and was sent home to England, where he received a pension. Horsley after all died a natural death in Portugal, at least if hunger and fatigue can be so denominated.[17]

On the evening of the 28th, being still on the same ridge, and near to the ground where the action was fought, orders were issued to light as many fires as possible, which being done we immediately marched off in the dark. Travelling the whole night, we passed through Coimbra next morning, where, having crossed the river, the bridge was blown up, in order to retard the progress of the enemy, who were in close pursuit of us. At Condeixa we were in quarters during the night, and left it early in the morning, accompanied by the whole of the inhabitants, who were flying from the enemy.[18] Next night the brigade lay in the convent at Pombal, where the monks were busy all night in preparing for the road in the morning, and who opened their wine and provision stores to us, with which we made ourselves very comfortable and happy.

By the time the division reached Leiria, the road was so crowded with the flying inhabitants that the troops could scarcely move on. It was a most distressing and lamentable sight, to see a whole people leaving their houses and homes to the fury and rapacity of the cruel invaders. Numbers of children were seen crying for the parents they had lost in the crowd, and parents bitterly wailing for their children; while many of the aged, who had dragged on until their feeble limbs could do no more, sat by the wayside in sad anticipation of the doom that awaited them. My attention was forcibly attracted by the situation of a respectable looking old lady, who was seated in a sort of open carriage, drawn by a pair of oxen, one of which, having dropped down dead, lay on the road. The lady was blind, and as we passed the carriage I could perceive the tears fall fast from her glazed and darkened orbs; but sympathy was all we had to bestow, for we ourselves were retreating in front of an overwhelming and victorious enemy. I thought at the time if our victories produced such ruinous results, that a defeat in its effects must be dreadful.[19]

17 Not quite correct. Three of the quartet perished during the war or shortly thereafter – Edward Perrott was killed in action at the storming of Ciudad Rodrigo in January 1812, Joseph Freeman died of sickness in Portugal on 15 February 1813, and the irascible Thomas Horsley died of consumption at the General Hospital on the Isle of Wight in August 1815. Joseph Norman was the one who lost an arm, but at Badajoz rather than Busaco, and survived to collect his Chelsea Pension in 1813 and his General Service Medal in 1847.

18 This was Condeixa-a-Nova. Notwithstanding Wellington's victory at Busaco, it had interrupted rather than prevented Massena's invasion of Portugal. The troops and civilians did not comprehend the reason for the retreat, but Wellington had a cunning plan, and he was not in the habit of sharing his plans with the lower ranks.

19 William's footnote at this point reads: When Ministers in Parliament were holding forth on this occasion, and expatiating on the success of our army, a most pertinent question was put by a noble

On reaching Leiria, we were as usual quartered in a convent, where the monks like their brethren at Pombal, opened their stores to us, which caused abundance of wassailing the whole night. Being not to march so early as usual, I walked into the town, which I found in the utmost confusion. Most of the inhabitants had left the place, and the soldiers commenced the work of plunder. As I stepped into a house I met one of our men coming out with a bundle of dried fish on his shoulder, which he seemed to regard as his own. On entering the place, I found it to be a grocer's shop, in which were a number of soldiers very busy. One man had seized a sack of rice, but it was so heavy he could not carry it, yet would allow no one to participate with him, until another ripped the sack with a knife from top to bottom, when a general scramble ensued for the contents on the floor. A cask, containing butter, was surrounded by another squad, who, disagreeing about the spoil, tore the cask into staves, and in the contest most of the butter was trod underfoot. The happiest fellow I saw in the whole group was one with his cap full of cayenne pepper, with which he seemed well pleased, and in secure possession, as nobody appeared to envy him of his prize. On entering a room above stairs, I found two women, belonging to our army, deliberately folding up the bed-cloths, which they had appropriated to themselves. In another apartment a parcel of fellows was endeavouring to break up a chest with a large stone, with which they ever and anon came thump upon the cover.

In returning towards my quarters at the convent, a short distance from the town, I met a Portugue leading a heavy laden ass. He had not proceeded far ere he came in contact with two soldiers, who immediately seized the animal and led him away, while the poor peasant stood confounded and amazed; and when he saw his property at a considerable distance he exclaimed, 'Adeus, adeus, pauvre borico!'[20] So saying he turned himself round and walked away. Such is the fate of a country where war spreads his desolating wings. The inhabitants are robbed and plundered by friends and foes, and fall an easy prey to the victors and the vanquished.

> Eternal powers! what ravens from afar
> Mark the fell track of desolating war.[21]

Leaving Leiria, we proceeded on our march in the direction of Lisbon, at which port it was generally believed we would embark, as the necessity for evacuating the country appeared to be very pressing.[22] But in this we were mistaken. There was much to do – and it was done – ere that event took place; and thousands, nay tens

Lord, (Grenville). 'Are we then,' said his Lordship, 'arrived at that melancholy situation of our affairs, in which disasters are to be called victories, and the cypress that droops over the tombs of our gallant defenders, whose lives have been uselessly sacrificed, to be denominated laurels?'

20 'Farewell, farewell, poor ass!'

21 From Falconer's *The Shipwreck*; although the original text is 'Eternal powers! What ruins from afar...'

22 Vide my earlier comment about Wellington not sharing his plans. He had absolutely no intention of abandoning Portugal.

of thousands, who had not then entered the country, served to mature the soil of the Peninsula before the close of the war.

In the course of this day's march, we passed a wine pipe by the wayside, in which was a soldier, in an inverted position, fully accoutred, with his knapsack on. Probably when reaching for liquor he had over-balanced himself, and thus drowned his cares in wine at the expense of life. At night we encamped as usual, marching early next morning; and in a few days after, reached the lines in the vicinity of Torres Vedras. These lines, strong by nature and improved by art, extended to a distance of thirty-five miles, flanked on one side by the sea, and on the other by the Tagus; while long ranges of batteries were erected, completely protecting the four passes that lead through the mountains to Lisbon; besides, in many places the roads were undermined and trains laid. On Massena's arriving at Torres Vedras, he reconnoitred the British lines, but finding their position impregnable, thought it prudent not to make an attack; and in a short time our army was put into cantonments. The enemy fixed their headquarters at Santarem, a short distance from our position.[23]

The ridge at Busaco in Portugal, where in 1810 four companies of the 45th halted a French column. (Anne S. K. Brown Collection)

23 The construction of the Lines of Torres Vedras was Wellington's cunning plan. They comprised a series of overlapping defensive fortifications, built by 7,000 paid labourers superintended by 17 Engineer officers between October 1809 and August 1810, completely defending Lisbon from the north. The French knew absolutely nothing of their existence.

Chapter 8

Again Falls Sick – Meets an Old School Fellow – Philanthropy of a Portugue – Portuguese Surgeon – Reflection – General Doctor – Staff Surgeon – Lisbon – a Procession

> Want and incurable disease, (fell pair)
> On hopeless multitudes remorseless seize
> At once; and make a refuge of the grave.
> How groaning hospitals eject their dead!
> What numbers groan for sad admission there!
>
> YOUNG

We were but a short time in quarters ere I was attacked by my old enemy the ague, and sent to the regimental hospital. After remaining there a few days, I was, together with a number more, ordered for Lisbon. Accordingly, I was once more laid on one of those engines of torture, a Portuguese car, and the same day arrived at Villa Nova, a town on the banks of the Tagus, from which we were to be removed in boats to Lisbon. Our quarters at this place was a stable, into which we were stowed like so many herrings in a barrel, lying with belly to back, and nearly suffocated with heat, and the effluvia arising from the filth and nastiness of the place, which was full of bullock and mule's dung. There being no boats ready to carry us away, we were detained in this execrable place the whole of the next day, during which period a number died.

While here I met with a townsman and old school-fellow, whose condition was analogous with my own, being ill with the ague and bound for the hospital. When at home and at school, we were but slightly acquainted; but meeting in a foreign land, and in the circumstances we were placed, we embraced as brothers. Our first meeting being over, we crawled to the banks of the river, where we sat and conversed of home, our boyish days, and the times that were long past. 'Oh man! William,' said he, 'What would I give to be as near the banks of the Irvine as we are to those of the Tagus! But I shall never see home more – I know I shall die in this hateful country, and my body be left to rot above the ground, or fill the hungry maw of dogs!' I endeavoured as well as I could to dispel the despondency that seemed to prey upon his mind; but it was of no avail, a deep and rooted melancholy had seized upon his spirits. His anticipation's were but too true, for he died at Lisbon a short time after. Poor James! He fell another victim to ambition's shrine.

The boats having arrived, we went down the river, and landed at Lisbon, the same night we embarked, at a late hour. Here we lay in a grand square, under a piazza, until daybreak next morning, when a Portuguese gentleman happening to pass, his attention was attracted by the groans that issued from beneath the piazza. He evinced great concern at our wretched condition, and while stepping over us as we lay shivering on the cold pavement, he uttered many pious and fervent ejaculations, invoking the whole saints in the calendar to have compassion on us. But he did not leave all for the saints to perform. After a short absence he returned, accompanied by a servant bearing a large pitcher of chocolate and a basket of biscuit, which he distributed amongst us.

Shortly after this we were conveyed in cars to the convent of St. Francisca, where I was put in charge of a Portuguese surgeon. This son of Esculapius was a firm and true disciple of the Sangradian school.[1] The first time we met he took a large quantity of blood from me, when, God knows, I had more need of a beef steak, or some other cordial; and at the same time prescribed I should not drink anything stronger than barley or rice water. This surely, thought I, cannot be Sangrado himself, nor even his worthy pupil Gil Blas! No, no, it cannot be: this worthy gentleman must be successor to that great master of the healing art, and can only have got a receipt of the sovereign remedy, by which his celebrated predecessor acquired such fame, and which eased so many patients of their pains. Having a vivid recollection of Dr. Sangrado, I determined to make my stay with this leech as short as possible. Accordingly, next day, when he asked 'Commo estra?'[2] I looked as well as I could and replied 'Monte Bon.'[3] He shook his head, which was as much as to say, I know better; 'but', said he, 'I have no doubt that you will be so in a few days, provided you attend my prescriptions.' Of this I had little doubt, for my doing so, I would certainly have been very soon released from all my troubles. I, however, put such a good face on the matter, that in the course of eight days I was discharged from the hospital, and sent to the depot at Belem; and though scarcely able to stand on my feet, yet I felt happy at having escaped the hands of such a butcher.

When but a few days at Belem I was taken extremely ill with dysentery, while my former disease continued with all its enervating effects. In a short time, I was so

1 Today, we would say – a quack. Doctor Sangrado was a fictional physician in the popular novel *Gil Blas* whose panacea was copious bloodletting and drinking of hot water.

2 'How are you?'

3 'Very well.'

exhausted I could not stand on my feet, and was again carried to the hospital. By this time, I was almost weary of life, and began to loath my very existence. Seeing no termination of my troubles but by death, I began to retard the grizzly monarch with a kind of favourable feeling, although at the same time I saw much to fear; for, as Blair expresses it, 'Sure tis a serious thing to die.'[4] Notwithstanding, while I lay on the wagon, writhing with pain, I wished I might be carried again to the Franciscan convent, that Golgotha, where, under the management of my old friend the Portuguese, I might be quickly dispatched; for I expected never to emerge from the precincts of the hospital more, unless when carried out un-shrouded, even without a shirt, (that article being generally appropriated by the attendants,) and thrown into a hole promiscuously with many others like so much carrion.

While engaged in this melancholy train of thought, the wagon halted in front of the Estrelle convent;[5] but it was a matter of no interest to me, for I conceived I was going the way of all flesh. I was, however, carried into the house, and as I could neither stand nor sit, was laid on a bed in one of the passages, until such time as the surgeon inspected me. It was not long before two surgeons hurried past, but hearing me groan deeply, immediately returned. The oldest of the two, a most benign looking man, asked me in a soothing tone, what was the matter; and after informing him of my ailments, he ordered me to be instantly removed to the fluxed ward. Here I was stripped of my clothes, which, along with my arms and accoutrements, were put into a large room, occupied as a store for the arms of the sick.

The apartment I was now in, was one of a range that went entirely round the building, and which had, no doubt, in better times, been occupied as cells by the holy fathers; but were now sadly polluted by the profanity of heretics, and occupied by them as a lazar-house. The apartments, however, did not accord with my ideas of a cell; they were large, spacious, and lofty, with a handsome window in each, and altogether such as a person who had renounced the devil, the world, and the flesh, might live very comfortably in, and doze through life in all the luxury of indolence and sloth, especially when supplied abundantly with the greater part of the good things of this world, and made certain of enjoying all in the next. From the window of the apartment the greater part of Lisbon was seen, with its spacious harbour, and the numerous shipping that crowded the port; while the high ground on the opposite side of the river bounded the view, with numerous towns, villages and convents; the whole interspersed with fields of maize or Indian corn, orange groves, and vineyards. But it was a long time ere I could reach the window, being unable to walk across the room for two months after entering it.

At this hospital, things were managed in a very different manner from what I had seen in any similar establishment. The greatest attention was paid to the

4 From Scots poet Robert Blair's poem *The Grave* published in 1743.

5 This probably refers to the Basilica da Estrela in Lisbon.

cleanness and comfort of patients. Each day while ill, I had a clean shirt and pair of sheets; and everything was procured that was deemed beneficial, or tending to expedite the recovery of the sick. The general doctor was kind, feeling, and humane, and fulfilled the high and important duties of his profession with honour to himself, and benefit to the whole of his care; while the surgeon, to whom the more immediate charge of the ward was consigned, was a young man of an equally amiable and humane disposition; and to him, under Providence, I owe my life.

Notwithstanding the care and attention bestowed upon me, however, three months elapsed before I was discharged; and then I returned to Belem barracks. During the time I remained there, which was a considerable while, I had many opportunities of visiting Lisbon, which I found remarkable for little, save the filth and nastiness of the streets! What attracted my attention most, was the numerous processions, crowding the narrow thoroughfares; and the shoals of itinerant and begging friars, some carrying bags, and others boxes, perambulating the city. those carrying bags enter the houses, and fill their wallet for the love of God and St. Antonio; while the others keep the street with their box, which contains some canonised and sainted personage, and ever and anon holds it up to the lips of the passenger, by whom the mendicant is rewarded, in the name and for the love of his tutelary saint.

A stranger, when walking the streets of Lisbon, is apt to imagine himself amongst a pious and devout people, and the place where he sojourns the holiest of cities. When he hears the tolling and sounding of bells from morning till night, and from night till morning; when he views the numerous images, composed of stone, wood, or wax, enshrined at the doors of the nobles, and the houses of the plebeians daubed from the street to the chimney top with the blessed sign of the cross; and when his eye meets with that emblem of Christianity indented on the top crust of every loaf he may chance to see, he will be ready to cry aloud, 'Surely this is a blessed people, and zealous of good works.' But he will find, when better acquainted, that all this is but washing the outside of the platter.

Amongst the number of processions, I witnessed was one termed the anniversary of the crucifixion. By it was meant a representation of the Jews leading the saviour from Jerusalem to Calvary. As this was a pageant on a grand scale, I shall endeavour to give as distinct an account of it as possible, without making any comment on the gross impiety and superstition displayed on the occasion, but will leave the reader to form conclusions for himself.

The whole being assembled in and about the courts of a large convent, situated by the river side near Belem, the front of the cavalcade, consisting of a strong detachment of cavalry, issued from the great gateway, at twelve o'clock noon. Immediately in the rear of the horse marched a body of infantry, with arms reversed, consisting of about seven hundred men. Next followed a dark and dense column of priests and friars, walking four by four, with white staves or rods in their hands. This body might amount to five hundred. After them came a tall gaunt figure, wrapped in a dark gown, which trailed on the ground; and over him was suspended a species of network, supported by four men with poles. I never could learn who this personage was meant to represent. A second body of clergymen, equal in numerical strength to the first, followed this great unknown, walking in the same order, and bearing staves as those preceding them. Next came twenty children, nearly of one size and age, (about seven years). The apparel they wore was a dress of white muslin, fitted close to the body, and on the back of their shoulders were displayed expanded wings, deeply gilt: these were imitation angels. Following the children who formed the centre of this triumph of holy mother church, came six men, supporting a bier, shoulder high, on which stood a figure of the saviour. This figure appeared above the middle size, and was habited with brown pantaloons, a green striped vest, and a blue cloak. Instead of a crown of thorns, a good Kilmarnock cowl covered his pate; and on his shoulder he bore a large wooden cross. In the rear of this there followed, in the same order and number as preceded, the different squads of angels, priests, monks and friars, while the military detachments of horse and foot closed the rear.

At this, as at all their other processions, the immense crowds assembled were on bended knee in the mud. The most profound silence prevailed. All seemed deeply impressed with the scene before them, which was truly imposing, and well calculated to work upon the minds of an ignorant and superstitious people.

Map 2 Route of the 45th Foot in 1810.

Chapter 9

Embarks for Figuera – Commences Servant – Dreadful Tempest – a Scuffle

The wounded bark, thus smarting with her pain,
Scuds from pursuing waves across the main;
While dash'd apart by her dividing prow,
Like burning adamant the waters glow;
Upheaved behind her, in tremendous height,
The billows frown, with fearful radiance bright!
Now shivering o'er the topmost wave she rides,
While deep beneath the enormous gulf divides.
Now, launching headlong down the horrid vale,
She bears no more the roaring of the gale;
Till up the dreadful height again she flies,
Trembling beneath the current of the skies.
FALCONER

Being perfectly recovered in health, and in high spirits, I was ordered, along with eight hundred more, who, like myself had been sick, to join the army, which, in consequence of the retreat of the French, had advanced to the northern frontier of Portugal.[1] In order to facilitate our march, we were put on board a thirty-six-gun frigate, to be conveyed to Figuera,[2] and from thence to march to our respective regiments. Upon getting on deck I heard someone calling on me by name, and on turning round I perceived it to be Mr C[harles] C[ook], second surgeon to our regiment.[3] Being shown to him, he came forward and requested me to attend him on the quarter-deck, as soon as my arms were put up. When I met him again, he

1 Whilst William had been absent from his regiment, the French had given up their hopeless siege of the Lines of Torres Vedras and retreated northwards, starving.

2 Figueira da Foz.

3 Charles Cook joined the 45th in Portugal in May 1811 as assistant-surgeon.

told me, that having just arrived from England, he was in want of a servant, and asked if I had any objections to the situation. I replied I had none, but that never having been in service was afraid I would not please. He, however, being willing to try me, I was installed in the office, of what in the army is termed a Dog-rubber or Bone-polisher.[4]

Having cleared the Tagus, we proceeded along the coast, and cast anchor in Mondego bay, after a pleasant voyage of a few days. We had not, however, been in the bay a few hours, ere it blew a brisk gale, which soon increased to a hurricane. Although a second anchor had been let go, the vessel began to drift, and would soon have been on a rocky cape that formed one side of the bay. The captain immediately ordered the cables to be cut, and again put to sea. Night coming on, and the storm still gathering strength, the soldiers were ordered below, where we were kept under hatches forty-eight hours. This precluded us from witnessing the storm above, but there was enough of it below. It is scarcely possible a just conception can be formed of our situation, while below in this floating dungeon, except by those who may have been similarly situated. The hatches being down, and the port holes shut up, left us at once in total darkness, and much in want of air, which produced such a suffocating heat, that it was with the utmost difficulty we could find breath. In a short time most of them got sick, and from the filth and vomiting that ensued, the place became intolerable. Our situation, in fact, became so truly appalling, that numbers were seized with a kind of frenzy, who, running through the place, beat down and trampled all in the way; at the same time shouting and roaring, and venting the most dreadful imprecations on those whom they conceived to be the authors of their distress; some even went so far as to wish the vessel were blown up, with all it contained, or sunk to the bottom. Others again, more calm, prayed fervently to be delivered from their distressed situation; and that their supplications might prove more efficacious, endeavoured to bribe the Deity with a promise of perfect obedience to his will in future; while others, seemingly lost in stupor, lay in a torpid state, deprived of all motion, except from the impetus given by the heaving of the vessel, which rolled them about like as many shuttlecocks.

On the afternoon of the second day of our confinement, the storm being somewhat abated, we were permitted to get on deck, which formed a great contrast to the scene below. Instead of being suffocated for want of air, we had the utmost difficulty in keeping our footing on deck, from the heavy gale that still continued to blow. Sometimes we were in no little danger of being washed overboard, by the heavy seas that were shipped, and which rolled in quick succession over the deck from stem to stern. Previous to this I had often read of mountainous seas, stormy billows, and the raging main, but all my ideas had never pictured to my

4 Each officer was allowed one servant. An assistant surgeon ranked more or less as a lieutenant in terms of pay and hierarchy. The term 'dog-rubber' probably refers to the act of looking after an officer's pet, whereas 'bone-polisher' suggests hours spent polishing bone-handled cutlery.

imagination anything like what I now beheld. Here, indeed, were seen no waves running mountains high, no mermaid sitting on the rock, with comb and glass in hand, presaging to the fear stricken mariner the coming storm, but all the horrors of the contending tides of the Bay of Biscay rose at once on the astonished view, and struck the inexperienced landsman, and soldier, and the veteran tar, with equal terror and dismay. Around the labouring vessel arose the foaming ocean in aquatic spires, and in terrible array menacing us with instant destruction. During the night the scene was awfully sublime, at the same time astounding and terrific. From the broken nature of the water the ocean appeared as an immense boiling cauldron, or a great furnace filled with liquid metal. In fact, I could not avoid comparing the scene before me, to the description I had heard of the lake that is said to burn with fire and brimstone; for all around appeared as one sheet of that vivid element.

Meantime, our gallant ship, like the presiding genius of the storm, continued her devious course; and as she ploughed her way through the briny element, appeared at times deeply immersed in the foaming tide; and again, as if impatient of the pitiless tempest, bounding from the summit of the passing billow, and cleaving at once the snowy and hissing crest of the coming wave. While poised thus high in air, and again suddenly descending to the yawning depths below, my mind was highly excited; and when borne alone the swelling surge with such amazing velocity, the sensations I felt are indescribable. At this distance of time I can hardly tell whether hope, fear, joy, pain, or pleasure, were most predominant.

The storm being considerably abated, we once more bore away for the mouth of the Mondego, which we gained on the morning of the sixth day after leaving it. We were immediately put on board five small transports that were in the bay, for the purpose of being carried to the harbour. Accordingly, at high water in the afternoon, we made for the port; but the van ship having hung upon a sand bank that crossed the harbour mouth, the others were deterred from making any farther attempt, and all again returned to the bay.

The vessels we were in were loaded with military stores, which precluded us from getting below; and having neither provisions no water for such a number as we amounted to, we were carried alongside the frigate, in order to be taken on board again, until such time as the tide served, or at least to get some provisions, for night was now approaching, and we had tasted nothing since morning. But that was nothing to the honourable Captain D----, commander of the frigate, who swore that we should neither come on board, nor have provisions; and if we did not immediately sheer off, he would sink us to the bottom. It not being safe to argue much with a man having thirty-six pieces of cannon at his command, and especially with one so willing to use them as the honourable captain seemed to be, we immediately sheered off, as he termed it; and during the night kept at a respectable distance from this man-of-war.

Having no other resource than patience, which, by the by, is a virtue rarely found in men, exhausted by want and fatigue; and especially when galled and borne down with heavy burdens on their backs – for we were still standing accoutred, with our knapsacks on and arms in our hand – there being no place to sit, but were so closely jammed that we had difficulty in standing. Having no alternative but to wait the coming tide, the night was got over surprisingly quiet, with the exception of a few philippics against the captain of the frigate; at which, although a countryman of my own, I was nothing sorry.

The morning's dawn found us all in good spirits, and with sanguine hopes of being landed at high water. Immediately at full tide we once more made for port, but owing to a dangerous surf on the bar, all our efforts at landing proved unavailing; so that after an equally unsuccessful attempt with that of the preceding day, we were under the necessity of again returning to the bay.

Our situation was now become truly alarming. Twenty-eight hours had elapsed since we had tasted victuals, and the prospect before us afforded no hope of getting any. The surf which prevented our landing, might continue for days, nay, even for weeks; and the captain of the frigate, having once got rid, now swore that he neither had, nor would, take anything ado with us. Having returned to the bay, the men consulted amongst themselves for some time, and murmurings, 'not loud but deep', were heard, which in a short time increased in strength, till the smouldering flame at last burst forth, when cries of 'The frigate! The frigate! Let us board the frigate!' were heard on all sides. This was a bold and daring proposition, but which, I believe, would have been attempted, had not a boat appeared, as if making towards us from the shore, to which all eyes were instantly and eagerly turned, every one anticipating it a harbinger of good tidings. As it drew near, it was perceived to contain three men, two of which were Portuguese. The third by his dress appeared to be an Englishman, and was acting steersman; but, when within a few yards of our vessel, veered off towards the frigate, which considerably lengthened every countenance amongst us. They were instantly hailed by a number of voices at once, to which they paid no attention. Enraged at such conduct, an officer belonging to a Scotch regiment, seized a rifle from a man standing near him, swearing he would shoot the fellows if they did not come alongside. Having loaded the piece, he laid it on the railing of the vessel, in order to take a good aim; but, recollecting himself, he gave the piece back to the owner, telling him he was a better marksman; that he was to take a good aim, and shoot the fellow at the helm through the head. The soldier fired, but instead of shooting the steersman as desired, the ball entered, and shattered an arm of one of the Portuguese. The boat immediately lay to.

On coming alongside, a great altercation took place between the officer and steersman, who proved to be an Englishman employed in the commissariat department. The officer demanded to be taken ashore in the boat. The other swore he would report the officer to the commandant at Figuera. At this our champion got enraged, and without more ado, leapt into the boat. A scuffle immediately ensued, during which the boat upset, and all that was in it precipitated into the sea.

Prompt and speedy assistance being given, our fiery Scot, and his opponents, were quickly extricated from their untoward situation. The parties received no other damage than a hearty ducking and the loss of the boat, which had gone to the bottom. At the Englishman's request, a boat was given to take him on shore, on condition that he would state our situation to the commandant. He faithfully executed his mission; for by two hours after he was gone, a number of boats came alongside, into which we immediately entered. Instead of making for the port we sailed along the coast about a mile, where we were obliged to leap waist deep into the sea, and after plunging and wading, amongst rocks and sea-weed, we at last most joyfully set foot on 'terra firma.'

On arriving at the town, my master was quartered in a respectable house, where, over a good dinner, to which a pitcher of most excellent wine lent its cheering influence, I soon forgot the privations and fatigue I had been exposed to. Next morning, we left Figuera, and proceeded to Montemor; and on the following day we entered the city of Coimbra,[5] where the surgeon was lodged in the house of a priest, named Senior Padra Manuel de Lima.

5 Coimbra was Portugal's former capital, with a preserved medieval old town and a fine university.

Chapter 10

A Bachelor – Three Old Maids – an Anecdote

> Thus to relieve the wretched was his pride;
> And even his failings lean'd to virtue's side;
> But, in his duty, prompt at every call,
> He watch'd and wept, he prayed, and felt for all.
> GOLDSMITH

As I will at a future period have occasion to speak of the good old father, and the individuals composing his household, I will proceed with my narrative, without making mention of the kindness and pleasure I experienced in his house. Let it therefore suffice, that we left Coimbra with strong injunctions from our venerable host and his amiable sister, that if ever we came that way again, to make their house our home during our stay in Coimbra, assuring us at the same time we would meet with a hearty welcome.

Proceeding on our march, we soon entered a ragged and mountainous region, but agreeably diversified with fertile valleys, and numerous villages, which at a distance bore a romantic and beautiful appearance. On entering them, however, they were invariably found wretched places of abode; their streets choked full of mud and filth. The mode adopted by these villagers to avoid the mud with which their streets abound, must be confessed a rare and ingenuous contrivance. As they never so much as dream of removing the nuisance, the roads through the villages sometimes get absolutely impassable. At which time a number of cars are dispatched to the mountains, to collect heath and broom, a stratum of which being laid on the streets, serves for a time to cover the mud. As soon as this is trod under foot, and the roads become again impassable, another dose of broom is repeated; and so on, one layer above another, until I believe they would get completely buried, if the heavy rain which falls at times did not wash part of it away.

On account of a deficiency of surgeons at Celorico, my master was detained there to assist in attending the sick who were very numerous in that place. When he had been ten days there, he was ordered to Coimbra with a party of invalids, consisting of about three hundred men. We accordingly proceeded on our way, my master walking along with the cars, humanely attending and assisting the sick, as occasion required; while I was mounted on a stout donkey, with which I ambled along the road in great style.

Having reached Riva, four leagues above Coimbra, the sick were embarked in boats, in order to go down the Mondego to that city. The boats being crowded and no convenience found for the animal I rode, I was ordered by my master to proceed by land. Intending to avail himself of the invitation given by the reverend father, I was desired to go direct to the house of Senior [sic] Padra Manuel de Lima.

I had not proceeded above a league on my way, ere a considerable river, on which was a ferryboat, crossed my path. No person being near to take me over, I attempted to ford the stream, driving Dickey before me. When nearly midway through, the water began to assume a deep and rapid appearance, by which the animal was carried off his feet, and instantly borne along with the current. Being apprehensive of the danger the animal was in, I immediately plunged into the depths, and with difficulty gained the opposite bank. Following the stream, I soon overtook poor Dickey, who had got to the side, but owing to the steep nature of the shore was unable to effect a landing, although he made great exertions. Afraid of losing the creature altogether, I laid hold of his fore legs, in order to assist him, when he again fell back into the river, drawing his master after. Having rolled over each other several times, I caught hold of a bush, and extricated myself from the soft embraces of my companion. A short way below this the stream joined another of a larger size, at the confluence of which a beach was formed on the side I was on, where the poor animal was carried, and managed to crawl out in a very exhausted state. Here I rested two hours that he might recruit his strength. I then set forward, and arrived in the evening at my old quarters in Coimbra, where I found my master, he having arrived a few minutes before me.

About a week after, my master fell ill of a lingering fever, and in consequence was detained above three months in the city, which time I passed very pleasantly in the family of our reverend landlord. But that the reader may have an idea how I spent my time, and the pleasure I experienced, I must give a brief sketch of the individuals composing the family, they being the sole company I kept, having intercourse with no other in Coimbra.

The Senior Padra, as master of the mansion, and on account of his virtues, well deserves the precedence in this review of his household. He might be said to have arrived at the utmost verge of human existence, being at the time three score and ten. As canon of the cathedral of La Trinidad, he had for many years enjoyed a rich and fruitful benefice; a large portion of which he expended in alleviating the distress of the unfortunate, and ameliorating the condition of the necessitous and indigent. He was a firm adherent to the Church of Rome, giving implicit belief to holy mother church, yet had none of that bigotry and zeal which excludes all sects but his own from the favour of heaven. Though living in the daily practice of the virtues and duties incumbent on the Christian, yet he disclaimed anything like supererogation, a favourite tenet with his church. He seemed to count his own righteousness as filthy rags, living in the lively hope of a blessed immortality, through the merits and atonement of a divine intercessor.

His mode of living was simple and temperate, even to a degree that might have vied with the most abstemious anchorite. Wholly abstaining from animal food, he confined himself to a vegetable diet, a large portion of which was fruit. Wine he seldom or never tasted; but at night, previous to retiring to rest, he generally partook of a glass of negus,[1] and while sipping it, frequently smoked a segar,[2] being very fond of one. In stature he was above the middle size, slenderly made, and when young I doubt not must have been handsome. But now, borne down by age, he stooped considerably; while his thin and silvery locks, partly shading his pale and furrowed cheek, gave an air of reverence to his person, which, when arrayed in the sacerdotal robe, was dignified and commanding. Such was Manual de Lima, of whom it might be truly said, he was a man according to Gods own heart; who, living in the fear of his Maker, had peace and goodwill to all men.

Being affable, easy of access, and fond of conversation, I passed many a pleasant and agreeable hour in his company. Previous to this I had acquired as much of the language as enabled me to converse with tolerable fluency. Our conversation turned chiefly on common-place subjects, but never on religion. He never once hinted at the merits of his, or the demerits of mine: which was a fruitful topic with the generality of his countrymen, who perhaps, having more zeal on their tongues than he, had less religion at their hearts.

Senora Agatha, sister to the good canon, and residing with him, was a vestal of fifty-seven. Though arrived at this advanced age, with her maiden sweets inappropriate, she was no snarler, nor yet devotee, a common channel through which disappointed damsels vent their spleen. On the contrary, she was cheerful and content with her state; and was mild, gentle, and affable to all. She seldom went abroad, but devoted the most of her time to the needle. the whole proceeds of which was bestowed on the poor and necessitous; and scarcely a week passed but she assisted in clothing the widow and orphan.

Theresa and Joanna, were sisters, and the only domestics retained in the family. They were both held in high estimation by their master, for their fidelity. They had been many years in the family, and were regarded more as companions and relations, than servants. Theresa was still a maid, although fifty summer suns had passed over her head; and time, that all potent destroyer of power, strength, and beauty, and indeed, of all the world can afford, had plucked the virgin bloom from her cheek, which was now blanched and pale; and her once raven locks were fast assuming a silvery hue. She was fond of conversation, and gave vent to her ideas with all that volubility so peculiar to women. Although so corpulent that she had not been down stairs above once for a number of years, yet she was healthy and

1 Port mixed with hot water, spices and sugar.
2 Cigar.

cheerful, to a degree seldom found in people of her age and condition. Joanna, her sister, was strong and masculine in her person, yet had many amiable traits in her character, being modest, mild, and good natured. Having seen two score years pass over her, without having been once solicited to accompany anyone through life in the holy bands of wedlock, she had relinquished all hopes of matrimony; and with a resolution worthy of herself, had determined to die as she had lived, a pure and spotless virgin.

In the company of this triumvirate of old maids, I passed my time most happily; conversing with one, dancing with a second, and singing Scottish airs to a third; and was by all regarded and treated as one of the family. Once, while sitting conversing with Senora Agatha, I chanced to ask if she and her brother had remained at Coimbra, when the French entered it, after the Battle of Busaco? In a hurried and agitated tone, she replied, 'Oh Senior Gulliame, (Mr William) that was indeed a dreadful time – the ruin of many, and nearly proving fatal to our family in particular; for we were in the hands of those that sought to do us harm, whose tenderest mercies were cruelty. But we were saved by the goodness and mercy of that being, who guides and protects them that put their trust in him, from shame, and death, when it seemed inevitable.' I begged her to relate the particulars of her history at this eventful period, to which, after some hesitation she consented. The following is the substance of what she stated.

Upon the reduction of Almeida, and the subsequent advance of the enemy on Coimbra, the inhabitants of that city were thrown into the utmost consternation. Numbers left the place 'pon receiving the first intelligence, while others, having more confidence in the valour and prowess of the British arms, remained with fear and trembling. Amongst the latter was our host, Senior Manuel, and his family; who, hoping for the best, remained at home, without securing any of their effects. On the arrival of our army at Busaco, which is but a few leagues from Coimbra, the intelligence of our having made a stand, in order to oppose the farther progress of the enemy, inspired the people with confidence and hope; but, when the result of the action was known, and the British columns began to pour through the town, all were seized with terror and dismay, and those that were able fled from the fury of the advancing foe. The canon and his family not being prepared for such an event, hastily packed up a few necessaries, and left their peaceful home to the rapacious and cruel invaders of their country. He arrived in time to witness the destruction of the bridge, which was blown up by the retreating army, but which at the same time, deprived him of the means of escaping. There was no other way he could retire by land, and as for the river, every boat had been put in requisition by the fugitives, who had long since moved down the Mondego.

Being in a sad dilemma, and not knowing what course to pursue, he stood on the street consulting with his family, when the piercing cry arose from the crowd 'The enemy! the enemy!' and immediately the advanced guard of the French, which were cavalry, rushed down the street towards the bridge, cutting down all that stood in the way. At this critical juncture, the good canon sought refuge in the cathedral, where he had for many years officiated; and where, in his ministerial capacity, he had so often imparted the consolations of religion to his flock. Having secreted himself and family in a recess, or cavity, behind the grand altar, he there waited the issue of this eventful day. They had not been long in their hiding place, ere they saw the cathedral filled with the French soldiery, who apparently meant to make their quarters good in this place of worship. In a short time they kindled several fires on the floor, and in order to supply them with fuel, pulled down all the wood they could reach. Not content with what they had got, they proceeded to the altar itself, which they immediately stripped of its images, and ornaments, and committed them at once to the devouring element. As they went on with the work of destruction, the whole of the altar was brought down, which exposed to view the dismayed Canon, and his no less terrified family, who were immediately dragged forth from their place of refuge, into the body of the Church. After the myrmidons of rapine and bloodshed had vented the most gross invectives and dreadful imprecations on their unoffending and guiltless victims, they proceeded to adopt still more brutal and sanguinary measures. While one party abused the females with all the malice and fury of demons, another branded the old man for a hypocrite, and one who richly deserved death for the lies and impositions he had for so many years practiced upon mankind; and that he might not have it in his power to do so again, they would instantly hang him up for a spectacle to the world in general, and to his order in particular. This threat they put into immediate execution. A silken cord which hung from the lofty and vaulted roof, to which a large chandelier was attached, being thought a proper and ready instrument, was fastened round the shrivelled neck, of the pious and benevolent Priest, who had already taken a farewell look, (for he was not permitted to speak) of his weeping sister and domestics, who were about to be exposed to the two extremes suggested by appetite and cruelty. His soul he had committed to the care and keeping of his maker, from whom he mentally prayed for forgiveness to his enemies and executioners, who drawing tight the rope, their victim hung suspended. At that instant an officer of high rank entered, and immediately ordered the sufferer to be cut down; and who, when he had informed himself of the affair, sent the now grateful old man and his overjoyed friends under a safe escort to his own house, which they found occupied by two French officers, who protected them from further injury.

My master's health being again firmly established, we prepared to march, in order to join the army, from which I had been a long time absent.[3] When taking leave of my friends, which I did with the utmost regret, and which I have the vanity to believe, was reciprocal, I was presented by Senora Agatha, with a small ivory crucifix, richly ornamented with silver, and on which was an image of the Saviour, composed of the same precious material. 'This Trifle', said the amiable woman, 'I give in token of the esteem I have for you. But why do I call it a trifle? – may I be

3 Indeed! About ten or eleven months by this point.

forgiven for so doing! The blessed cross, though it be composed of the basest materials – of stone, wood, or even straw – is in price far above rubies; and is of inestimable value to all true believers. May this which I now bestow, have a tendency to avert all danger and difficulty the receiver may ever be menaced with. May the God of armies protect and guard you in the hour of battle; and when the sanguinary conflict, which has so long distracted the world, and been so ruinous to our beloved Portugal, is ended, may you be returned to your country, and once more enjoy the society of your parents and friends. Farewell! May He bless you who can and will do it, if asked in sincerity and truth – farewell! Farewell!'

Leaving Coimbra, we passed Condeixa, Pombal, and Ponto Marcello, and arrived at Abrantes, seated on a hill by the banks of the Tagus, over which at that place was a bridge of boats, which we crossed on our way to Villa Valha,[4] where we re-crossed the same river by a similar conveyance. At Castel Branco we halted for two days, when we again set forward, and after a long and fatiguing march, joined our regiment, then quartered in the village of Al de Defont;[5] but from which we removed in a few days after to another about a league distant. In this latter village my feelings were destined to undergo a great change – a change which has had an influence on my conduct ever since. The cause and effect will be found in the next chapter.

4 Vila Velha de Rodão, on the Tagus River north-east of Lisbon.

5 Aldeia de Ponte, on the Spanish border just south of Fuentes d'Oñoro. This would fix his return to the 45th as being in August 1811.

Chapter 11

Albergaria – Love a la Mode – Skirmish

Love should be pure –
Harmless as pilgrim's kisses at the shrine
Of virgin martyrs – holy as the thoughts
Of dying saints when angels hover o'er them
Calm and serene – the zephyr, and not
The Whirlwind of the soul.
ANONYMOUS

Albergaria,[1] the village now occupied by the regiment, was situated in Leon, once an independent kingdom, but long since politically attached to, and forming one of the extensive provinces of the Spanish Dominions. The village itself was small and straggling, and bore a very mean appearance. The inhabitants were poor, and had been made still more so by the predatory excursions of the garrison of Ciudad Rodrigo, which fortress was but a few leagues distant. Although but three miles from our late quarters in Portugal, a considerable difference appeared in the customs and manners of the two people. The Portuguese were slovenly in their dress, in the interior economy of their household, and indeed in everything else – the lower orders lousy in the extreme. But here the young Spaniard appeared gaily and neatly dressed, with sashed doublet, and scarlet, or leathern, girdle round his waist. Instead of the heavy 'sapato', or shoe, sandals were worn, made of undressed leather, with hair and all on, just as it came off the animal. But unlike 'Bryan O'Lins' breeches, which had the woolly side in, the Spaniard, with his sandals, wears the hairy side out. The interior of their houses displayed a degree of cleanliness unknown to their neighbours the Portuguese.

Fernando Silvero, in whose house my master was quartered, rented at a low rate a few acres of land; on which, by the industry of himself and two sons, his family were enabled to live in tolerable ease and comfort. Besides his two sons, he was

1 Albergaria is modern La Albergueria de Argeñán, just across the Spanish border from Aldeia da Ponte.

the father of a lovely daughter named Rosa, the pride and joy of her parents. This pretty village maid was yet in her teens, possessing all that glow of health and beauty which innocence can bestow. The day I first beheld this charming girl, was that on which I first entered her native village. As I approached her father's house she stood on the threshold. When I drew near, and could discover the mildness of her countenance, and the grace of her person, new and strange sensations affected me. My mind was confused and flurried; I felt the crimson current mount my cheek, and when I essayed to speak my tongue refused its office. The contour of her face was oval; her complexion of that hue which is termed brunette, but inclining to a light olive. Her soft, moist, and cherried lips, when opened, displayed a case of teeth that rivalled the finest ivory; and the bloom that sat upon her cheek, which vied with the rose in beauty; and her dark sparkling eyes, with the black glossy ringlets which shaded her high and polished forehead, were enough to warm the heart of the most rigid ascetic: while;

> A native grace
> Sat fair proportioned on her polished limbs
> Veil'd in a simple robe, their best attire,
> Beyond the pomp of dress; for loveliness
> Needs not the foreign aid of ornament,
> But is, when unadorned, adorned the most.[2]

As a minute detail of the progressive intimacy that ensued between us, and which kindled in time to a mutual flame, might prove uninteresting, I will pass over the incidents of this endearing period. May it therefore suffice – in a short time I found her sentiments reciprocal with mine, and I basked in the sunshine of her smiles, and revelled in all the luxury of a chaste and genuine passion, 'with joys that guilty pleasure never felt.'

> O ye! whose melting hearts are form'd to prove
> The trembling ecstasies of genuine love;
> When, with delicious agony, the thought,
> Is to the verge of high delirium wrought;
> Your secret sympathy alone can tell
> What raptures when the throbbing bosom swell;
> O'er all the nerves what tender tumults roll,
> While love with sweet enchantment melts the soul.[3]

2 From James Thomson's poem cycle *The Four Seasons*, published in 1730. The extract is from 'Autumn'.

3 From *The Shipwreck*, poem by William Falconer, dated 1762.

But sublunary joys are vain and of short duration – a potent rival soon appeared to disturb my dream of happiness. This intruder on my peace was no less a personage than the first surgeon of the regiment. He was a native of the sister kingdom, and was in the habit of arrogating great importance to himself, on account of a long line of ancestors from which he had descended; being, as he represented himself, a scion of a noble house, whose family name is preceded by the letter O – a most appropriate designation for this their relative, for he 'owed' everyone who was credulous enough to believe his promises of payment. But notwithstanding the airs he assumed, his pedigree might easily be traced – the vulgarity and grossness of his manners furnishing ample proof of his mean extraction. His conversation was truly disgusting, being interlarded with oaths and imprecations – a vice unworthy of any man, but particularly of one walking in the sphere, and laying claim to the title of a gentleman. In his professional capacity he was unfeeling and brutal; in proof of which I will give an instance witnessed by myself. He was about to perform an operation of phlebotomy,[4] and having got his instruments prepared, he turned himself round to the poor fellow, who stood behind him, and in a scowling manner ordered the sick man to come near for a b------r, till he would bleed him like a bullock!

Being mess-mate with my master,[5] this Surgeon O'[Connell][6] generally dined at our quarters, and had many opportunities of seeing my landlord's daughter. His base mind having suggested the idea of destroying the peace, and sullying the purity of the innocent Rosa, he accordingly put in practice every method his sensual appetite could devise; but all in vain. Her nobleness of soul withstood all his blandishments and promises, and meeting with a rebuff he little expected, at length gave up his unhallowed attempt.

He was irritable to an extreme degree, and when under the influence of passion his countenance had more the appearance of a fiend than a human being. Rosa had seen him in such a state more than once, for which she despised him; and it is more than probable, if he had known how much she abhorred him, he never would have attempted what he did. Having discovered the intimacy that existed between us, he entirely attributed the failure of his machinations to me, and from that hour marked me for his victim. But I foiled him in all his schemes, and escaped the snares he had the meanness to lay for me. But I was no longer the mild and timid boy I had hitherto been. Love had imparted to his votary a new impulse, and armed him with resolution and courage, to repel every aggression that tended

4 The act of drawing blood, or 'bleeding'.

5 By this comment, William confirms that he was acting as a man-servant to an officer, a capacity in which generally only steady and reliable men were selected.

6 Surgeon Richard O'Connell, the surgeon of the 1/45th from April to August 1813. There is a problem with the timing here. The 45th were quartered at Albergaria in the periods August 1811 and February to May 1812, a full year before O'Connell joined the regiment. It is likely that William compounded several later memories into the one.

to violate against the virtue, or disturb the peace of his mistress. Regardless of all consequences I had formed the resolution, at some convenient season, if this miscreant persisted in his endeavours to injure either of us, to make him bite the dust, and seek the shades below. In a short time after, however, he left the regiment; since which I have never heard of him.[7]

About this time, I was near encountering a foe of another description, but whose nature, perhaps, was not so savage as that of my late adversary. One day, while employed in cutting forage in the vicinity of the village, and finding the grass short and thin, I mounted a wall in order to look round for better. In doing so I perceived a large wolf amongst some bushes, within twenty yards of me. He sat upon his hind legs and eyed me eagerly. I grasped the sickle firmly which was in my hand, determined to defend myself as well as I could. He seemed to get animated, and to my imagination his eyeballs began to roll and glare most terribly, and every moment I expected him to seize me for his prey, for I was well aware it would be an unequal combat. At length rising, he turned himself round, and walked leisurely away, growling deeply as he went. These animals were very numerous in the neighbourhood, and at night frequented the place where our cattle were killed, voraciously devouring the offal left on the ground.

In a short time after this, a more formidable enemy than either of these appeared, which caused me to leave behind all I held dear on earth. Intelligence having been received, that a great quantity of provisions, ammunition, and other stores, escorted by a strong convoy, were on the road from Salamanca to Ciudad Rodrigo, intended for the supply of that place, it was determined we should advance, and endeavour to intercept the enemy before they reached their destination. Orders being given to march in the morning, I past the greater part of the preceding night with her my mind adored; and after exchanging vows of eternal love and fidelity, we tore ourselves asunder in all the agony of despair.

With grief o'erwhelmed, we parted twice in vain,
And urg'd by strong attraction met again.
At last my cruel fortune torn apart,
While tender passion stream'd in either heart;
Our eyes transfix'd with agonizing look,
One sad farewell, one last embrace we took!
Forlorn of hope the lovely maid I left,
Pensive and pale, of every joy bereft![8]

7 O'Connell joined the medical staff of the Peninsula army in August 1813, and served in Netherlands and France during 1815 without being present at Waterloo. He lived in County Antrim and went on half-pay after 1815; he did not receive the Military General Service Medal which suggests he was probably dead by 1847.

8 Also from *The Shipwreck* by Falconer.

At dawn of day I left Albergaria, (a spot I shall ever remember with lively regret,) and in company with the brigade, proceeded on the march in a state bordering on destruction, almost unconscious of what I did – and it was several days ere my mind recovered its former elasticity. Advancing on our march, on the 5th of September 1811,[9] we passed Rodrigo, putting that fortress in a state of blockade, for we had now got between the garrison and the army. The division was put into cantonments in several villages, where we remained during the day, but in order to make sure of our prize, we encamped during the night. On the 21st the French advanced in great force from Salamanca, towards the same place, when Lord Wellington took up such a position with his army, as might enable him accurately to ascertain the strength of the enemy, and to resist their attack, or retire, as he might judge most prudent. On the morning of the 25th the French attacked and drove in the light posts on the left of the British lines, and in consequence of this partial success they ventured to cross the Aguada,[10] but were in turn attacked and compelled to retire. This morning we were not permitted to return to our quarters as we had hitherto done, but making a retrograde movement, were drawn up on a height above Rodrigo, with that fortress directly in our front. We soon perceived issuing from the town, a strong column, consisting of thirty-five squadrons of cavalry, followed by fourteen battalions of infantry, the whole supported by eighteen pieces of cannon. With this overwhelming force the enemy made a furious attack upon the left brigade of our division, when the greater part of the Portuguese brigade of artillery,[11] attached to the division, were taken, the men standing by their guns until literally cut down by the sabres of the enemy. They, however, did not long retain their prize, for the 5th regiment, having made a prompt and gallant charge, almost immediately returned the cannon, along with some prisoners. Finding it impossible to cope with such a force, and no reinforcements near, being some leagues in advance of our army, we formed squares by regiments, and retired unbroken before the enemy.

A more singular spectacle than that we now exhibited perhaps did not present itself during the whole war. While retreating the French advanced corps surrounded us on all sides, but being inferior in numbers, did not dare to attack, only endeavouring to retard our progress as much as possible until the main body would come up. They kept so near, however, that on riding past one of them struck my elbow with his foot. When marching across the plain from Albedon,[12] the enemy, on a rising ground on the right, brought their cannon to bear upon our

9 In August 1811 the 45th were headquartered at Aldeia da Ponte on the Portuguese/Spanish border; therefore, some companies must have been cantoned at Albergaria, about five kilometres to the east and inside Spain proper.

10 The river Agueda.

11 These were two companies of Portuguese artillery commanded by Major Victor von Arentschildt attached to the 3rd Division, who in fact lost only five men wounded in the affair.

12 This is the celebrated action at El Bodon on 25 September 1811

squares, which annoyed us considerably. But keeping the most admirable order, though for two hours surrounded by our enemies, we at last arrived in the vicinity of Fuente Ginaldo,[13] where part of our army having come up, the French fell back.

By this day's encounter the division had several killed and wounded; while at the same time the enemy carried off a quantity of our stores and baggage, together with the greater part of the women belonging to our brigade. Their co-mates, however, did not seem deeply affected at this circumstance. The same night when seated round the fire, an Irishman, who had lost his wife, being condoled with on the occasion, replied, 'Faith, boys, I would not have cared a straw about it at all at all, but Jenny the b---h has got my pipe away with her.'

We continued in camp the whole of the next day, during which the greater part of our army arrived. It was then expected we would engage the enemy, who were still in our view, but when evening was come, we marched off, and continued to retreat the whole night. Next morning, we halted to cook some victuals, which we immediately set about. Numbers were employed hewing wood, while others were drawing water, and not a few kindling fires and getting the kettles in order. In the midst of all this preparation for breakfast, the enemy, whom we imagined had been deceived by our nocturnal movements, now menaced us with an immediate attack, when we stood to our arms, and were once more obliged to decamp. After retreating about half a league we halted, and forming line advanced under cover of the artillery, which were posted on a height in front of the village of Alfeatte. The enemy sustained the attack with great courage and intrepidity, and continued to fight for two hours bravely. At length British valour prevailed against all opposition; the French fell back, and were pursued by our cavalry and light troops to the banks of the Aguada. The enemy then filed off towards Salamanca and Placentia, and our army went into cantonments.

At this time our brigade was quartered in a small, mean, dirty village;[14] and being extremely crowded, our situation was very uncomfortable, while our allowance of bread was by no means calculated to improve it, being curtailed from sixteen ounces to eight, and that of mouldy biscuit. This supply was very inadequate for the subsistence of young men, such as the army is in general composed of; and especially to us, who were undergoing so many hardships and fatigue, and exposed almost continually to the open air. But I suppose it was our commander's intention to whet our appetite, and render us ferocious at the approaching siege and storming of Ciudad Rodrigo, for which preparations were in train; a number of the men being employed making factions and gabions for that important event.

When we had been a few days in quarters, the women who were taken in the late affair at Albedon,[15] were escorted to our outposts by a party of the enemy's cavalry,

13 Fuenteguinaldo, about fifteen kilometres south-west of Ciudad Rodrigo.

14 Probably Fuenteguinaldo in Spain, or somewhere very close to that place.

15 El Bodon.

and were thus again restored to their 'loving' husbands. Many a course joke and broad surmise were passed regarding the treatment they had experienced during their captivity.

In a short time, our regiment left this detested village, and returned to Albergaria, where we occupied our former quarters. I had the happiness to find my Rosa kind and true, and for a time enjoyed all the felicity an ardent, mutual, and chaste love can bestow.[16]

16 This would be the period October to December 1811.

Map 3 Route of the 45th Foot in 1811.

Chapter 12

A Miser – Capture of Ciudad Rodrigo – Pillage

The trench is dug; the cannon's breath,
Wings the far kissing globe of death;
Fast whirl the fragments from the wall,
Which crumbles with the ponderous ball;
And from that wall the foe replies,
O'er dusky plains and smoky skies,
With fires that answer fast and well.
BYRON[1]

In Albergaria the regiment remained three months, during which I was often perplexed in mind respecting the line of conduct I ought to pursue in regard to Rosa Silvera. At time I was resolved, whatever might be the consequence, to unite my destiny with hers and run all hazards. But, upon mature reflection, my heart sickened at the recollections of the privations, fatigue and danger, she would be exposed to in following the army. I therefore, by the time we had orders to march, resolved to defer that important event to a more distant and auspicious period. Having exchanged vows of mutual fidelity, I left her father's house, in which I had passed so many days of delight, and in company with the regiment proceeded on the march, during a heavy snow storm which continued nearly the whole day. Arriving at a village long after dark, my master was quartered, with three other officers, in a most uncomfortable lodging. On entering the house, we found it nearly dark, and to appearance deserted by its inhabitants, for we could discover no one in or about it. The only intimation of it having been recently occupied, was a few embers that still gleamed in the hearth, but not affording sufficient light to discover any object.

When advancing towards it, a squeaking, tremulous voice, that issued from beyond the fire place, demanded what we wanted? Being civilly informed of what

1 An extract from Byron's *The Siege of Corinth*, published in 1816.

we were, and what we wanted, our landlord (for so he proved to be) got into a rage, and swore he had no accommodation for such numbers as we appeared to be; he having neither wood for firing nor anything else. At length he was prevailed upon to light the cruise, which he did with much growling and grumbling, muttering all the while about the expense of it, when we beheld a most woeful figure indeed. The very prototype of misery and wretchedness stood before us in the person of our landlord. In stature, if standing upright, he might be about the middle size, but stooping considerably, he had a dwarfish appearance; while his body resembled a pole stuck into a bundle of rags. His countenance had such a squalid and cadaverous hue, so meagre and thin, with eyes full of rheum, and edged round with red, that we readily believed the assertions he continued to make of his poverty. His habitation had no better appearance than himself, being nearly void of anything in the shape of furniture; the walls were tapestried round with spider's nets; and the floor, which was clay, was both cold and damp. This house of misery was indeed poor cheer for us, who had been marching all day under a heavy fall of snow. But there was no alternative, so we began to make the best of it, by gathering wood, which we took where we could find it, and soon had a comfortable fire, a thing, I dare say, had not been in the house for many a day before. After supper we rolled ourselves in the blankets, masters and men, and stretched on the floor, slept soundly till day-light. In the morning I learned from a neighbour, that, notwithstanding the semblance of poverty that surrounded the old Don, he possessed considerable property in the village, and was supposed to have treasure hidden somewhere. Be that as it may, it was at all events a dead letter to him, for he could not, or would not, make use of it.

Leaving this prince of misers to perish with his gold, we proceeded on our march, and next day crossed the Aguada, and took up our quarters in a village two leagues east of Rodrigo. Next day, being the 8th of January, 1812, it was announced to us by an order from the Commander-in-Chief, that, in order to execute the plan of operations he had formed, it was necessary to gain possession of Ciudad Rodrigo, which we were now on the eve of investing; and on this arduous and important occasion he felt assured we would signalize ourselves like men and Britons, as we had done in former times. A severe frost having set in, which rendered the season unfit for camp, the divisions engaged at the siege were to remain in quarters, and take the duty twenty-four hours alternately. On the evening of the same day, a detachment of the Light Division stormed and carried the redoubt on the hill of St Francisca, took some prisoners, and put the rest to the sword; themselves having six killed, and fourteen men and three officers wounded. In consequence of this success, our troops were enabled to break ground within six-hundred yards of the place, and notwithstanding the heavy fire of shot and shell from the garrison, continued to push on their operations with great vigour.

On the 11th of the month, and third day of the siege, our division took its turn of this hazardous duty. At our quarters was heard the sound of cannon growling like thunder; but as we approached the scene of action it became loud and discordant.

On our way thither, the road crossed a height, from which we descried the city of Rodrigo; where

> Like hills th'aspiring ramparts rise on high,
> Like valleys at their feet the trenches lie;
> Batt'ries on batt'ries guard each fatal pass,
> Threat'ning destruction; rows of hollow brass,
> Tube behind tube, the dreadful entrance keep,
> While in their wombs ten thousand thunders sleep.[2]

From this height we could perceive thousands of our troops busily employed in deepening the trench, strengthening the breastworks, and rearing batteries, that were to open a passage into the town, from the ramparts of which issued volumes of smoke and fire; while the hissing ball and the crashing bomb, dealt death and destruction to the besiegers, who had not got their guns to bear on the massive wall.

As we approached the trench, I began to reflect on the fatigues and dangers my inconsiderate folly had exposed me to – a cold clammy sweat bedewed my limbs; I got sick at heart, and in a word, sincerely wished myself at home. I conceived myself like one plunged into a whirlpool, and now fast approaching the centre of the vortex in which I was to be engulfed. These reflections, I must confess, partly arose from fear, and from the novelty of the scene I was about to be engaged in, for a siege is a different affair from a field engagement. On entering the works an accident occurred, which was in no way calculated to allay the perturbed state of mind I then laboured under. When passing two Portuguese soldiers, who were carrying a box of ammunition, a shell from the enemy alighted on their burden, by the shock of which they were thrown to the ground. The box was shivered to pieces, and its contents strewed about, amongst which the bomb continued to whirl a few seconds with amazing rapidity; then with a horrible crash it exploded, by which nineteen men were killed and wounded. This was an awful spectacle. Some of the sufferers were dreadfully scorched and burned by the explosion of the powder, while other were shockingly cut and mangled by the pieces of shell that flew in all directions. One man lay completely decapitated, his head being some yards distant from his body. I was not long in the trench, however, until I recovered my natural buoyancy of spirit, and laboured hard at throwing up a breastwork, which was oftener than once levelled by the shot and shell of the garrison. During the day I was several time literally buried with the earth thrown up by the bursting of shells. A considerable number were killed and wounded, although not near so many as I anticipated. After being twelve hours exposed to eminent peril and hard labour,

2 From *The Campaign*, a poem written to celebrate the Duke of Marlborough's military successes in 1705, by Joseph Addison.

we were at midnight relieved by the other half of the division, which, during the day, had been stationed in the rear, and occupied their ground for the night.

As I stretched myself on the hard and frozen ground, I thought it very cold cheer for an 'Old New-year's day' morning.[3] On this day, thought I, will my townsmen celebrate the commencement of the new year, with every demonstration of joy. Even at the very hour many a juvenile party will issue forth to hail the infant year, and in company with their neighbours and friends pass the day in jollity and endearing conviviality; while I, doomed by thoughtless folly, lie shivering on the bare cold ground, exposed to all the rigours of a winter morning, in the midst of strangers, and in the front of enemies. While thus ruminating on the disasters my folly had launched me into, and as I turned me on my icy bed, I cursed the imprudence that had made me the tool and dupe of ambitious and designing men, whose cabals and intrigues lay waste the world; for whose aggrandizement rivers of human blood has flown, and who are as callous to the sufferings of humanity, as if their victims were inanimate, void of all sensation and feeling, and altogether of a different species from their rulers. But not withstanding these galling reflections, the chilling and piercing cold, the roar of cannon, and the noise and tumult that surrounded me, I soon sunk into the arms of Morpheus, and in the embraces of the sleepy God enjoyed that in vision, which, while awake, I had regretted the absence. In fancy I was far from the scenes I had been engaged in the preceding day; far distant from devastation and bloodshed, and at home enjoying the sweet company of friends, relations, and companions. My happiness too was greatly enhanced by Rosa Silvera being the principle personage in this drama of fancy. But awaking at dawn of day, sorrow returned, and I found myself so stiffened with cold that I could scarcely rise.

Our next turn for duty being on the 15th, we moved on to the scene of action, but being for the night work, we remained in camp until evening. I was attached to the covering party, which consisted of three companies, and sent in advance of the works, there to remain until daylight. The ground we occupied was a hollow that intervened between our batteries and the town, being about a hundred yards distant from either. Our duty here was to keep a sharp lookout for the enemy, and in case of a sortie by the garrison, to give an immediate alarm. Along the side of the town we occupied, was stationed a cordon of double sentinels, with orders to be on the alert, but at the same time to keep stretched on the ground, for fear of discovery by the enemy, and to be relieved every hour by the companies in the hollow. I was posted along with a young Englishman, who might be about my own age, with whom I lay close for some time, viewing the astounding scene; a scene which none but those that have been similarly situated, can form a just conception of. On each side were employed above fifty pieces of heavy cannon, the balls of

3 An old custom from the Julian Calendar, and obviously still practiced in Scotland in 1812, where New Year was celebrated towards mid-January.

which passed over our heads with a hideous noise, spreading death and devastation wherever they went; while the hissing bombs, as they winged through the air, and their subsequent explosions, the deafening roar of cannon, their gleaming flash, contrasted with the darkness of the night, the shouts of the parties at work, and the cries of the wounded, formed altogether such a scene as resembled more the works of devils, (if devils do fight, which is something problematical), than the works of men. While thus engaged, my companion started to his feet, at the same time swearing he would suffer to be shot, rather than be frozen to death, lying on the ground. We therefore rose, and after walking about some time, a volley of grape-shot fell amongst us, when my companion exclaimed, 'Oh God! I am wounded; run for assistance to carry me off.' Having brought up from the hollow a non-commissioned officer and two men, it was discovered the wounded man had received a shot in one of his knees, which had broken the bone, and shattered his limb considerably. He was accordingly carried away by the sergeant and one of the men, while the other, an Irishman of the name of Murphy, was left with me as a substitute for my former associate, who was scarcely gone, ere another volley of grape annoyed us, and my new companion fell to the earth exclaiming, 'Ah! By Jasus, I am killed!' When assistance was brought, it was found the ball had entered his head behind the left ear. Being still alive he was carried off, and a third man left to bear be company during the remainder of this eventful hour, in which thirteen volleys of murdering grape fell amongst us, from the whole of which I had the happiness to escape unhurt. The hour being at length expired, we were relieved from our perilous situation, and joined the companies in the hollow, which were withdrawn at daybreak.[4]

It was generally supposed that the breaches would be practicable by the 19th, which was our next day for duty; and it was expected our division would have the sole honour of storming the town. In this we were partially disappointed, for on leaving our quarters, the Light Division were seen coming down from theirs. This circumstance, however, assured us we were to participate in the glory of wresting from the enemy on of the strongest fortresses on the Spanish frontier. Being thus confirmed in our expectations, every heart beat quick in the anticipation of high daring, this being the first essay made by the British troops in the Peninsula, to storm a regular fortification. Their valour had often been tried in the field, and had nearly been uniformly victorious; but now a very different mode of warfare was presented, in which their courage and intrepidity might find full scope. Instead of the long drawn line, the bristly column, and other comparative sports of the field, – twas theirs to cross the broad and deep fosse, to surmount the high and lofty wall, on which were arrayed their fierce opponents – twas theirs to force the

4 Based on casualty returns it looks like 25-year-old Private James Fogg from Nottingham was hit in the knee; however the Murphy may be either a Patrick or a Michael; the details available do not allow us to distinguish.

deadly breach, and pass the hidden and slumbering mine, about to wake and hurl destruction on the hardy adventurers. A person given to reflection would very naturally have shrunk from such appalling dangers, but the present was no time for reflection. All seemed animated as with one spirit, and appeared determined to conquer or die.

When arrived at the camp ground, a covering party was sent to the trenches to keep the enemy in play, while the remainder bivouacked in the vicinity until evening, when the whole prepared for action. A short time after dusk, the troops, in five different columns, composed of the Third and Light Divisions of the army, and of General Pack's brigade, were ordered to advance. The Light Division was to gain the rampart on the opposite side of the town by escalade, while the Third Division under General Picton, was destined to storm the breach. On debouching from the trench, the enemy received us with a most galling fire of musketry, round-shot, and bombs; notwithstanding we advanced at double quick time to the outer ditch, and was about to leap into it, when a magazine near the breach blew up with a tremendous explosion, by which a great number of our men were blown to pieces.[5] By this dreadful catastrophe I lost my eye lashes, which were completely singed, and my whole face was scorched by the sulphurous flame. For a few seconds I was deprived of the power of vision, and in this state was pushed into the ditch by the troops that now came rolling on like a flood. We then ascended the breach amidst a shower of earth, stones, bones, and rubbish, which had been raised and whirled into the air by the explosion. After an arduous contest the rampart was gained, when the enemy retired to the adjoining houses, and commenced firing from the windows, while a strong body of them remained on the street. These were charged by our men to the square, or market place, where they were met by another party, pursued by the Light Division. On perceiving themselves surrounded they threw down their arms.

Thus, in the short space of ten days, one of the strongest holds on the Spanish frontier was taken from the enemy. A place which, but two years previous to this, cost them much loss and labour to take from the Spaniards, an enemy they affected to despise. The loss on both sides was very severe; that of the British was estimated at 1200 killed and wounded.[6] The chief of our brigade, Major General M'Kinnon having led his troops up to the breach, was unfortunately blown up by the explosion of the enemy's magazine;[7] and Major General Crawford[8] was severely wounded. The garrison who submitted on this occasion, consisted of 1700 men, besides officers. The fruits of the victory were a hundred and fifty pieces of

5 In fact the French had detonated a massive mine under the breach, which probably killed defenders as well as attackers.

6 Wellington's losses were 568 men in the storm, and another 553 men in the siege.

7 Major General Henry McKinnon was literally blown to bits by the mine at the head of the breach.

8 Light Division commander Major General Robert Craufurd was hit by a sniper and badly wounded; he died on 23 January 1812. It was a grievous loss to the army.

cannon, and large quantities of military stores. To express their grateful sense of this achievement, the Spanish Cortes conferred on Lord Wellington the rank of Grandee of the First Class, with the title of Duke of Ciudad Rodrigo; while his grace was graciously pleased to reflect back, as it were, the rays of his glory on the troops, by intimating to them in general orders, his grateful thanks, and the high estimation in which they were held by him, for the courage and valour displayed at the late glorious occasion; thus bountifully bestowing the shadow while he retained the substance. But such is the remuneration the poor soldier generally receives, for the toils and dangers to which he is exposed; confirming the truth of the poet's song, that;

> Glorious honour crowns the toil,
> And that's the soldiers fee.

Numbers, being aware of this, endeavoured to indemnify themselves by plunder. No sooner was the enemy disarmed than all seemed intent on having something for their trouble. The houses, which were in general shut up, were soon broken open, to the ruin of the terrified inhabitants, who stood aghast while they saw their houses pillaged, and their property carried away by their friends and allies, the generous British. Some, more outrageous than the rest, proceeded to even greater extremities; by insulting the men, and subjecting the wretched females to that, which to mention, would make humanity shudder, and wound the delicate ear of virtue. All order and subordination for the time being lost, I spent the early part of the night in rambling the streets, which were crowded by our men, many of whom were deeply intoxicated, and seemed as happy as if they had all been created dukes of the place. Others, again, more provident, or perhaps more covetous and rapacious, groaned under loads of spoil, which, to any but themselves appeared in vain, as they were not able to carry them off.

At last, getting amongst some of our company, I entered a house with them, the inhabitants of which were absent, having most probably fled from the horrors of the time. There not being sufficient room for us on the hearth, a fire was kindled in the midst of the apartment, around which we got seated, and being supplied with abundance of brandy and wine, which was brought up in large water buckets from a cellar immediately under, we all got as merry and happy as belted knights. While some displayed the rich silks and costly drapery which they considered their lawful prize, others held up to view more precious and glittering articles, such as silver watches, gold repeaters, diamond necklaces, a variety of gold chains, hallowed rosaries, with splendid crucifixes, chalices, and other vessels long ago sanctified and set apart by the benediction of some holy father, for the exclusive use, and sacred purpose of holy Mother Church. Some, again, were busied counting into their caps a shining store of Spanish dollars, and rich doubloons. Others, less fortunate, affected to despise all this show of wealth, and paid fervent adoration at the shrine of Bacchus; or, in other words, kept plying hard at the brandy buckets, from which they ever and anon poured deep libations in honour of the rosy God, to the degradation of themselves, until at length overpowered by the effervescence and fervour of devotion, sunk down victims of their folly and fanaticism. Neither was cooking forgot – materials for which lay around in abundance. A quantity of flour was made into cakes, each something more than an inch thick, and laid on the fire to harden. A large brass kettle full of rice was likewise put on to boil, with a variety of other things. Four whole hams of bacon were laid on at once, from which issued a spiral blaze that nearly reached the ceiling above. In the midst of all this preparation for festivity, the floor, which was composed of wood, gave way – when, as if by enchantment, the fire and all that was on it disappeared, and 'like the baseless fabric of a vision, left not a wreck behind.' All who were able to make a scramble for the door, which having gained, they looked back with astonishment on the sudden change of affairs. Those that were left on the floor, insensible to the danger they were in, were seized by the heels and dragged out, their heads coming thump on the steps as they descended the stairs. Next morning, we assembled on the camp ground, and about mid-day returned to our quarters.[9]

9 Wellington's army gained no credit in the sack following the fall of Ciudad Rodrigo. True, it did not befit a professional army; but can we really judge, given the men were often weeks (even months) behind in pay, miserably provisioned much of the time, and so dressed in patched-up uniforms as to look like scarecrows?

Chapter 13

Siege and Storming of Badajoz – Sacking of a City – All for love – Gets Discarded – Duties of a Servant

> Once more unto the breach dear friends,
> Or fill up the wall with English dead.
> SHAKESPEARE

We had been only a few days at rest when we were ordered to Badajoz, a strong fortified town of Spain, distant from Rodrigo one hundred and fifty miles. On the third day of our march we arrived at Albergaria, where I was received by my dearest Rosa in the kindest and most affectionate manner; but parted in the morning with vary faint hopes of ever meeting again. Twice had Badajoz been invested during the war, and both attempts had failed to reduce this strong fortress. A powerful army, with a numerous and well-appointed battering train, were now on the way for a third investment, in which it was supposed, all their art, strength and courage, would be required. In order that the siege might be pushed on with the utmost vigour, Lord Wellington determined to superintend the operations in person. On the 15th March we crossed the Guadiana by a bridge of pontoons, and same day took up our ground before Badajoz, on the left bank of that river. On the evening of the 17th operations were commenced on the north-west side of the town, which happily was not discovered for some hours by the enemy, when the parties at work were comparatively under cover of the breastworks.

My master, having been during the night engaged in his professional capacity in the trenches, I went with breakfast to him in the morning, when the garrison was keeping up a heavy fire on our works. Just as I had spread a cloth on the ground, and in the act of laying out the breakfast materials, a shell from the enemy alighted on the breastwork immediately in our front, which exploding, covered both master and man with the earth it threw up. We crawled out as well as we could, looking very sillily at each other, without, however, sustaining any injury, except the loss of breakfast, which was buried in the earth. On the second day of the siege the weather became broken, and rained very heavily for about eight days, which was a great annoyance to the men, who stood the whole time in the trenches, to the knees in mud and water. In the 19th, as I lay on the tent floor, I heard an unusual firing at the works, and the cry of 'Sortie! A sortie!' was heard from all quarters. Immediately standing to our feet, every man seized his pouch and musket, and without order's rushed to the works. The enemy consisted of 2,000 men, part of whom had actually entered the trenches. Amongst the rest I perceived one fellow, a grenadier, with a handful of iron rods and a hammer, with which no doubt it was intended to spike our cannon, but they were soon driven into the town with considerable loss, when a heavy cannonade was commenced from the ramparts. On leaving the trenches a man of our company had a narrow escape from a cannon ball which passed over his head, so near that it took away the crown of his cap as neatly as if it had been done with a knife, and so dextrously, that the cap was not removed from his head.

Whether a presentiment, or foreknowledge of things in the womb of time, be given to some or not, I cannot determine; but an occurrence happened at this time which almost made a convert to the belief that there was. One morning, when the parties turned out for work, a grenadier belonging to our regiment betrayed great reluctance to go to the trenches, declaring he would never return. Being an old soldier, and having seen much service, in which he never evinced any symptom of fear or cowardice, but was well respected in the company, on seeing him so disheartened, one of his comrades, who was cook for the day, volunteered in his stead, provided he would act for him in his absence; which offer the poor fellow joyfully accepted. At the dinner hour he went to the trenches with the men's victuals, where he remained until they had finished their meal; but when rising to come away, a shell from the enemy fell at his feet, which instantly bursting, a large piece struck his body, and laid him completely in two.[1]

On the 25th, at the distance of six hundred yards, our artillery opened their batteries, and continued to bombard the town with a heavy and most destructive fire. On the night of the same day, a detachment, consisting of seven hundred men, from our division, stormed and took Fort Picarina, a strong out-work, nearly in line with our batteries. The assailants encountered great opposition in the attack, but eventually proved victorious, when most of the garrison were put to the sword. Neither did our men escape unhurt, they suffered severely in the assault, and afterwards. No sooner were they masters of the place, than the garrison from the town turned their guns upon it, by which a great number of our men were killed and wounded. Amongst whom was Brigade-Major Wade, who was killed by the bursting of a shell.[2] He was a brave, gallant, and valuable officer. By the 6th

1 Private Robert Wilson was the only Grenadier Company man killed at that time, so it seems likely this is he.

2 There was no officer named Wade killed at Badajoz. Possibly this refers to a Captain Leonard Potter of the 28th Foot, who served as brigade major and was wounded in the siege but died of his wounds a

of April, three breaches, which were regarded as practicable, were effected in the bastions of La Trinidad, and St Martha, and Wellington determined to commence the assault that night. Our division, under General Picton,[3] was ordered to attack the castle by escalade, which was considered the most dangerous point of attack; Major Wilson with a detachment of the Fourth Division, was to assail the ravelin of St Roque; Major General Colville, with the remainder of the Fourth, and the Light Division, was to attack the breaches; while the conduct of a false attack was committed to General Leith, with instructions to turn it into a real one, if circumstances should prove favourable.[4]

At ten o'clock at night our division left the camp and proceeded towards the castle of Badajoz, the rest of the divisions following close in the rear. Having filed through the trenches, we gained the main road, along which we moved in the most profound silence. This was a most impressive and interesting moment, being now on the very point of assailing the strong fortress, which was immediately in our front. The high and lofty battlements, and the gloomy and massive towers, seemed to frown as it were on the advancing troops, who were already near the foot of the cliffy rocks which they surmounted. The serene stillness of the night had likewise a tendency to inspire the contemplation of things very different in their nature from the enterprise in which we were engaged. Above, the azure and spangled vault of heaven shone forth with resplendent lustre; while the spheres, each in their respective orbits, rolled on in regular and uninterrupted succession through boundless and infinite space, a scene at all times admirably calculated to infuse into the mind an awe and reverence for the Great Architect,[5] raising us above all sublunary trifles, and teaching us to look up through nature's works to nature's God. Below all nature stood still, as if waiting the result of the great event which was momentarily expected to commence; not a zephyr arose to disturb the calm and balmy air; not a sound, nor voice was heard, but the momentous 'gaura vow' of the French sentinels,[6] which was incessantly echoed round the ramparts. Even the firing had ceased on both sides – the murdering and deafening roar of cannon, which had for twenty-one days and nights been employed in ruin and devastation, had given place to the anticipation of more close and perilous combat. All round a dead and death like silence prevailed, not even a whisper was heard – the very breathing of the troops was suppressed – when lo! As Etna pours her liquid and overwhelming masses on the adjoining country – as when Vesuvius belches forth her burning stores on the neighbouring provinces, the impetuous garrison

month later. This officer might have had connections to other officers in the 45th, which leads me to suspect it is the man so described.

3 The Third Division.

4 All this is much more information than would have been available to a private, so this knowledge is clearly written after the fact.

5 Evidence that William was probably a Freemason.

6 Presumably 'Gare à vous!' Watch out, or take care.

now hurled death and destruction on their assailants, who rushed forward with the utmost intrepidity. From the blazing ramparts, which now seemed enveloped in flames, issued volleys of round-shot, while numerous bombs winged their way through the air, alighting with fatal precision amongst our troops. We were now crossing the broad moat, filled with water, in which the bullets fell so fast as to resemble a shower of hail, and where all that were wounded perished in the liquid element, while showers of grape and canister continued to pour from the town. Numerous fire-balls were thrown out by the garrison, in order to show in what direction we were advancing; then hand-grenades were poured forth in appalling numbers on our men,[7] the van of whom had now gained the covered way, and were making great exertions to break down the outer palisading, which being at length effected, they gained the ditch.

Our regiment, being on the right of the division, might be termed the forlorn hope, and suffered accordingly. The point at which we descended into the ditch was between two bastions, from both of which we experienced a most dreadful fire of musketry; while from the body of the wall, the enemy continued to pour, by means of boards placed upon the parapet, whole showers of grenades, which they arranged in rows, and being lighted with a match, the whole was upset, exploding amongst us in the ditch with horrid destruction. Coils of rope, in a friable state, strongly impregnated with tar, pitch, and oil, were likewise employed by the enemy as a means of annoyance, which completely answered the purpose intended, by scorching and scalding numbers in a dreadful manner. Two men of our company received each one of these coils upon the head, which next day exhibited a horrid spectacle. From the extreme swelling that ensued, the whole of the skin burst and came off their head and face. They were deprived of sight for a long time after, but both ultimately recovered.

The ladders, by some mistake, were not brought up in time, and the period passed in waiting for them, I shall never forget. The fosse was full of men, and the remainder continuing to pour in, so condensed the whole that we stood in great danger of being crushed to death; while the flanking fires from the bastions, and the destruction that fell from the parapet above, were beyond description.

> The wild confusion, and the swarthy glow
> Of flames on high, and torches from below;
> The scream of terror, and the mingling yell –
> For swords began to clash, and shouts to swell –
> Hung o'er that spot of earth the air of hell.[8]

7 Probably more like improvised bombs similar to 'Molotov cocktails' than the grenades we know today.
8 From *The Corsair* by Lord Byron, published in 1814.

The men fell like stubble. At one time three that were wounded had hold of me, endeavouring to prevent themselves from falling, which was certain death, and which I had nearly participated with them, for borne down with their weight I was fast sinking. A number of ladders being brought up, however, caused a general movement, when I extricated myself from their grasp. Our men rushed up the ladder with the greatest impetuosity, but when near the top the whole broke down, and all that were on them were precipitated on the points of their comrade's bayonets, by which many received their death. We were then ordered to unfix our bayonets, and sling the firelock on our shoulder, which being done, and a number of ladders brought, we immediately began to ascend. The ladder I chanced to be on, was laid to the bottom of an embrasure, in which were a number of the enemy ready to receive us, and in front of whom stood an officer with a pistol in each hand, ready cocked. On the ladder a grenadier officer of our regiment preceded us, who, when his head was nearly on a line with the enemy's feet, was fired at by the officer in front. Missing the contents of the pistol, he instantly gave his opponent a back slap across the legs with his sabre, who fell over into the ditch. Our officer then leapt onto the embrasure, cutting down all that opposed him, and was immediately followed by the men, who became directly masters of the ramparts.[9] The enemy retired beyond the court of the castle, to a gateway that communicated with the town, where a number of prisoners were taken. All endeavours, however, to get into the town proved of no avail, so that we were obliged to remain in the castle during the night.

About the same time the castle was taken, the ravelin of St Roque was carried by Major Wilson, but the Fourth and Light Divisions met with much more serious obstacles. They advanced as far as the covered way before they were perceived, and two of the bodies descended into the ditch, and proceeded to storm the breaches; but the enemy made so determined a resistance that the assailants found all their efforts in vain to establish themselves within the place. At length despairing of success in this quarter they were drawn off, after having sustained very great loss, both in officers and men. The intended false attack under General Leith was more fortunate. The troops engaged in it, having turned an outwork, gained the ditch, and climbing the adjoining bastions, established themselves in the town itself. The French governor, General Philippon, with his staff, retired into Fort St Christoval, and surrendered next morning. The garrison, which amounted originally to 5,000 men, had lost 1,200 killed and wounded in the previous operations, besides those that fell in the assault. The British loss was likewise very severe, amounting to 51 officers killed, and privates in proportion, with 213 officers, and upwards of 2,000 privates wounded.[10]

9 This officer was probably Lieutenant Hans Stevenson Marsh, commanding the Grenadier Company in the absence of the wounded Captain Alexander Martin, but we cannot be totally sure.

10 Oman, *History of the Peninsular War*, Vol. V, pp.594-595, Table IX [B] gives the official loss as being 3,713 during the storm and 957 during previous operations, or 4,670 in total.

The bloody but successful siege of Badajoz in April 1812, in which the 45th played a significant role. (Anne S. K. Brown Collection)

Badajoz thus fell into the possession of the allied armies, and notwithstanding the severity of the loss, was considered a valuable and important acquisition. It was captured at a very critical conjuncture of affairs, Marshal Soult being fast approaching to its relief with all the forces he could collect in Andalusia and the neighbouring provinces, while Marmont, in the north, was threatening Ciudad Rodrigo. No time, therefore, was to be lost in the reduction of this fortress, and it may be safely asserted, that on no occasion was British valour manifested to greater advantage, or more necessary than in the capture of Badajoz. The Garrison, under the direction of General Philippon, had almost exhausted the means of defence, which were of such a formidable nature as would have appalled most troops, and rendered all their efforts unavailing.

When the garrison surrendered, leave for two hours was given us to go to the town, camp, or wherever we pleased, but the town was universally preferred. All rushed to the gate that communicated with it, which caused a deal of noise and squabbling, for the enemy had built up a gateway as a means of defence, leaving only a narrow passage, through which but one man could pass at a time. They all, however, got to the town soon enough for the inhabitants, who were by many of our men shamefully and barbarously treated. There was not, I believe, a house in the whole town that was not ransacked from top to bottom – murder, rape, and robbery, were committed with the greatest impunity. The first building I entered was a church, which the French had occupied as a provision store, and was at the time well filled with bags of flour, bread, biscuit, and leaf tobacco. On one side were piled casks of liquor to the very roof. Each soldiers, as he entered, seized one for himself, and having set it on one end, staved in the other with the butt of his flintlock, then knelt down and drank what he pleased, which in many cases was not a little. In a short time, numbers got intoxicated, when all became confusion and uproar. The casks were upset, and the liquor poured on the floor, until the church was nearly knee deep, into which some in their folly threw themselves, that they might have it to say they had swam in rum, brandy and wine. During the day, I entered many genteel houses, all full of our men, who were busy pillaging; and what could not be carried away they in mere wantonness destroyed. But all this was harmless, and might be termed as nothing, when contrasted with some of the atrocities perpetrated in this devoted town. Happening to go through the passage of a genteel house, I got into a small court, surrounded by stables and other offices belonging to the house. Looking round the place I perceived a man, apparently naked, walking to-and-fro in one of the buildings in front of me. Prompted by curiosity I stepped towards him, and having asked how he became reduced to the state he was in, he informed me that being master of the house he had endeavoured to repel the lawless aggressions of my comrades, but being unable to withstand such numbers, they had stripped and turned him out of his own house, which they were then busy plundering. As I stood commiserating his misfortunes, and ashamed of the rapacity and cruelty exercised by my countrymen, two of the 88th Connaught Rangers made their appearance, who coming forward, audaciously demanded from the Spaniard his money. The poor man solemnly protested he had none; that they might perceive he had no means of secreting anything about his person; that his all was gone; his house had been robbed and plundered; his property carried away and destroyed; himself stripped and turned out of the house, which called him master, and into which he durst not enter, as it was still occupied by the deprecators. But all this was lost upon the two ruffians: he might as well have told his misfortunes to the winds. They still insisted he had money hid, and if he did not immediately produce it, they would find means that would make him glad to do it. This threat they put into immediate execution, by coming to the charge with their firelocks, and holding the points of their bayonets to the naked man's breast, who, with despair in his looks, still declared his inability to give what they wanted. Seeing things coming to a crisis, I began to remonstrate with the villains on the absurdity of demanding a thing they might see the poor man had not to give. They immediately turned upon me like two hellhounds, swearing by Jasus I had nothing ado wid it at all at all, and if I did not keep myself aisy they would run me through. As if in defiance of the remonstrance's I continued to make, and the threat of reporting their conduct to the commanding officer of the regiment, they seized the Spaniard, and dragging him forth, plunged him headlong into a deep draw-well that was in the centre of the court. Sickened at heart, and detesting the depravity of such murderous wretches, I left the place. In going through the passage I heard a great noise in the house, which I entered, and found it full of soldiers, who were tearing and turning everything upside down. By the fire-place was seated a respectable old woman, whom I considered the mistress of the house, and wife of him I had seen murdered. On her knee she held a child of some months old, which, in the midst of all the noise and tumult that surrounded it, apparently enjoyed a calm and serene sleep, while its nurse cried and sobbed bitterly. Poor woman, thought I, you have enough before you here to grieve for, but you little know the extent of your misery and loss. But this is not your child – you are too old to be the parent of such an infant – I will ask where its mother is, and try to console the old lady in her calamity. Thus thought I, as I stood near the door; but endeavouring to pass those that were on the floor, I happened to turn myself round, when – Oh! Horror of horrors! I saw, laid on a bed, a young woman, whom I immediately conceived to be the mother of the babe, surrounded by demons in human shape, who were satisfying their unbridled and sensual appetites, at the expense of everything held sacred, and violating the laws of God, of nature, and of man. One fellow held up in triumph a pair of red morocco boots he had torn from her feet; while another wretch displayed a rich necklace he had stripped from her bosom. But I turned from the revolting scene in disgust, and rushed out of this most unfortunate and ruined house.

Determined to leave such a scene of riot and outrage, I proceeded along the street, in which were exhibited every crime that could render man contemptible, and disgrace human nature. At last arriving at the ground of the preceding nights encounter, a very different scene presented itself from that which I had just left. There, lust and rapine were perpetrating every crime, and at the moment trampling upon every principle sacred and civil, moral and religious; at that very instant, were the demons of rage ruining everything held good and virtuous, destroying the properties, and violating the rights of every family, and of every habitation. But here reigned a still and solemn silence; not a sound was heard, not a voice arose to disturb the awful pause, save the faint groans of the wounded and the dying. From the blood stained rampart, I beheld thousands of my fellow creatures immolated on the altar of ambition:

Fatal Ambition! say what wond'rous charms
Delude mankind to toil for thee in arms?
When all thy spoils, thy wreaths in battle won;
The pride of power and glory of a crown;
When all war gives, when all the great can gain,
Ev'n thy whole pleasure, pays not half thy pain![11]

11 From Nicholas Rowe, *A Poem Upon the Late Glorious Success of Her Majesty's Arms &c.*, published in 1707.

Amongst the slain, I saw many of my comrades and associates, with whom I had travelled many a long and weary mile. Some with whom I was intimately acquainted, and with whom but yesterday I had conversed freely, now lay stretched in their gore. In reviewing this tragic scene, my mind sickened at the contemplation of so much misery, and could not help wondering that such should be the works of reasonable creatures; that there could exist any who took delight in beholding it, or to follow war solely from ambition. Yet such things are, and by such men has Europe been rendered a slaughter-house! The inhabitants of Britain may complain of what they have suffered, they may dwell upon the evils which still assail them, but have their eyes seen, has their country witnessed, the storming of a town, the sacking of a city, or the carnage of a battlefield? Compared to these, the evils which assail them, are but as a grain in the balance.[12]

Leaving a garrison in the captured city, the army advanced in quest of the enemy, who, under Marmont, had entered Portugal, in order to make a diversion in favour of their beleaguered countrymen in Badajoz. Passing Camp Mayor and Olivenza, we reached Nisa the third day of our march, where I met a townsman and old school fellow, who was then in the 79th regiment. With him I passed the greater part of the night, and over some wine, we talked of our boyish days, youthful frolics, friends, relations, and of sweet home; none of which poor Duncan was ever permitted to see again, for he died some months after in the hospital at Salamanca. Crossing the Tagus at Vila Valha, we soon reached Castel Branco, to which place the enemy had advanced, but had left it on the day previous to our arrival, retracing their steps towards the northern frontier, and in the true French style, destroying everything that came in their way. Passing Penamacer, Alpederinha,[13] and other towns along our line of march, we found the inhabitants had fled, leaving their all to the invaders of their country. As we approached Albergaria, I was all impatience to know the fate of that village, and its inhabitants. On entering this hamlet, in which were centred all my hopes, and which contained all I held valuable on earth, it was also found to have undergone the fiery ordeal of the enemy, who had laid it completely in ruins, while the whole of the inhabitants were fled to the mountains. On perceiving the devastation and ruin that had been committed, I flew to the dwelling of Fernando Silvera. What my sensations were, may be more easily imagined than described, when I found all ruined, the inmates fled, and no one near that could inform me when, or in what direction they retreated. The walls were dismantled of the roof, and divested of all the doors and windows; and when I passed the threshold I found the furniture broken and destroyed, the shattered pieces of which lay strewed on the floor. As I stood on the once happy, but now deserted and desolate hearth, contemplating the

12 Wellington eventually stopped the sack of Badajoz by sending a Portuguese brigade in to round up all looters, and by erecting some gallows in the Cathedral Square.

13 Penamacor and Alpedrinha, north-east of Castelo Branco.

foul outrage that had been committed on innocent and harmless people, I heard footsteps in the passage, and to my ravished and enraptured view, my dearest Rosa entered, who, when she beheld me, exclaimed, 'Mina Gulliame!' and in a moment we were in others arms. When the emotions this unexpected meeting had raised were somewhat subsided, the lovely girl informed me that on the approach of the enemy, her parents, with a number of their neighbours, retired to a sequestered spot, about two leagues distant, where they had then been ten days; but having heard of the retreat of the enemy, and the subsequent advance of the British, she, in company with a few belonging to the village, had come down to ascertain the truth of what they had heard.

Impatient to let her parents know what had taken place, Rosa resolved to go to their place of refuge that evening, and I being determined to accompany her, we left the village. Proceeding about half a league on the road leading to Fuente Ginaldo, we struck to the right, and having passed through a large wood, got upon a heath of great extent, which seemed to have no boundary but the horizon. As I looked over this broad and barren waste – this is, thinks I, a love adventure, which many would think deeply tinged with Quixotism, but I will go through it. Passing over a great extent of moor, ere I was aware we stood upon the margin of a narrow and deep ravine, the almost perpendicular sides of which were clothed with bush and bramble, from the base to the very summit. From the high ground poured a considerable rivulet, which rolled down the steep precipice, and dashing from rock to rock, formed a beautiful cascade; then falling into a large basin, worn smooth and highly polished by the friction of water, it again issued forth from the deep and boiling caldron, and gurgling with great impetuosity over its rocky and channelled bed, it wound its rugged course along the bottom of the romantic dell, until lost in the superior waves of the Aguada. On this charming and beautiful spot I stood riveted for some time, enjoying with ecstatic pleasure the surrounding scene. The soft and balmy twilight was fast succeeding the glaring blaze of a May-day sun, whose setting glory still gilded the high and distant peaks of Portugal. Through the faint and dubious light was seen on our left, the lofty battlements and towering turrets of Rodrigo, which, in the gloom of evening, seemed to frown on the broad and rolling torrent of the Aguada, as it swept along their base. The profound depth of the glen, over which we stood as if poised in air; the sombre and darkening hue of the spreading foliage on its steep and rugged banks, between which the curling smoke now ascended from the evening fires of the fugitives we were in search of, who were bivouacked at the bottom; and even the surrounding and expansive waste, yielded peculiar charms. In the company of those we love, every object assumes a pleasant and delightful aspect. The place, the hour, and the adventure I was engaged in, raised my mind to an exalted pitch of enthusiasm; and that the illusion might continue, I fondly wished I had been born a Spanish shepherd, and destined to attend my flocks in company with my lovely shepherdess.

Having indulged ourselves in the contemplation of the surrounding scene, and devoting a part of our time to the mysteries of love, we descended into the hollow, where, on the banks of the impetuous stream, I found, seated under the shade of a large cork tree, Rosa's father, old Fernando, his wife Theresa, and their two sons, Diego and Lopez, by all of whom I was most kindly and joyfully received. After remaining the greatest part of the night with my kind but unfortunate friends, I prepared to depart, by taking a sorrowful farewell of her on whom my soul doted, deprived of whose company I thought life not worth preserving. At this moment my mind was assailed by strong contending fears and emotions. I felt as if parting, and that forever – for I had a presentiment that we should never meet again – and about to be cast an isolated being on an unfeeling world, without a home, or a single individual interested in my welfare, to sympathize, or soothe me in the various fatigues and dangers to which I was daily and hourly exposed. For a moment the thought crossed my mind, of at once renouncing my country and my engagements with the army, and of uniting my destinies with the family of Silvera. But the thought only lasted a moment, and tearing myself from the embraces of my friends, I rushed up the rocky steep.

As the morning dawned I entered the village of Albergaria, to which my friends were to remove in the morning, and found the troops already preparing for the march. My master, being in the utmost impatience on account of my absence, interrogated me concerning it. I informed him of the whole particulars, at which he was very much displeased, and threatened to give me my leave if ever I did so again. But being resolved to join my company, and do my duty as a soldier, I told him he need be under no apprehension of me repeating it, for I wished him to furnish himself with another servant. He accordingly did so, and I joined my company.

The leaving such service I counted no sacrifice, for the situation of servant to a subaltern in the Peninsula, was often attended with much extra fatigue and toil. After the most tedious and harassing marches, it was his duty to assist in unloading his master's baggage, the whole of which he had to unpack for the use of the night. His master's tent was then pitched, and wood and water sought after, which frequently was very difficult to be got, and when obtained, the next thing was the making of a fire-place; then to set fire to the fuel, which being always green, he had to puff and blow until his eyes were starting from their sockets, and nearly suffocated with smoke; then he commenced cooking; but what was worse, there was sometimes little or nothing to cook. Dinner being on the fire, he cleaned his master's clothes, boots and shoes, &c. Then he attended table, and officiated in the quadruple capacity of valet, cook, and butler. When the cloth was drawn, he retired to the outside of the tent, and robbed the dogs of their prey, by devouring the bones his master had left. When the great man signified his desire to retire to rest, the servant then acted as chambermaid, by making the bed, and performing several little offices; for all which trouble he was often saluted with a volley of oaths, on account of the chilliness of the air, or the hardness of the ground. All being retired to rest, he then wrapped himself in his single blanket, and over-powered and faint with fatigue, threw himself on the hard ground. There perhaps he had not been long, until his ears were assailed with the swelling notes of the bugle, warning him to rise and load the baggage. Then cups, saucers, tumblers, and glasses, and all the paraphernalia of the table had to be collected and packed up in the dark; the tent struck, the baggage loaded, and he fall in with his company and march with the division. Such was the daily routine of the poor servants in Spain, and to make the matter worse, all that has been enumerated was often done in the open air, and under heavy rains.

Chapter 14

Battle of Salamanca – Narrow Escape – Enters Madrid

At once the wide extended battles move,
At once they join, at once their fate they prove!
The roar ascends promisc'ous; groans and cries,
The drums, the cannon's burst, the shout supplies
One universal anarchy of noise!
ROWE

The enemy having retired into the interior of Spain, our army was put into quarters on the frontiers, where we remained until the beginning of June, when the whole army crossed the Aguada, and on the 16th arrived in the vicinity of Salamanca. The enemy's cavalry being driven in by our advanced corps, Marmont evacuated that city, leaving a garrison in three forts, which he had constructed on the ruins of some convents. These forts commanded the passage of the Tormes, by the bridge of Salamanca, in consequence of which the army passed the river, on the morning of the 17th, at some fords in the neighbourhood of the place.

The Sixth Division, under Major General Clinton,[1] being left to invest the forts, our army occupied the heights in front of the city, while the enemy retired in the direction of Toro, but on the 19th again advanced on Salamanca, when a variety of skirmishes took place. Meantime the operations against the forts were pushed on with great vigour, and by the 27th a breach having been effected, orders were given for an assault, when the whole were carried in the most gallant style. Seven hundred and six prisoners, and thirty pieces of cannon were taken, with a considerable quantity of clothing and military stores. Upon the capture of the forts, the enemy fell back in the direction of Toro and Tordesillas, and passing the Douero,[2] took up a position on the north bank of that river. Our army was on the opposite

1 Major General Henry Clinton, son of General Sir Henry Clinton of American War of Independence fame.

2 The river Douro (in Portuguese) or Duero (in Spanish).

bank, the left at Pollos, the centre opposite the bridge at Tordesillas, and the head-quarters at Rueda. While in this position, the men composing the two armies bathed in the river promiscuously, mingling with one another with the greatest confidence and cordiality. But operations of the first magnitude, and events of the greatest importance were now approaching. Marmont having assembled all the disposable force in that part of Spain, the army under his command, amounted to 60,000, which was now reinforced by 10,000 under General Bonnette. Joseph Bonaparte himself was in motion, and was marching with the greatest haste to join him with the army of the centre, consisting of 12,000 infantry, and 3,000 cavalry. A series of the most masterly movements now commenced on the part of the enemy, in which all the skill and judgement of those tactics which had so long alarmed and defeated Europe were exerted to the utmost, against the skill of the British Commander. Marmont, whose force was now much superior in numbers to the British, wished to bring Lord Wellington to a general engagement, and if possible to cut him off from the possibility of a retreat, or if they declined the combat compel them to retreat into Portugal. For this purpose, all his art, all his judgment collected from twenty years' experience in the fields of war, were now exerted upon a large scale, which in time brought on the sanguinary conflict and general battle of Salamanca.

Salamanca, the capital of the province of that name, in the kingdom of Leon, is an ancient, rich, populous city, and a bishop's see, with a famous university, consisting of twenty-four colleges. Besides the cathedral, which is accounted one of the handsomest in the kingdom, there are twenty-one parish churches, thirty-three convents, and six hospitals. The city is partly built on a plain, and partly on three hills, and contains 700 houses, with 24,000 inhabitants. Over the Tormes, which washes its walls, is a bridge built by the Romans, consisting of twenty-five arches. The Tormes is a tributary stream of the Douero, and is here a considerable river. During the upper part of its course it runs north, passing by Alba de Tormes and Huerta, but about nine miles above Salamanca it bends in a circular manner, and then continues its course almost due west to the Douero. It was within this bend, between the city and Alba de Tormes, that the memorable battle of Salamanca was fought.

On the afternoon of the 21st, Marmont crossed the Tormes, between Huerta and Alba de Tormes, with the greater part of his army, the remainder being left at Bablafuente.[3] Continuing his movement upon the left, he endeavoured to gain the roads, which led to Ciudad Rodrigo. Our army also crossed the Tormes, by the bridge at Salamanca, with the exception of our division and some cavalry, which were left on the right bank to oppose the enemy at Bablafuente. Still continuing to press forward in furtherance of his favourite plan, Marmont, during the night of the 21st, occupied the village of Calvarras de Arriva, and the heights near it,

3 Babilafuente, about ten miles east of Salamanca.

called Nuestra Senora de la Pena. Our cavalry occupied the village of Calvarrasa de Abaxo, and early in the morning of the 22nd, detachment from both armies attempted to obtain possession of one of the two hills called Dos Arapiles, which was most distant from the right wing of the British position. The superiority, however, of the enemy's forces enabled them to gain this hill, the possession of which materially strengthened their position, and gave them additional means of annoying the Allies. All this time the light troops of the First Division, and the 4th Cacadores,[4] were engaged with the enemy upon the height called Nuestra de Senora de la Pena, where they maintained themselves throughout the day, notwithstanding every effort to withstand them. Previous to the general attack by our troops, the village of Arapiles was occupied by the light battalion of the Brigade of Guards, supported by two companies of fusiliers. These troops maintained this post against every effort of the enemy. Here Lieutenant General Cole, with the Fourth Division, was posted. Major General Packenham, who commanded our division, on account of the absence of General Picton from ill health,[5] was directed to move across the Tormes with the troops under his command. At the same time General Bradford's brigade of Portuguese infantry, and Don Carlos de Espana's Spanish infantry, moved up between the Third and Fourth divisions.

After a variety of evolutions, about two o'clock on the afternoon of the 22nd, Marmont, under a heavy cannonade, extended his left and moved forward his troops, with the intention to embrace the position of Arapiles, which our army occupied. With the eye of the eagle in search of his prey, Wellington perceived the moment had arrived, the consequences of which would rebuke the pride of Marmont. The extension of his line to the left, and his advance upon our right, notwithstanding the ground his troops still occupied, and his position being well defended with cannon, gave our Commander an opportunity of attacking him, for which he had been long anxious. This long expected and critical moment was seized with energy and skill by the British general – that unfortunate moment, which destroyed the result of six weeks of wise combinations and methodical movements, the issue of which had hitherto appeared certain. As it was denominated by Marmont, that 'unfortunate moment' was immediately taken advantage of. The spirit of the British soldier, long checked by the judgement of their General, was now given full play. From the hazardous nature of the duty, and the long series of fatiguing movements in which we had been engaged, to attack the enemy at all points, heedless of their position or numbers, had long been the wish of every individual. That order was now given, and it was obeyed with alacrity. Officers and men, like lions, rushed to the combat.

4 Cacadores were Portuguese light infantry, dressed all in brown and black.

5 Edward Michael Pakenham was Wellington's brother-in-law. He died commanding the British forces at the battle of New Orleans in 1815.

The grand attack began at four o'clock in the afternoon, and was irresistible. The troops on the left, commanded by General Packenham, gallantly supported by the Portuguese cavalry, and two squadrons of the 14th Dragoons, overthrew everything that opposed them, defeating completely every attempt of Marmont to retrieve the disaster on his left, and all his endeavours to annoy the flank of the eighth division.[6] It was on the centre, however, where the attack was most determined, and the defence most obstinate. The divisions, under the command of Generals Bradford, Leith, and Cole, with the cavalry under Sir Stapleton Cotton,[7] performed prodigies of valour. They attacked and stormed the enemy's 'inexpungable post, which completed their position,' and drove them from one height to another, bringing forward their right, so as to gain strength upon the enemy's flank as they advanced. General Pack, in the meantime, made an attack upon the front of Arapiles. In this, however, he was foiled, after every effort, which advantage gave the enemy an opportunity to detach from this point a considerable force to the assistance of that part of his line pressed by the Fourth Division under General Cole.[8] The British troops, under a tremendous cannonade, descended from the heights they occupied in silence. At the bottom of the valley, before they began to ascend the height occupied by the French, while grape-shot and shells poured against them as thick as hail, they met the sharpshooters of the enemy, whose incessant fire greatly annoyed them.

Ascending the hill in a firm and determined mass, they came in close contact with the enemy, who, perceiving that the British columns were resolved to come to close quarters, immediately sent their guns to the rear, and in solid squares waited the approach of their antagonists. The British were now within forty yards of their front, without having fired a shot, when the French, with the front rank kneeling, commenced a general discharge of musketry upon them. It was received and answered in a moment. With three cheers, and fixed bayonets, the British column advanced against the enemy's masses. Terror struck they fled; at a distance they again rallied, but being again charged by the Fifth Division, they turned and fled. One division, however, more courageous than the rest, and which had been reinforced from the post of Arapiles, after the failure of General Pack's attack, bravely maintained its post against all efforts of the Fourth Division, who were compelled to give way. Marshal Beresford,[9] who was on the spot, immediately ordered a brigade of the Fifth Division, in the second line, to change its front, bringing its fire to bear upon the flank of the enemy's division; but while engaged in this service he received a severe wound. How hot the engagement was at this

6 It is not clear what William meant by this, since Wellington commanded divisions numbered one to seven, plus the Light Division.

7 Lieutenant General Sir Stapleton Cotton, later Lord Combermere, Wellington's cavalry commander in 1812.

8 Major General Sir Galbraith Lowry Cole.

9 Marshal William Carr Beresford, the Irish-born commander of Wellington's Portuguese troops.

place, may easily be inferred from the number of General Officers that fell. In a brilliant charge of cavalry against a column of infantry, which they over-threw and cut to pieces, the gallant and victorious General Le Marchant was killed;[10] General Cole had already been wounded; Marshal Beresford next shared the same fate; and much about the same time General Leith was wounded,[11] and obliged to quit the field. On the side of the enemy General Bonnette, second-in-command, was wounded and taken prisoner, and many other officers fell.[12] The enemy's division at this point continuing to remain firm, the Sixth Division, under General Clinton, was ordered to relieve the Fourth, when the enemy were overthrown, and the battle restored to its former success. In the meantime, the enemy's right, reinforced by the troops which fled from their left, and by those who were driven from Arapiles, still continued to resist. The First and Light Divisions, which had been placed in reserve, together with some brigades of the Fourth Division, were ordered to turn the enemy's right; while they were also attacked in front by the Sixth Division, supported by the Third and Fifth Divisions. After an obstinate conflict, the French were driven from their position. The route became general. In consternation, the enemy fled through the woods towards Huerta, and the fords of the Tormes, pursued by the British cavalry, and part of the infantry, as long as they could find any of them together. The darkness of the night saved the remains of the French Army from total destruction. In their flight they were completely broken; the cavalry penetrated their ranks, and made dreadful carnage.

During the action, as our brigade were marching up to attack a strongly posted column of infantry, a furious charge was made by a body of cavalry upon our regiment, and not having time to form square, we suffered severely. Several times the enemy rode through us, cutting down with their sabres all that opposed them. Our ranks were broken and thrown into the utmost confusion. Repeatedly our men attempted to re-form, but all in vain – they were as often cut down and trampled upon by their antagonists. At length, however, the enemy were driven off by some squadrons of our cavalry, who came up in time to save us from being totally destroyed.[13] Numerous and severe were the wounds received on this occasion. Several had their arms hacked from their shoulders; and I saw more than one with their heads completely cloven. Among the rest, I received a wound, but comparatively slight, although well aimed. Coming in contact with one of the enemy, he brandished his sword over me, and standing in his stirrup-irons, in order to have more purchase, prepared to strike; but pricking his horse with my bayonet, it

10 Major General John Gaspard Le Marchant, commander of the British heavy cavalry brigade.

11 Major General Sir James Leith, commander of the 5th Division.

12 Général de Division Jean Pierre François Bonnet was in fact third in seniority, although was seriously wounded. He was not taken prisoner.

13 William may be over-stating the seriousness of the charge. Total losses in the 45th were 55 men for the entire day. The two battalions of the nearby 5th Foot collectively lost 150 men and may have suffered more at the hands of the French cavalry.

reared and pranced, when the sword fell, the point striking my forehead. He was, however, immediately brought down, falling with a groan to rise no more.

The strength of the armies engaged on this memorable occasion, has been variously estimated; but the most current report stated the amount of the French from 60 to 70,000 and that of the British from 50 to 60,000; all agreeing that the French had 10,000 more than the Allies.[14] In a conflict so obstinately contended, the loss on both sides may justly be supposed to have been severe. That of the French was dreadful. Several accounts rated their killed and wounded from 10 to 12,000.[15] Marshal Marmont, the General-in-Chief, was severely wounded in the arm, and was afterwards under the necessity of having it amputated.[16] Bonnette, second-in-command, was wounded and taken prisoner;[17] 3 Colonels, 3 Lieutenant Colonels, with 130 officers of inferior rank, and 700 privates, were made prisoners. Twenty pieces of cannon, 2 eagles, 6 standards, and a considerable number of baggage wagons, also fell into the hands of the victors.[18] The battle of Salamanca, with the operations that preceded and followed it, from the time that the French crossed the Douero, until they re-crossed that stream in their flight, cost their army 20,000 men. The loss of the Allied army amounted, during the same period, to nearly 6,000 killed and wounded, with 572 missing, the greater part of whom were most probably amongst the first number. For this achievement, Wellington was raised to the rank of a Marquis of the United Kingdom, and received the thanks of the British Parliament, who at the same time declared, that the gallant troops under this illustrious General, deserved well of their country. Whether some of them got their deserts or not, will be seen in the sequel.

Next morning, after the battle, our victorious army commenced the pursuit of the enemy, who in dismay fled towards the Douero. Our advanced corps harassed their rear guard, consisting of 2,000 infantry, and a considerable body of cavalry, who, upon the approach of the British, abandoned their infantry and fled. The whole of the infantry were destroyed, 1700 were taken prisoners, and about 300 killed and wounded.[19] The Allies continued to advance, their light cavalry hanging upon their rear, and taking prisoners daily. On the 30th they entered Valladolid, having taken 300 prisoners in the neighbourhood, and 800 sick and wounded in the place; with 17 pieces of cannon, and a considerable quantity of stores. After various severe skirmishes, and a long march, rendered very fatiguing by the extreme heat of the weather, our army reached the vicinity of Madrid, which

14 In fact, the French had around 50,000 men and Wellington's force 52,000.

15 French losses were probably about 12,500 men.

16 Marmont was indeed seriously wounded, but the arm was in fact saved.

17 See prior note concerning this point.

18 The Eagles were those of the 22e and 101e Ligne, although no two accounts agree precisely on this point, since given the disgrace, the loss of an eagle was not something regiments liked to disclose.

19 This was the famous incident at Garcia Hernandez, where the heavy cavalry of the King's German Legion broke two squares of French infantry – something which rarely happened.

Field Marshal Arthur Wellesley, Lord Wellington. The cool respect rather than affection the author had towards his commander is in keeping with other memoirists of the era. (Anne S. K. Brown Collection)

the enemy had evacuated, leaving a garrison in Buen Retiero, once a royal residence, but converted into a fort by the French. On the 12th of August, the Allies entered the Spanish capital, amidst the joyful acclamations and benedictions of its grateful inhabitants. In two days after, the garrison left in the Retiero capitulated, their number amounting to nearly 3,000 men. In the place were found 189 pieces of cannon, 3,000 barrels of gunpowder, 20,000 stand of arms, large magazines, clothing, provisions, and stores. Amongst the latter were 3,000,000 of ball cartridges, 7,000 bayonets and two eagles.[20]

20 These were the eagle of the 13e Dragons and the other a 'decapitated' eagle of the 51e Ligne. Both were left there by their units, which were at the time operating in scattered detachments against the guerrillas.

Chapter 15

An Execution – Bull Fight – Retrograde Movement – Perilous Situation – Hair-breadth – Escape – Harassing Retreat – Fuente Ginaldo

> But when a soldier, said I, ain't please your reverence, has been standing for twelve hours together in the trenches, up to his knees in cold water; or engaged, said I, for five months together in long and harassing marches; harassed perhaps in his rear today; harassing others tomorrow; detached here – counter-marching there; – resting this night out upon his arms – beat up in his shirt the next; – benumbed in his joints – perhaps without straw in his tent to kneel on; – he must say his prayers how and when he can.
>
> STERNE

Madrid was for six weeks occupied by two divisions, while the remainder of our army were employed at the siege of Burgos.[1] This period I passed with pleasure, in examining, as far as I had opportunity, the buildings and curiosities of this great capital. Not having the means of purchasing admittance to the theatres, and other places of amusement, I contented myself with perambulating the broad and magnificent streets; in witnessing the numerous processions of monks and priests; in attending the public exhibitions of fire-works, which were given in the Plaza Mayor; or in mixing with the crowds, which, from all quarters, resorted to the Prado, on foot, or in carriages, to meet and breath beneath the shade of the long alleys – the air freshened by waters spouting from the fountains, and embalmed by exhalations from the fragrant flowers. This promenade is nearly two miles in length, and is ornamented with beautiful fountains, statues, and vases, and planted with trees. This is the scene of many a love adventure; where measures are often

1 The 3rd and Light Divisions, which had perhaps earned a vacation following their exertions at Badajoz and Salamanca, remained in Madrid.

concerted to deceive the vigilance of a mother, or the jealousy of a husband. This splendid promenade approximates the ancient Palace of the Retiero.[2]

While in Madrid, I witnessed the execution of a Spanish nobleman, convicted of carrying on a correspondence with the French. In the square, destined for the criminal's exit, an immense concourse of people was assembled on the morning of his execution. Having waited for some time, the unfortunate man arrived at the spot, preceded by the municipal authorities, and accompanied by several monks. He mounted the scaffold with a firm and intrepid step, and for a few minutes prayed with apparent fervency. He was then placed on a kind of seat, in the back of which were two holes, through which a chain was passed. The chain being put over his head, the executioner, with a pole at the back of the board, gave it a wrench, and the neck of the sufferer was in a moment made flat with the board.

Having heard much of the famous bull-fights, for which the Spaniards have such an unbounded attachment, I resolve to gratify my curiosity, by visiting the theatre devoted to this species of amusement. I found it lined with a number of benches, some of which were sumptuously ornamented with crimson velvet, and other rich stuffs, belonging, as I supposed, to noble Dons, who were amateurs and patrons of this noble science of brutal cruelty. In the centre was the arena, or scene of action. It was surrounded by a railing six feet high – light being admitted from the top of the building, which was open. To witness the exhibition a vast concourse were assembled, amongst whom were a number of our officers and men. The most of the latter, however, I dare say were greatly disappointed; for soon after the commencement of the entertainment, or rather the disgusting spectacle, many of them rose and left the place. Imitating their example, I went home to the convent in which our regiment was quartered, completely disgusted with the cruelty displayed, and even with the puerility of the thing itself, for in reality the 'picador's, matador's' and what-not, ran little or no danger whatever.

But we were soon to be engaged in combats in their nature very different from those far-famed Spanish fights. The French, under Joseph, Soult and Jourdan, had been reinforced with all the disposable troops in Spain, with which overwhelming force they were marching on the capital, to compel the British to abandon Spain, and once more establish Joseph on his throne. A French force, consisting of 50,000, under General Souham, compelled Wellington to raise the siege of Burgos, who

2 At about this time the 45th recruited some Spaniards into the battalion – thirty-two in all suggested by the muster rolls. The experiment was a disastrous failure; all but one deserted or died within four months. Twenty-four deserted in a single day, 16 November 1812. The last one deserted in July 1813, rejoined in October and (after tasting British military justice) went sick in France and was finally struck off the roll in March 1815.

retreated towards the Douero;[3] while General Hill,[4] with whom were Generals Espana and Villemar, after destroying all the military stores which could not be carried away, abandoned Madrid, and marched towards Arevala.[5] On the 20th of November the French troops again entered Madrid, to the sorrow and regret of its inhabitants. The situation of the people of Spain at this time was truly pitiable. The events of the war were such, that they could hardly tell who was ultimately to be their master, and the severity of the French was of the most unmerciful kind, against everyone who showed the smallest satisfaction at any misfortune that befell their armies. It may well be conceived that were the feeling of the people of Madrid, when they saw their oppressors again return, at whose expulsion they had lately shown such striking marks of satisfaction.

General Hill continuing his retreat from Madrid in the direction of Salamanca, several skirmishes took place, in all of which the enemy were worsted. On the 8th of December[6] he occupied Alba de Tormes, and same day formed a junction with the main army from Burgos, which occupied the heights in front of Salamanca. The army under Joseph, with Soult from the south, and the army under Souham from the north, having effected a junction on the 7th near Arevala, their united forces 90,000 strong, with 200 pieces of artillery, marched directly after the British army to Salamanca. We continued several days in front of that city, in which time various skirmishes took place between the contending hosts. That of the 10th was particularly severe. On the morning of that day the enemy made a furious attack upon Alba de Tormes, with a force of 15 squadrons of cavalry, 6,000 infantry, and 20 pieces of cannon; but from the gallant conduct of the 51st, 71st, and 32nd, regiments, and Major Howard's brigade,[7] the enemy, notwithstanding the greatest efforts, were foiled in all their attempts. Their light troops advanced to the very walls of the place; but after having fired 1,500 cannon shot on this point, without being able to dislodge our troops, the French withdrew their force. At last threatening to turn the British army, and cut it off from Ciudad Rodrigo, we broke up from St. Christova[l], and moved on the 14th to the former positions at Arapiles. The enemy having crossed the Tormes at three fords above Alba, our Commander-in-Chief moved with the second division of infantry, and all the cavalry he could collect, in order to attack them. They, however, were by this time too strongly posted, and too formidable in numbers, to be attacked with any prospect of

3 Général de Division Joseph Souham was an aged and veteran warrior. The siege of Burgos and subsequent retreat was perhaps Wellington's least-distinguished campaign of the entire war.
4 Lieutenant General Sir Rowland Hill, commander of the 2nd Division, who was commanding a multi-division force. He was probably Wellington's most trusted subordinate.
5 Wellington did not consider the occupation of Madrid crucial to his campaign aims; it was too far removed from his supply bases in Portugal and too easily surrounded. The Spanish saw it differently.
6 Actually 8 November.
7 Actually Brigadier General Kenneth Howard, whose brigade included the 1/50th (not 51st), 1/71st and 1/92nd (not 32nd) Regiments of Foot.

success: and after reconnoitring their position, Wellington decided upon a retreat to Ciudad Rodrigo.

During the night of the 14th, the greatest part of our troops moved through Salamanca. On the following morning our division forded the Tormes about a league above that city, and moved down the left bank of the river, in order to gain the road that leads from Salamanca to Ciudad Rodrigo. It was now our sorrows commenced; the rain that had begun early in the morning descended in torrents. When we gained the road it was completely cut up by the numerous baggage, and the whole army which preceded us, for on this memorable retreat our division formed the rear guard. We were not long in this puddle, which was nearly knee deep, ere the majority were bare-foot. To add to our distress, the enemy's cavalry came furiously upon both our flanks, and annoyed us considerably with a smart fire from their carbines, until a body of cavalry came to our assistance, who kept the enemy at bay, while we moved off as well as we could. Having dragged through this slough of despond until long after dark, we fled to the right, and encamped in a wood at a short distance from the road. The ground destined for our quarters during the night, was low and flat, and when we stepped over the ditch that surrounded it, we were immersed to the knees in water. This was, to be sure, more pleasant than the mud we had marched in all day, yet it bore a very cheerless aspect, when we reflected that it was our bed for the night. Previous to this the hatchets for cutting wood, had been thrown away; but as fires were necessary to preserve our existence, the branches that hung over our heads were caught hold of, and by main force torn from the trunks, and laid on the ground, until they were above the surface of the water. This was our fire place, but how to get it lighted no one knew; everything was soaked with water, and the rain continued to fall in torrents. Opening our knapsacks, each man, for his own comfort and the public weal, contributed something to the furtherance of our object. For my share I gave one shirt, three brushes and a button stick; but ere our efforts were crowned with success, forty such lots were consumed by the company. Some will be inclined to think this a very expensive fire, but such must be similarly situated as we were, before they can duly appreciate such luxury. The worst, however, of all was yet to come. On the morning as we passed the bridge at Salamanca, we saw the Tormes choked up with stores, that had been thrown over the bridge, that they might not fall into the hands of the enemy. Such care was surely superfluous, when thousands were passing with empty haversacks, and I may add, empty stomachs to boot, who would have been happy in carrying what they could of it away. But so anxious were our rulers that none of it should fall into the hands of the French, that we were prohibited from touching any part of it; and it is more than probable, if any individual had had the hardihood to have done so, the old salve of four dozen from the Provost-Marshal would have been his portion.[8] Be that as it may, we had now the

8 The Provost-Marshal was the head of the army's military police. A corps of Assistant Provost-Marshals was created and eventually grew to 24 men, all hand-picked serjeants, who wore a red scarf around

horror of pale famine before us, which to contend with for any length of time, was likely to prove a more dreadful foe than the French, who were hanging on our rear.

Next morning at daybreak we again moved on, and keeping to the right of the road, we passed through many woods of oak, the acorns of which were picked up by officers and men, and eaten with as much relish as if they had been the greatest dainties. Extensive sandy plains, which we had traversed but a few months before, and on which we had suffered much by the intense heat that then prevailed, and the scarcity of water, were now literally broad and deep lakes, through which we dashed, the water often reaching above our waist. When we essayed to halt for a few minutes, the enemy, who were close on our rear, sent their shot and shell amongst us, so that we were obliged to decamp.

On the afternoon of this day we encamped in a wood, but were scarcely halted, ere the enemy's cavalry made a furious attack, when we moved on until it was long after dark. We then had leave to lie down on the ground, from which numbers never again rose. On the daybreak of the 18th, we were aroused long before morning from our watery beds, to commence another day of hunger, hardship and fatigue. Numbers however, were exempted from this – their toils, and pains, and dangers were no more – their souls had fled from the scene of misery and woe into which they had been plunged, and their spirits had returned unto God who gave them. When the bugle had sounded I awoke from a deep sleep, and found myself embedded in sand and gravel, which had been washed round me by the heavy rains that fell during the night. With great difficulty I got upon my feet, but found myself scarcely able to move, while the division being formed up, was ready to march off. Oh, Heaven! is it then my lot at last, thought I, to be left in this wretched and desolate spot, to die unheeded and uncared for? On this spot is my flesh to be torn by the ravenous wolf, and my bones left to bleach and moulder in the winter's blast. Or, however horrible this may be, is there yet in reservation a more dreadful doom? Yon brazen trumpets, which, like the knell of death sounding in my ears, is now assembling the Gallic legions, who in a short time will hurry over this very ground – then woe to me, and all that will be so unfortunate as to become their prey.[9] As I stood, as it were, riveted to the ground, bewailing my fate, and anticipating evils that were yet to come, I heard the tramp of the division, which had marched off, getting fainter as it receded from me. For a time, I became bewildered in thought; sweet home, and all its early and endearing recollections, flashed on my memory. Albergaria, to which a few more days would have brought me, was not forgotten; – that emblem of innocence and purity – the magnet of attraction,

their right shoulder as identification. They were permitted under military law to inflict punishment to any enlisted man they found in breach of regulations. The title Assistant Provost-Marshal carried with it the pay and entitlements of the rank of ensign, although such men remained serjeants on their muster-rolls, and in the eyes of their officers.

9 William's footnote at this point reads: In Spain it was a common practice with the French to shoot their prisoners, when unable to march.

by whose laws I was moved and governed – the creature of all my hopes and wishes – at the thought of her, my heart chilled and warmed, the sanguineous current resumed its wonted course, and inspired me with fresh courage and animation. Life, death, heaven and hell, time and eternity, all whirled through my brain with wonderful velocity, when all at once I was roused from my reverie, by the sudden and quiet advance of a large body of cavalry, who were within a short distance of the spot where I stood. A number of poor fellows who were laying around me, vainly flattered themselves that it was the last of our rear-guard advancing; but overhearing their language, and the often repeated 'Sacra vutre',[10] I dropped my knapsack, darted into a thicket, and in a moment after I heard the screams and cries of the poor men I left on the ground, who, I make no doubt, were by the enemy butchered in cold blood.

Making what haste I could, I gained the opposite side of the thicket, where my progress was arrested by a broad ditch. Being unable to leap it, I endeavoured to sound it with my musket, but could find no bottom. As there was no time to spare, I immediately threw over my firelock, and seizing a long pole that very opportunely lay on the spot, I swung myself over, and dashed through thick and thin, until I reached the division, which I overtook when passing a village, where was a large garden well stocked with cabbage. These seemed, as if by a miracle, to have been preserved from all the ravage that preceded us; but which now, as if by a counter miracle, were as suddenly plucked up by the roots, for every man seized a head that could, and shared with his comrades who had none. As there was no time for cooking, the whole were eaten, or rather devoured, in a few minutes, rough and raw as we found them; and was, I dare say, considered by all the sweetest morsel they had ever tasted. Previous to this the majority had fasted forty-eight hours, and excepting a windfall like the present had fallen in the way, we were in a fair way of fasting for a much longer period. The acorns indeed, already mentioned, served the turn with many, but they brought so vividly to my recollection the prodigal son and the husks, that they actually stuck in my throat, and would not go down. But as a detailed account of the fatigues and hardships which our troops underwent in this arduous retreat might prove tedious, and even uninteresting to many, I will waive the subject. Let it therefore suffice, we reached Ciudad Rodrigo on the 19th, after suffering unparalleled and unheard hardships. Many men who had been under General Moore, during the disastrous retreat to Corunna, avowed they had undergone more fatigue, and suffered greater privations on the retreat from Madrid, than they had ever done the whole of their lives.[11]

10 Presumably 'sacré foutre', or 'holy f--k'. Suggests that perhaps the French were as surprised to find the slumbering troops as the reclining redcoats were at being overcome.

11 William is drawing a long bow here. Moore's retreat was through a mountain range and in the depths of winter. The retreat from Burgos was conducted over much flatter country and in heavy rain.

Notwithstanding the severity of the weather, and the want of provisions, the loss of our army was comparatively small. The total loss of the British and Portuguese, during the whole retreat was stated at 857 killed and wounded, and 421 prisoners; a trifling loss indeed, considering the nature of the operations, and the overwhelming force brought against them. This is the British statement of the affair: the French accounts estimated our loss at 12,000; perhaps a medium might be drawn between the two.[12] On reaching the vicinity of Ciudad Rodrigo, we encamped, when the enemy stopped short in their advance, and even fell back on Salamanca, and other parts. Our army was then put into cantonments on the frontiers of Spain, and our brigade quartered at Fuente Ginaldo.

12 Oman, *History of the Peninsular War*, Vol. VI, pp.747-748, Table IV gives the losses between October and December as 189 killed, 753 wounded, and 4,752 'missing'. Many of the latter were stragglers who subsequently re-joined. According to official returns, Wellington's army lost 1,011 men dead in the period 25 November to 25 December 1812, with most of the missing men back in the ranks by Christmas.

Chapter 16

Dreadful state of the men – Hopes and Fears – A Disappointment – Court Martial – Winter Quarters

A MEDLEY[1]

We remained eight days in this town, during which I suffered much from the want of my blanket, which I lost with my knapsack on the retreat, and a smart frost having set in, rendered our situation truly miserable. Our regiment was quartered in a dark cell of a chapel, the dreary walls of which were cold, damp and clammy. This was very uncomfortable lodgings to men worn out with fatigue and hunger; while our fare was still very scanty, and had no means to procure any more than what was served from the stores. But indeed, though our pockets had been full of money, it would have been to little purpose, for everything was scarce, and what was to be had was at an extravagant price. Bread sold at one dollar a pound, and salt went for half as much, while everything else was in proportion.[2] After walking about all day, like so many spectres, at night we lay down on the pavement of the wretched sepulchre, for in Spain and Portugal the churches are the only place where the dead are interred. Under the floor on which we lay, were, perhaps, all the people that had died in the town for centuries past. This I do not mention as being any grievance or annoyance; they did not disturb us in the least – there being more likelihood of us joining them, than of their joining us.

If it had been possible for a dandy volunteer, or even a militiaman, to have got a glimpse of us at this period, it would never have entered his brain that we were the heroes of the Peninsula, whose victories he had so often seen emblazoned in the public prints. Instead of being the stormers of garrisons and towns; or of being the victors of Salamanca's proud field, our appearance would have made him believe

1 It is not clear why William chose to title this chapter thusly.

2 The Spanish Dollar (real de a ocho), also known as the eight-real coin, or the piece of eight, was the closest thing to a universal currency in the Napoleonic era. The exchange rate was 5 Spanish Dollars to the Pound Sterling.

we were deserters from the tombs, or a set of miserable wretches about to be sent there. The whole of my garb at this time consisted of my red jacket, which, during part of the retreat, had no sleeves, having been torn to tatters amongst the bushes and briers; but which deficiency I had since made good, by stitching to the precious article the legs of my only pair of stockings, the colour of which were light blue, forming a fine contrast with the jacket, which by tear and wear was approximating to a dark brown. My trousers, which once belonged to a Frenchman, I picked up in the Retiero at Madrid. They were originally black, but had so often been mended with patches of divers shades, that it could not be distinguished. As for a shirt – ah! 'Pauvre homnio!'- He had none. A rag of what was once a shirt, hung down before and behind, having much the resemblance of a que, and the whole so stiffened with nits, of so shining a quality, that anyone at a little distance might have thought it richly embroidered with silver lace. At this time, I could have boasted of being the sole proprietor and governor of a population, far exceeding in numerical strength the dominions of the Grand Porte, or of the Emperor of China. But finding their ruler an illegitimate sovereign, having no divine right, my subjects considered me a usurper – one that wished to infringe upon their sacred rights and liberties – and so became seditious, often rising in open rebellion against me, when much loss and bloodshed was sustained on both sides. Shoes and stockings I had none, having left them far behind on the deluged plains of Leon, but which were soon replaced by new ones, received as a gift from the Marquis of Wellington, who so generously bestowed upon every individual of the army, a pair of shoes, in consideration of the arduous service in which we had lately been engaged. This was the second pair I had received in the manner; his lordship having been graciously pleased to order, upon the capture of Badajoz, a pair to each man engaged at that place; but for all this, our situation at this period was truly grievous. We were but meagrely fed, and as has already been mentioned, most wretchedly lodged. While we were in this place, a man of our regiment, wishing as I suppose to extricate himself from the accumulated evils by which we were assailed, attempted to cut his throat, but was by his comrades prevented from completing it. He, however, had given himself a severe wound under the chin, in consequence of which he was carried to the hospital, where his wound was dressed, and put to bed. Not being satisfied with what he had done, he attempted with a razor to sever his hand from his arm, and before anyone discovered what he was doing, he had cut and mangled his wrist in such a manner, that the surgeons found it necessary to amputate his arm under the elbow. What his motives were in thus endeavouring to destroy himself, he would never explain, but if he expected to get rid of the army by it, he was most egregiously mistaken. When recovered from his wounds he was severely punished, and was retained in the service until the termination of the war. He was in all the fights and feuds in which the regiment was engaged – a sufficient punishment – being obliged to stand and be shot at, while he was unable to defend, or avenge himself on his enemies.

Amidst all the difficulties I had at this time to encounter, my mind was greatly supported by the hope I entertained of soon meeting again with my dearest Rosa, which occurrence I fondly anticipated would be a full indemnification for all the toils and dangers I had been exposed to since I last saw her. On the march from Madrid, every step I considered as bringing me nearer to the object of my wishes; and now when only two short leagues intervened between us, I almost felt as if already with her. From the height on which stood [Fuente] Ginaldo, our present quarters, could be seen the valley, where lay her native village, the curling smoke of which I watched for hours, as it rose from the lowly hamlet, and which was regarded by me with as much reverence and satisfaction, as ere the smoking sacrifice was regarded by the most devout and zealous, or the most penitent of sinners. It being generally supposed we would winter in Portugal, whither most of the troops had gone before us, I made sure of passing through Albergaria.

The long wished for order at length arriving, we left Fuente Ginaldo for Portugal. As we descended the hill on which the town is situated, and entered the much loved valley containing all my hopes, my heart throbbed quick, my pulse beat high; and as we drew near the village, I felt overpowered by the contending emotions of hope, fear, and joy. I was indulging myself in all the feelings so peculiar to love, and which none but lovers feel. I thought, perhaps she may be dead! or, what is worse, she may have changed her mind, and already bestowed her heart and hand on some more fortunate lover! But this thought lasted only for a moment – it passed o'er my mind like a summer's cloud. No, thought I, my Rosa's sentiments will still be found the same as when I took the last farewell embrace; in a short time I will be cheered by her smile; in a few minutes I will be transported by her soft and endearing caresses! Her angelic form will be conspicuous in the crowd assembled to witness our entry into the village, from which we cannot be far distant. On raising my eyes to ascertain what the distance might be – Oh! what were my sensations? How did I feel in that awful moment? My very heart withered within me, as I saw the front of the column file to the right, and move on in the direction of Villa Fermosa. To have the cup of bliss thus dashed as it were from the lip – to see my long cherished and most sanguine hopes all at once blasted, was more than I was capable of supporting. A thick film came over my eyes – I reeled and staggered, and falling out of the line of march, I sunk upon a bank that skirted the wayside. I was immediately asked by a non-commissioned officer what was the matter, and making no answer, he ordered me, with an air of authority, to get on. Summoning all the recollection and strength I was master of, and springing upon my feet, I made towards the captain of the company, from whom I solicited leave to go round by Albergaria, promising to be with the regiment ere night. But all my entreaties failed in having any effect on this gentleman; he declared my request was more than it was in his power to grant. Conceiving it of no avail to urge my suit any longer with him, and my mind being now raised to a state bordering on distraction, I was determined to use all the means in my power for the attainment of my object. I therefore left this officer, and with the rapidity of lightening, flew to the head of the column. In a hurried and incoherent manner I addressed the colonel,[3] but, judging by my demeanour, he believed I was intoxicated, and ordered me to my company. Still persisting in my request, which was now assuming the nature of a demand, I was ordered to be seized and taken to the rear-guard. On hearing this order, my mind, which was before sufficiently excited, now rose to the utmost frenzy. I raved, I cursed and swore, and endeavoured to resist those that were about to carry the order into execution, but was ultimately made prisoner, and marched as such, until we arrived at Momento de Beira, where the regiment was to remain during the winter.[4]

When we had been a few days in quarters, I was warned to prepare for trial, and next day was arranged before a court-martial. The crimes alleged against me, were no less than insolence to the commanding officer, and others, and disobedience of orders. Being asked if there was any evidence in my favour that I wished to bring forward, I answered in the negative. My defence being called for, I frankly stated that, considering myself guilty of the crimes laid to my charge, I had none to make, but threw myself on the mercy of the court. At this the escort was desired to withdraw, and conduct me to the guardhouse, for in military courts the award of the council is known but to themselves, until such time as the prisoner is brought out – then the proceedings are read in front of the regiment. On the afternoon of the same day, I was taken out, when a sentence of three hundred lashes rung in my ears, to be carried into execution, at such time and place as the commanding officer should think proper. This was an awful moment – the three 'fatal sisters'[5] which no man embraces, but dearly feels the smart, already stood in grim array before me.

The dread words of 'strip sir', were given. On raising my eyes, which I had hitherto kept fixed on the ground, my former master stood before me, and was to superintend the punishment. I immediately implored his to exert his influence with the Colonel on my behalf, which he promptly complied with, by advancing to our commander, and having conversed together a few minutes, the latter turning round, was pleased to say, that 'in consequence of the high recommendation he had just heard of my general conduct, he forgave me at this time.' I was then dismissed with a caution to take care in future; that if ever I was again arraigned, it would not fare so well with me.

Owing, as it was generally supposed, to the hardships and privations we had lately undergone, we had not been long in quarters when a most malignant fever made its appearance amongst us, by which in a short time numbers were swept away. The nature of the disease being so fatal and contagious, men could not be got to attend the sick, and it was found necessary to take the first for duty. By this

3 Lieutenant Colonel Henry Ridewood.
4 Moimenta da Beira, in the Viseu district of Portugal.
5 William's footnote reads: The triangles.

expedient, I was compelled to attend one of the wards in hospital; which duty I managed above three weeks, but was then seized with the distemper. My head was immediately shaved and blistered, but being insensible, and in a high brain fever, I tore the plaster off, and threw it out of the window. Another was directly applied, while my hands were secured down to my sides; in which state I lay several days. Six weeks elapsed before any symptom of recovery appeared, at which period I was so weak and emaciated I could hardly walk across the room. While here I had an opportunity of being present at the opening of several men who had died of this disease. It was observed, that the lungs were thickly covered with small black spots, which resembled grains of gunpowder; and of all that died, their face in a few hours after, assumed a dark livid hue. When perfectly recovered I was discharged from the hospital, and quartered on a family, in tolerable circumstances, with whom I remained the whole time we lay in Momento, and was regarded and treated as one of the family.[6]

6 87 men of the 45th died whilst cantoned at Moimenta da Beira in January and February 1813.

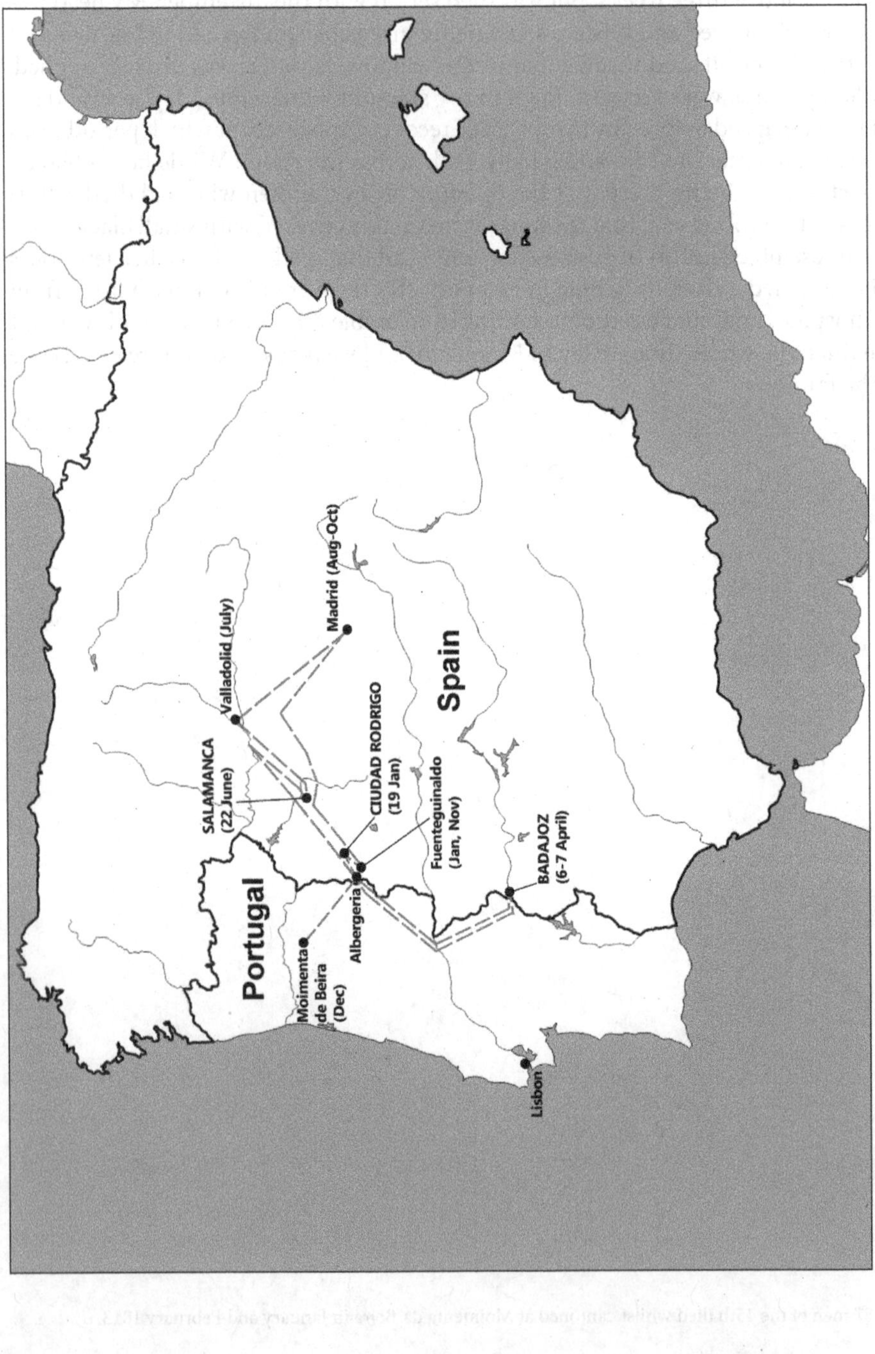

Map 4 Route of the 45th Foot in 1812.

Chapter 17

Advance into Spain – Battle of Vittoria – Narrow Escape – the Misery of Riches – A Robbery – a Row

But now the trumpet, terrible from afar,
In shriller clangours animate the war;
Confed'rate drums in fuller concert beat,
And echoing hills the loud alarm repeat.
ADDISON

During the winter, our army received a great accession of strength, by numerous reinforcements from Britain; while every attention was paid to recruit and re-organise the army after the fatigues of the last campaign. Another of great difficulty and danger was yet to take place, for which supplies of men, and every necessary, continued to be forwarded with the utmost dispatch; so that by the time the season arrived for active operations, the Marquis of Wellington found himself at the head of the most numerous and best-appointed army ever seen in the Peninsula.[1]

The commencement of the month of May, 1813, saw our army in high spirits, and completely equipped for the arduous campaign, which was now about to open. We were abundantly supplied with every necessary and comfort that in the nature of things could be expected. Tents were also provided for the whole army, which were a great convenience, and of infinite service on many occasions. All things being in readiness, our regiment, on the 16th, in conjunction with the rest of the army, left its cantonments, in order once more to try its fortune in Spain.

Having crossed the Douero in boats,[2] near the Portuguese frontier, our army issued from the deep valleys and narrow defiles of that kingdom, and like a flood

1 True at least for the non-French armies – the British contingent of Wellington's army had swelled from 37,146 in January to 47,927 in May 1813; the Portuguese contingent had likewise grown to 30,000 troops. But the French still had over 250,000 troops in the Iberian Peninsula.

2 Douro.

rolled on with great impetuosity, driving the enemy before us, who retreated with the utmost expedition by Valladolid, in the direction of Burgos. By the 13th of June their army reached that town, but finding themselves unable to make a stand, they blew up the fortifications of the place, and retreated across the Ebro, which river our division, with the left wing of the army, under the gallant Graham, crossed at the same time at Avena. On the 16th our whole army crossed this famous river at Quintana; the French, under the command of Joseph Bonaparte, and Marshal Jourdan, continuing to fall back in the direction of Vittoria, at which place they, on the 20th took up a strong position, determined to try the fate of a general engagement. But long ere we reached that point we were much in want of provisions, being several days on half allowance of bread, which was not very agreeable to men on a fatiguing march during the day, and encamped at night. The country had been exhausted by the enemy during their retreat, so that no hopes could be entertained of a supply in that quarter; while our prospects in regard to the stores that were following us, were equally dark. By the 16th, our stores being completely exhausted, we had to subsist on what we could pick up in the fields where we encamped. The bean fields, which were very numerous in that part of the country, were now our only resource. The stalks were torn up by the roots, and carried in armfuls by our men to the camp, but not having come to maturity, nor indeed half grown, the hulls, leaves, and tender tops of the straw, were boiled and devoured with the greatest avidity. Such was our fare for five days preceding the battle of Vittoria.[3]

On the 21st, at an early hour, our division commenced the march, and proceeding along the road two leagues, we afterwards filed to the right and ascended a height, from the summit of which we had an extensive view of the valley of Zadora. It lay immediately in our front, intersected with corn fields and vineyards, and studded with many smiling villages, conspicuously among which stood the town of Vittoria, situated some miles to our left. The valley appeared about three miles broad in front, but extended to a much greater breadth on our left, and was bounded on the opposite side by a chain of hills of considerable height, on which were drawn up in battle array the legions of the France, confident of victory, and ready to receive us. Their confidence was not altogether without foundation – their hopes of success resting on the superior force they had to that of the Allies – the position they held was formidable, and indeed of such a nature, as might have appalled most troops. The dark, deep, and rapid Zadora flowed along the bottom of the heights they occupied, which were fortified with breastworks and redoubts, and strongly lined with cannon; while a broad and level plain intervened between the contending hosts, across which the assailant's had to pass in front of their most deadly foe. Such was the commanding and formidable position of the French army, in the morning of

3 The fact that Wellington's army fought at Vittoria in a state of starvation is not well known.

this ever-memorable day, on which they were driven before our army, like chaff before the wind, or like the thistle down before the autumnal blast.

Notwithstanding all these formidable obstacles, it was determined by our Commander-in-Chief, immediately to commence the attack. Being ordered to move forward, we descended the heights and advanced across the plain in the direction of the enemy. On gaining the river side, it was found unfordable, by reason of the strength of the current, and the depth of water. This was a very unfortunate circumstance, for we were now sorely galled by the enemies' cannon shot from the heights, and annoyed by the fire of their light troops, stationed on the opposite bank. We then moved to a bridge, some hundred yards higher up, but which was found barricaded with wood. From an isolated hill in front of the chain of heights, and about two hundred yards from the bridge, the enemy kept up a heavy cannonade, mowing down our ranks, and literally making lanes through our columns. The bridge being found impassable, to ford the river was once more attempted; but all our efforts in this proving of no avail, orders were given to counter-march, and force the bridge. Being hemmed in between a high thorn hedge and the end of the bridge, we had not space left for this evolution, so that the column got into confusion. This was a dreadful moment. From the enemy's cannon the shot flew quick, our men fell fast, and nothing less than total destruction seemed inevitable, when a round shot from the French struck the barricading, and threw the planks of which it was composed to a considerable distance. Our troops, like lions pursuing their prey, immediately rushed on the bridge, and without any orders being given, cheering as they went, flew up the road, climbed the height, and neither stopped nor stayed until they were on the summit and in possession of the enemy's redoubt, who, in their flight, left behind four pieces of cannon, and a quantity of arms and ammunition.

About the same time that our division, under General Picton, crossed the Zadora, the Fourth and Light Divisions, upon our right, crossed the same river by two different bridges, while the Seventh Division, under the Earl of Dalhousie,[4] followed the route we had taken. These four divisions were destined to attack the heights on which the right of the enemy's centre was placed; while Sir Rowland Hill, who began the operations of the day, by attacking the heights of Pueblo, and carrying the village of Subigan de Alava, moved forward to attack the left. The French were driven in disgrace from their commanding position, and commenced a retreat in good order towards Vittoria. While the efforts of the right and centre were thus crowned with success, General Graham,[5] with the left wing, consisting of the First and Fifth Divisions, with two brigade of Portuguese infantry, and

4 Lieutenant General George Ramsay, Earl of Dalhousie. His division in fact arrived late and attracted Wellington's ire.

5 Lieutenant General Thomas Graham, later Baron Lynedoch. The only subordinate apart from Rowland Hill entrusted with independent command by Wellington.

several brigades of cavalry, moved forward and attacked the enemy's right, which was strongly posted in several villages on the line of road leading from Bilboa to Vittoria; from the whole of which they were driven by the gallantry of our troops, and retreated with precipitation and confusion through Vittoria. Their centre and left, on abandoning the heights, moved through the valley, where they made an obstinate resistance at some villages, but from which they were ultimately dislodged by our troops at the point of the bayonet, leaving several cannon behind them. Retreating in open columns, and filing by companies, they occasionally halted, wheeled into line, and saluted us with several volleys of musketry, but they were instantly charged by our troops, who bore down everything that opposed them. The retreat of the enemy, which had hitherto been conducted in good order, now assumed the nature of a disorderly flight. Pressed hard on both flanks, and closely pursued in the rear by our victorious army, their main body reached the vicinity of Vittoria, when a scene of confusion and dismay ensued which exceeds description. In confidence of victory they had not removed the immense treasure, ammunition, and stores, which they had in and near the town of Vittoria; but when they saw their routed army flying in confusion, they, when it was too late, endeavoured to move it away by the Pampaluna road, the only one now left them. Artillery, cavalry, and infantry, officers and men, were promiscuously crowded with carts and wagons, and in their flight trod one another down; and so great was their fear, that they fled in the utmost consternation, leaving the whole of their cannon and baggage to the victors. Of the whole of their numerous artillery, only one gun and one howitzer were carried away by the routed army; and previous to their reaching Pampaluna, the former of these was taken from them. Joseph's private baggage, with the whole of his servants were taken, while he himself had a narrow escape, being obliged to abandon his carriage and seek safety on horse-back. Jourdan, in despair, threw away his baton of office, which was sent to Britain as a trophy of victory. Of the French force, which consisted of between 70 and 80,000, above 15,000 were lost on the bloody field of Vittoria; and there is not perhaps an instance upon record, in modern times, where an army of this magnitude, in one day, and at one place, lost everything they had which could distinguish them as soldiers.[6]

A short time previous to the flight of the enemy, in a charge made on them, by our brigade, Colonel Reidwood,[7] commanding our regiment, received a wound in his left arm; but brandishing his sword over his head, he exclaimed, 'never mind this, my lads, I will lead you on to glory!' When dashing across the field, our progress was arrested by a high and close hedge, while the enemy from a neighbouring field

6 According to Oman, *History of the Peninsular War*, Vol. VI, pp.754-756, 761-762, Tables X and XII, the French had about 63,000 men at Vittoria, and lost about 8,000. It was all too common to over-estimate the size of the opponent's force, and their losses.

7 Lieutenant Colonel Henry Ridewood.

kept up a most destructive fire upon us, by which our brigade suffered severely. Several of our company were killed. At this moment the balls flew as thick as hail, one of which struck my breastplate, which prevented any further injury. At the same time my comrade, while standing conversing with me, received one in the very centre of his forehead. He fell at my feet, and expired without a groan. He was a native of Ireland, a brave soldier, and had seen much service.[8] As I stood sorrowfully leaning over him, watching the last moments of his existence, I was pulled from behind by the belts, and on turning round, I was ordered by the Adjutant to go and assist in carrying off the Colonel.[9] Three others being ordered on this duty, we found our gallant commander apparently lifeless, stretched upon the green sward. In addition to the wound in his arm, already mentioned, a musket ball had entered his breast, from which flowed fast a crimson stream. Already his late flushed cheek had assumed a deathlike hue; his pale lip quivered, and gave every symptom of a speedy dissolution. This, then, thought I, is the coveted bed of honour, of which men talk so much. My sentiments, at this time, coincided with a certain knights, who thus expressed himself on the subject, 'If this be honour, I'll have none on't.' Having taken a blanket from one of our knapsacks, we laid our expiring commander upon it; and in the silence of grief conveyed him to a neighbouring farm house, where a surgeon attended, who, when he had examined the wound in the breast, pronounced it mortal. In a short time the Colonel's servant appeared, and taking charge of his master, we went to the garden, behind the house, in hopes of finding something to eat.[10] In our search we chanced on some bee hives, and upsetting one of them, we were immediately attacked in great force by the whole population of the kingdom we had invaded, who annoyed us considerably with their sharp and pointed weapons, and kept buzzing about our ears as thick as the French bullets had done lately. While thus engaged with our new enemies, the surgeon entered the scene of action, and perceiving how we were engaged, he began in a very gentleman-like manner, by bestowing upon us the soft, and perhaps as he thought, polite epithets of d-m-d scoundrels, plundering villains, skulking cowards, and many more compliments in the same style, all of which we took in good part. Having at last got through the whole of his vocabulary, we endeavoured to extenuate ourselves from the gross and unfounded charges he was pleased to load us with, by venturing to state that we were neither one nor the other of what he termed us; that we had been sent there on duty, which had been performed, and were now waiting until he pleased to give us farther orders. Upon hearing this, which this mighty son of Esculapius termed the grossest insolence,

8 According to casualty returns, this was Private John Mahoney.

9 The Adjutant was Lieutenant Charles Barnwell.

10 Ridewood's servant was Private George French, a middle-aged soldier who had transferred from the 52nd Foot to the 45th at the same time as Ridewood, in order to keep serving his master in his new regiment.

he got into a rage, and vowed he would have us severely punished when he joined the regiment, to which he ordered us to pack off instantly. This was exactly what we wanted. The afternoon of the longest day in summer was far spent, on which we had not tasted food, and for the previous five days what had fallen to our lot was but little. Now we fondly hoped that, when following our regiment over this field, where such an abundant harvest of honour and glory had been reaped, that a crumb of biscuit, or a crust of bread would fall in our way, with which we might ally the gnawings of hunger that now preyed upon our vitals; and we felt that being deficient in the 'one thing needful' it was of no avail to have our brows encircled with the glorious and unfading wreaths of victory.

Previous to leaving the place, we entered the house and took a last and farewell look of our brave commander, who upon the boarded floor, lay struggling in the agonies of death; and who, as we after learned, did breath his last ere the sun again gilded the eastern horizon.[11] Proceeding on our way, we followed the blood stained tracks, left by the contending hosts, which were then far in advance. The peal of cannon and the firing of musketry, which had since morning rolled like the loudest thunder, had then comparatively ceased. The obstinate and desperate combat had given place to a ruinous and disastrous flight, in which the once proud, but now humbled eagles of Gaul, were pursued and taken, by the victorious, and now no longer couchant, but rampant lion of Albion. But in all this there was much to deplore; victories, however, splendid, are the cause of much human misery. On the ground we trod, lay thousands of our fellow creatures, wrapped in their gore, who, but a few hours before, were young, gay, and animated. Numbers, who still retained the vital spark, but from whose bosoms the tide of life ebbed fast, faintly implored, (and often implored in vain) for the small boon of a drop of water to quench their parched thirst, and cool their burning tongues. But independent of these immediate victims to ambition, what woe, what anguish, and even fell despair, would their untimely fate impart to thousands of relatives – the loving wife, the tender mother, and kind indulgent father. But all this is often forgot in the blaze of victory, and what ought to be in the foreground of the picture, is too often thrown into the shade.

Passing over this field of blood and carnage, we came to a number of wagons that had been left by the enemy, all loaded with provisions, which at the same was more precious than fine gold. Numbers of our men were already employed in filling their haversacks, and drinking brandy, casks of which lay about in great plenty. My associates and I were no way backwards in entering the lists, when we

11 In fact Ridewood rallied and endured nearly three weeks of agony tended by Surgeon O'Connell and Paymaster Dalhunty, as well as his faithful manservant Private French. Shortly before his death, he wrote out his resignation from the army. His heavily-pregnant wife Charlotte anxiously waited for news in Lisbon. He died on 11 July. Charlotte soon after delivered a daughter, Henrietta, the couple's only child.

did great justice to the viands our enemies had so plentifully provided. Having for the present satisfied the cravings of nature, and laid up a store for the future, we left this spot, and soon after got upon the great road leading to Vittoria, from which we were then not far distant. On our way we passed a great number of carts and wagons, the whole heavily laden with provisions and stores; but which formed only a small part of the immense loss the French had sustained on this (to them) fatal day. On a field to the right of the road, we perceived a number of wagons, around which the greatest noise and tumult prevailed; numbers of men were seen on the top of the carriages, tumbling to the ground whatever was on them, while others ran snatching and tearing from each other what had fallen. Our party stepped up to this scene of confusion and bustle, and found it to proceed from the 'root of all evil', which has been the cause of much riot and strife to mankind, in mostly all ages and countries. The wagons were loaded with money, consisting of doubloons and dollars, packed up in boxes strongly hooped with iron, which the soldiers were now breaking open. A large stone being the only instrument they had to effect this with, it was regarded as the key to the treasure, and as such became an object of great contention. Happy was he, and lucky was he thought, who got hold of it; yet, after all, they that were thought so, seldom touched the box they had broken, it being immediately seized by those that stood around, when a most desperate scuffle and scramble ensued. In the confusion, I made shift to secure 500 dollars, and 90 doubloons, a sum equal to £549 sterling.[12]

At the foot of a tree I sat down, and reckoned my gains, but found myself far from being happy. This sum, which appeared to me immense, was far beyond what my sanguine hopes had ever anticipated. The transition from poverty to comparative wealth was too sudden. If it had been a few dollars only, I would have been at ease, nay overjoyed, and would have spent it the first opportunity; but the sum I now possessed was too great to throw away at folly's shrine, and how to dispose of it to advantage was more than I knew. To carry it with me was impossible, being to great an addition to the load I was already burdened with. Although this had been practicable, I would not have retained it long, for the very men I was amongst would have eased me of it; and for such a sum, without the least compunction would have served me as the Romans, under Titus, served the Jews. I knew full well the best and safest method was to send it home, but as far as I knew this was also impracticable. In fact I was in a complete labyrinth of care, and for the first, and I fear the last time in my life, I experienced the misery of being rich. My mind was so absorbed that I did not perceive that the shades of night had fallen, and I enveloped in her sable mantle. The noise and tumult which drew me to the spot had ceased, and been succeeded by a deathlike stillness, by me unheeded. The braying of a mule at last aroused me from my reverie, when I sprung to my feet, somewhat startled by the uncouth sound. I seized the animal, which I found to be

12 A sum equivalent to about ten year's pay for a private.

a French one, and mounting him, made the best of my way to the camp, which was a league in front of Vittoria, where I arrived long after midnight.

This night our camp exhibited a very different spectacle from what had been seen in it for some time past. Instead of the bean straw, which had been our only fare for a considerable while; the greatest abundance now prevailed, and that at the expense of the enemy. While their wagons and carts, which lay in every direction, were broken up for firewood, the blaze of which might have been seen for miles, numbers of our men who had gone back to the scene of action, now returned, driving before them herds of oxen and flocks of sheep, while others came galloping on, mounted on horses and mules, leading others behind them, heavily laden with spoil. On the forenoon of the next day, the division decamped, and followed the route of the enemy, who fled in the direction of Pampaluna,[13] closely pursued by our light troops of cavalry and infantry. We had not proceeded above a league on the road, when the division was halted, and the men ordered to open their knapsacks, which were immediately searched, and all the money found in them seized upon by our rulers, without asking any questions concerning how, where, or when it was got. Thus was all my treasure lost, as suddenly and as unexpectedly as I had found it; and whatever trouble and care it had caused me, while in possession of it, I felt no abatement of uneasiness when deprived of it. In fact, I considered the affair as a most flagrant act of injustice, and an extension of arbitrary power, that robbed me of what I conceived to be justly my own. If what I had got had been plundered, or wrung from the subject of an ally; or if when engaged I had stepped aside, or lingered behind, and commenced marauder, in either case I would have deserved, and in all probability would have been severely punished. But in this instance I had done neither. Situated as I was at the time, it would have been worse than folly to have declined lifting the money that in a manner lay under my feet; part of which I considered my due, as I had done what in me lay to force the enemy to abandon it. I had hitherto abhorred the numerous acts of cruel rapacity I had seen perpetrated by our men, but now grieved and irritated to the highest degree, in that hour I swore never to forego an opportunity of aggrandizement, whether at the expense of friend or foe. How faithfully I observed my vow will be seen in the next chapter.

13 Pamplona, the capital of the Navarre province in northern Spain.

Chapter 18

Vittoria – Major B[urton] – A Mistake – Provost Marshals Guard – Commissariat Store – Breach of Trust – A Hotel established by the Author – Bribery – Spanish Don – A Punishment – Marauding Party – Pyrenees

Now the rude soldier, with unsparing hand,
Robs the poor peasant, and despoils the land.
ANON

When about to move from the spot, where this licensed and general robbery was committed, an order was given for a number of men to be sent to Vittoria, in order to do the duty in that town, until such time as the Spanish troops would arrive, and relieve them. Thirty men from each regiment of the division were ordered for this affair, and the first for duty being taken, I was included in the number. We were immediately sent to our destination, which was two leagues distant. Our route lay along the road which the enemy in their flight had taken, the preceding evening. It was now blocked up by cannon, ammunition wagons, and other carriages, which they had abandoned in terror, and by which we now encountered considerable difficulty in passing. On entering the town, we remained on the streets while arrangements were making concerning our quarters, during which we experienced a most hearty welcome from the inhabitants, who assembling around us, displayed the greatest enthusiasm, and rent the air with shouts of 'Viva Los Engleses.'[1]

A number of young women began the 'Volera',[2] in which they assumed all the lascivious attitudes, and went through the most voluptuous movements, for which that dance is noted. The music they had was a pipe and tabor, which was played by a fellow very fantastically dressed, and the orchestra he performed in, was one

1 'Long live the English.'
2 Volero, more commonly spelled bolero.

of the wagons left by the enemy. This burst of joyful mirth and gladness, formed a striking contrast with the desolation and ruin that prevailed in the place, everything bearing the marks of recent warfare. Many of the houses were defaced; what was once the enemy's baggage still lay and obstructed the passage in the streets, where were strewed many of their slain, on which the Spaniards vented their fury and revenge, by mangling the lifeless and inanimate bodies. Having been two hours in the midst of this noise and tumult, we were lodged in an old barrack, which so recently as the day previous had been occupied by the French. We were in a short time joined by numerous detachments from the different divisions of the army, the whole placed under the command of that eccentric, or rather original character, Major B[urton], who belonged to a distinguished regiment of fusiliers, at that time serving in Spain.[3]

Many humorous anecdotes and blunders could be given of this meritorious and gallant officer, but perhaps if enumerated here would seem out of place. I shall therefore confine myself to the relating of a mistake that he made, when but a few days in command at Vittoria, and which happened as follows: Two men, belonging to the garrison, having committed some menial trespass, were confined by order of the Commandant, who swore in his ire he would make an example, by punishing them severely next morning. In the interim, however, it so happened that one of the prisoners was found to be innocent of the crime imputed to him, when the worthy Major, (who by the by, was a man of discernment, and could distinguish right from wrong), relented, and resolved within himself, that the innocent man should not be punished, but be relieved from durance vile in the morning. Accordingly, next day at parade, the prisoners being brought out, our Commander harangued the man that he supposed guilty, on the heinous and aggravated nature of his crime; and getting into a passion, without having patience to wait on the formalities of the court, he resolved to have the culprit punished through the mere summary medium of the Provost Marshal, who was immediately ordered to proceed with the punishment. The man accordingly received his quota, which was several dozen of lashes, and was then ordered to be taken down by the good commandant, who turning to the other prisoner, was pleased to say, that understanding he was innocent, he forgave him; but the Provost, knowing how matters stood, said it was the guiltless man who had been already punished – the worthy Major, with the greatest nonchalance, observed, that it was all right enough, for though he was innocent then, he would be guilty some time else.

The garrison were employed several days in the melancholy duty of interring the slain, and collecting together the wreck of the French artillery and baggage, which was drawn up and arranged in the fields near Vittoria. The front line consisted entirely of howitzers, of which there were 49. In rear of these were three lines of

3 Major Robert Haly Burton of the 7th Royal Fusiliers; a man who had worked his way up from the ranks.

brass cannon, the whole in most excellent order, amounting in number to 181.[4] Next followed several hundred wagons, all loaded with ammunition, 36 camp forges, 52 elegant coaches, said to have belonged to General Officers; a great variety of gigs and carts, belonging to sutlers and other followers of the army; while an amazing number of wagons closed the rear laden with provisions, clothing and other stores.[5] Amongst other curiosities was a portable corn mill, carried upon a sort of carriage about the double length of a cart – the machine was turned with the hand. The above I several times enumerated as they stood in line, and may be depended upon as correct. Eight wagons, laden with money, were said to have been left on the field, five of which I can vouch for, as I both saw and counted them, and likewise carried off part of their contents.

A division of Spanish troops having arrived,[6] the British detachments, after a stay of fourteen days in the place, left Vittoria in order to join the army, which was by that time on the summit of the high and lofty ridges of the Pyrenees. On the first day's march, owing to the extreme scorching heat of the weather, combined with the horrid stench arising from the putrid bodies of numerous horses and mules that lay dead on the road, I was seized with a loathing, attended by a violent reaching and vomiting, so that by the time we reached Salvatira,[7] where we remained for the night, I was so sick that I was hardly able to speak, look, or move. Next morning, I set out on the march, but not being able to keep up with the troops, I was with several others left in a small village, distant two leagues from our quarters of the preceding night. Here I was once more housed in an hospital, an appellation the place could scarcely lay claim to, being destitute of every comfort and convenience, and not even supplied with the most urgent necessaries. Of medicine, there was little or none, and instead of beds, the patients lay on the hard and cold pavement. A number of wounded were also in this wretched place of abode. The negligence with which these poor fellows were treated, might have served as a lesson to others not to be overly adventurous or fool-hardy in the day of battle. One poor fellow, who had got a wound in his throat, was in a miserable condition – a ball had entered immediately under his chin, issuing at his neck, and the wound having never been properly dressed, was now full of maggots. The consequence of which may be easily anticipated – mortification ensued, which cut the silver thread. He was then, according to custom, thrown out, and buried with as little ceremony as if he had been a dog, or some obnoxious reptile. For my own part I neither received medical aid nor advice, nature was left to work her own

4 Most histories put French losses in artillery at 151 pieces, considerably less than William's total. They escaped with just two pieces, which were captured the next day.

5 Sutlers were civilian merchants who followed the army, and often sold items at inflated prices.

6 Wellington had approximately 50,000 Spanish troops under his command in July 1813, although he rarely used them as first-line troops. The division relieving Vittoria was probably that of Capitan General Enrique José O'Donnell y Anatar, an officer of Irish descent.

7 Salvatierra, about ten miles east of Vittoria.

cure, which was perhaps as well for me, for I soon recovered, and at the end of eight days from the time I entered the place, was discharged as able for duty, and with four others sent forward to a village about four leagues distant, where I remained six weeks, during which I once more experienced the fickleness of dame fortune, who in her frolicsome mood at that time, seemed to make me the butt of her play.

The village was romantically seated at the bottom of a lofty chain of mountains, which, diverging from the Pyrenees, formed the boundary of one side of the fertile valley in which it lay. It was situated on the direct road from Vittoria to Pampaluna, and was exactly midway between them, being three days' march distant from either of these towns, both of which are very important places at that time. The former was the grand depot for our sick, wounded, and stores, while the latter was closely besieged by part of our army. These circumstances rendered this hamlet of great interest, as it was the only place where provisions could be drawn by the detachments and parties daily passing to and from the army. For that purpose, a commissariat store was established, and a guard of twenty-four men, under a Provost Marshal, stationed. To this guard I was attached, with which I remained all the time I was in the place; the duty was easy, and being abundantly supplied with provisions, the time passed pleasantly on, until an event occurred which once more sent me adrift from this haven of rest, which happened as follows:

Hitherto our guard had furnished a sentinel for the commissariat store, which occupied a small chapel, situated at a short distance from the village, but the commissary, wishing a detachment of our guard to be situated there, a corporal and three men; amongst whom I was included, were sent to do the duty of the place. This was by us counted a lucky hit, there being worse jobs in Spain than stationed at a provision store, for there we might safely calculate upon getting our rations regularly, and perhaps something more. Whilst thus congratulating ourselves on our good fortune, we took up our ground on a green in front of the chapel, on which, packed in bags, stood a pile of biscuit not inferior in size to the chapel itself, in the shade of which we now sought shelter from the intense rays of the sun. On the afternoon of the same day, a brigade of mules, laden with stores arrived, the conductor of which was an English sergeant, who being a little inebriated when he came in, very soon got more so, by sitting tippling with the store-keepers in the chapel, on whom the rum they consumed (which was not a little), had such an overpowering influence, that they retired to rest, the guard had to assist them upstairs. Having got the coast clear, the guard removed from their bivouac on the green, and entered the chapel, in which they took their quarters for the night, leaving a sentinel at the door, while the remainder stretched themselves on the floor to rest. In this position, I had not been long ere I was aroused by the sentinel, a man of the 40th Regiment, a queer, odd fellow, who kept pulling me by the arm, and in a low tone of voice desired me to rise, for he wanted to speak with me. Getting up on my elbow, he put a kettle of rum into my hand, saying, 'take a good swig of that, 45th, you will be much better of it, then I will want the help of your hand,' so saying he led me into the interior of the building, and on coming to a large skin of wine, 'now,' said he, 'let us get this upon my shoulder, and I will ease the house of it in a twinkling.' Having got loaded, we immediately made for the village, and deposited our cargo in a hay loft, immediately above our former guard-house, which was an old stable.

We again returned to the store, and made free with a bag of biscuit, which we laid alongside our wine. During the night, we repeated our deprivations several times, and at daybreak found ourselves possessed of such a quantity of provisions, as might have served us several months, independent of our allowance. But this was of no use to us – we were amply supplied from the stores, and at the time we were laying it up, we did not know what could be done with it. It was mischief, however, and that was enough; for, from the time I had been so gulled of my money, I was reckless, and ready to embark in any depredation whatever. Next morning, when the store-keepers got up, a portmanteau was missing, which belonged to the sergeant, who had arrived the preceding evening with the stores. The guard was immediately questioned concerning it, in the course of which they found out that none had been on sentry during the night except the 40th man and me, to whom the blame was directly attached. Of the portmanteau, I believe neither us knew anything, as I think it was lost before the conductor came there, in the midst of the interrogations, the Provost Marshal happened to come to the store; who, when informed of the matter, ordered us both to be confined and put in charge of his guard.

Thus was I deprived of a situation from which I had anticipated great advantage, and from the debauch of another, (for I believe the portmanteau was lost by the owner before he came), put in durance vile, from which, however, I was soon relieved. When about two hours confined, the Provost entered the guard-house, and ordered me to join the guard, desiring me at the same time to take my bayonet and stand sentry over that old rascal, pointing to my associate and fellow prisoner.

While on this service, numbers of sick and wounded (many of whom were in the village) frequently enquired where wine or spirits were sold, when the idea presented itself, that my charge and I might turn to good account the store we had secreted in the hay loft, by disposing of it, and commencing business on our own account. We were sure of having a quick market, and ready money, for as there was not a vintner in the place, we would have a monopoly of the business to ourselves. The thing was no sooner thought of than acted upon. The skin was brought down, and my companion seating himself in the manger, began to pour out the liquor, while I lifted the money with the one hand; the other, in virtue of my office, being armed with the bayonet, for I still preserved the appearance of a faithful sentinel. Things went on swimmingly; and word having gone abroad that wine was selling in the guard-house of the Provost Marshal, numbers poured from all quarters to purchase, who flocking around us, made a great noise and clamour to get served, as they perceived the wine getting low, which was reduced to a gallon. In the midst of the bustle in stepped the Provost, who, coming forward and seeing what was transacting, seized the skin, exclaiming, 'you must be a d-m-d old rascal,' and with it laid lustily round the chops of my confederate, who, without the power of motion, sat in the manger, like a criminal condemned; while I, terrified, and sure of a sound flogging, flew to my post at the door, at which our customers made their exit with the greatest possible dispatch. Although armed with arbitrary power, the Provost, (although a Provost) was a good fellow, and asked no questions; but after reprimanding me for allowing such numbers to enter the guard-house, he walked out with the skin in his hand, of which we never heard more. At this we were both well pleased, for if the affair had been inquired after, a severe flogging, or perhaps something worse might have been the fatal consequence. We were not, however, without our doubts and fears, for evil doers are always evil dreaders. We were afraid that this calm with our officer was only the prelude of a coming storm; but in this we were agreeably deceived. For in a few hours after the affray, the Provost entered, and ordered my companion to join the guard, which at once set our minds at rest.

On the evening of the same day, the commander announced to his guard, that he wanted three volunteers for a certain service which was to be performed next day. At this intimation, the whole guard sprang to their feet, offering their services, for soldiers are ever willing to embark in anything that promises novelty, or has the show of adventure. But the Provost had now a knowledge of our talents and address, and perhaps having a kind of fellow-feeling for us in our roguery, made their choice of the 'old rascal', as he had that very day termed my boon companion, the 40th man, to whom he gave the party in charge, which consisted of a young lad belonging to the 2nd, or Queens Regiment, and myself. The duty we were destined for was the pressing of mules, for the purpose of conveying the sick and wounded that were in the village to Vittoria. Hitherto the mules that were employed in the commissariat department, had been used for this purpose, when coming down unloaded from the army, and going to the rear for stores. They had been invariably seized by us as they passed through the village, and loaded with sick and others. Who were not able to walk; but the muleteers, who were Spaniards, although they had a dollar per diem for each mule employed, and provisions for themselves, eluded this duty, by taking another, although a more circuitous route. It was on this new route we were to lie in wait, and seize all that might come.

Next morning according to orders, we left the village at an early hour, and proceeded about a league across the valley until we came to a river, over which crossed a bridge, where we had been ordered to make our rendezvous. We accordingly halted, and established ourselves on the spot, by kindling a fire and commencing to cook our breakfast, at which we were busy, when a tinkling of bells was heard, and soon after a number of mules with their riders were seen shaping their way towards us. In order to keep from their view, and to make sure of our prize, we posted ourselves behind the parapet of the bridge, where we remained until they were within a few yards of us. Starting to our feet, they put about in all haste, galloping off in various directions through the fields, while our party continued the pursuit. Benson (that was the name of the man belonging to the

40th) and I continued to follow three of the muleteers who still kept together, at whom, to intimidate them, we fired a few shots, which caused them to halt; then seizing and mounting their mules, we left the owners to walk by our side. On our way back to the bridge, the Spaniards having consulted amongst themselves for some time, one of them came up and said that he and his comrades would give each a dollar, if we would let them away with their mules – which offer was immediately accepted by my companion and I. Having drawn from their scarlet girdles the money, and paid us our ill-gotten gains, by our directions they scampered off as fast as they could, to avoid discovery. That day no more mules made their appearance; and when evening came, we returned to our quarters as empty-handed as when we left them.

Early next morning we took the road we had been on the preceding day, but as ordered by the Provost, passed the bridge about half a league where we entered a narrow defile between two high ridges of mountains, both of which were thickly clothed with chestnut, and other trees to their summits. The road and river occupied the breadth of this deep and sequestered dell. On the side of the former farthest from the river, stood a small chapel, the grey and deserted walls of which, at a distance, almost appeared as one of the projecting rocky peaks, that everywhere jutted out from the swelling sides of the mountain. At this romantic hermitage, we had orders to halt, which was a most fitting place for our business, as neither man nor horse could pass without coming near us. We had not been long halted before two Spaniards made their appearance, each of whom had two mules. We immediately laid hold of them, to the utter consternation of the owners, who not being in the service, knew not what we meant or intended. In the simplicity of their hearts, they begged us to let them go on their way, for which kindness they would ever prey for our welfare and happiness. But perceiving we did not wish for any such thing, and that we were determined to detain them, though for what purpose they could not divine, they at last sat down in a very dejected state at the door of the chapel, almost persuaded they had fallen into the hands of the banditti, in which opinion I believe our subsequent conduct confirmed them.

We had scarcely tied the mules to a tree, when another Spaniard, belonging to our commissariat department, rode down the road on a mule, which we accordingly seized; but the rider, who seemed to know all the powerful influence of money, proffered a dollar for his liberty, upon which terms it was granted. When the other two saw that money was our hobby, they entered into a negotiation with us, which ended in their giving us a dollar for each animal, and promising to fill our canteens with wine, when they returned in the afternoon. About two hours after, a party of Spanish troops, consisting of thirty men, with a commissioned officer and two sergeants at their head, were seen coming down the way that our two friends, the muleteers, had taken. As they were about to pass, we were standing in front of the chapel, without any dread or fear, with our arms lying against the wall. In a moment, some of them sprung at our arms, while others seized our persons. This was but the work of a moment – we were in their power ere we were aware of their intentions. They then proceeded to rifle our pockets, from which they took all they found in them; our very knives were taken from us by these brigands; not even a flint was left, which, indeed, was now not material, as we had already lost our muskets. What money we had was also seized with avidity by the rogues. Fifteen dollars which I had, the proceeds of the sale of our wine, and the profits arising from the preceding two days, were all lost, and I once more left poor and penniless; which situation, perhaps, some of my readers will by this time think too good for me, and that I almost deserved hanging, which to tell the truth I very narrowly escaped at this time, as will be seen in the sequel.

Meantime, while our visitors were busy plundering us, we demanded to know by whose authority they treated British soldiers in such a manner, and what were their intentions by doing so; but all we could learn from them was, that we would know all about it soon enough. After having thus lost our all, we were marched off as prisoners by the Spaniards, who returned by the way they had come, and in the course of an hour, we arrived at a village, where a division of their troops were quartered, and where we soon learnt the cause of our capture. The two muleteers, who promised to treat us so liberally with wine on their return, upon reaching their countrymen, reported to the Spanish general that a band of English soldiers were lying in wait on the road, and were robbing everyone that passed the way; and that they themselves had been detained and plundered by the lawless heretics. It was upon the strength of this report that the party who seized us had been sent out.

On entering the village, we found the inhabitants, who had heard some vague report of the matter, all in a ferment; but when they saw the party advancing with us as prisoners, a great shout of exultation was given by the whole of the villagers, who came crowding around us, with looks and language that bespoke no great amity. They even pressed so close, that I believe they would have fallen foul of us, had not the guard restrained them, by using the butt end of their muskets, with which they laid so lustily about them, that I almost expected a scuffle would have ensued. We, however, at last got to the quarters of the general, but he being gone riding, we were detained on the streets until he returned, which was two hours afterwards. During the whole of that time, we had to bear the taunts and reproaches of all the men, women and children in the village. Of one woman, who stood near with a pitcher of water, I asked a little to drink, but she dashed the whole of the contents about me. Notwithstanding, I had no resource but patience; yet I thought, if ever an opportunity occurred, when time and place favoured, and of which I did not then despair, I would make some of her countrymen dearly pay for the insult.

When the general returned, he conversed with the officer a few seconds, and ordered a party of six men and a sergeant, to escort us to our quarters. It was deemed by this Don a necessary precaution, that three of his men should leave their firelocks, and carry ours, as it might have been attended with danger to have allowed us our arms on the road. We attempted to remonstrate with his 'Excellenza' against all these proceedings, and wished to know for what crimes we were treated in such a manner; but were struck dumb, when we perceived his heavy forehead lower and blacken, like a watery cloud in a thunder storm. His thick and bushy eyelashes almost his from view his small and animated eye, from which the lightening flashed. Part of his under-lip was drawn between his teeth, which were so compressed, that he appeared as if grinning at something horrible, just like what I conceive a tiger would be when about to pounce upon its prey; while his dark and strong mustaches, which had hitherto been curled, now stood erect and bristled up like quills on a porcupine. He walked about some time, seemingly greatly agitated with choler, which it was evident he wished to conceal, and at last gave a motion with his hand to the party, by whom we were directly marched off.

On entering the village in which we were quartered, we found on the street and standing together, the Commandant, the Commissary, two officers who were on their way from the army to the rear, and the Provost; the latter of whom had visited our post while we were absent, from which he concluded we were gone a marauding, in which he now supposed, we had been caught by the Spaniards. Upon being led up to him, he accosted us with 'well, gentlemen, I am happy to find you in such good company; I hope you can give a good account of yourselves!' But for this we got no opportunity; the Spanish sergeant took that upon himself, by relating to the officers the whole of our story, as far as he knew it, and something more, for however black our crime was, he took care it should lose nothing in the telling. He added certain items of a very aggravated nature, for which he had no foundation whatever, but which we were not permitted to contradict – it being the invariable practice with our officers in the Peninsula, to believe any charge that might be preferred against us by a native. But if the sergeant was lavish with his words, he was as niggard of his money; for, of thirty-two dollars that were taken from us, he gave only twenty to the Provost, which he, in our presence, had the effrontery to say, was all he had. But he did not get so easily away with this as he did with his false accusations. If we were not permitted to prove him a liar in the one instance, we made him a rogue in the other; for one and all declared he had retained twelve dollars, which being a money matter, and of interest, we were believed, so that the bluff sergeant after a deal of altercation, was obliged to give up the whole. This however by no means tended to extenuate or favour us. The Commandant having heard the extent of our guilt, declared he would have us soundly flogged, to which in his ire he swore by G-d! But the two officers already mentioned, having intimated that four men had, on the preceding week, been hanged at headquarters for a similar crime, our good Commandant again swore he would send us there, that we might share the same fate; at the same time ordering us to be confined, and a strict watch set over us.

When we reached the guard-house, I got into my old berth, the manger, where I sat for some time bewildered and confounded, for I looked on myself as one upon whom sentence of death was already past, and considered all things at an end – at least as far as sublunary affairs were concerned. I began to take a retrospective view of my life and transactions, when a faithful monitor within upbraided me for many a vile deed committed in folly and wantonness, at the recollection of which I now shuddered. When such were my reflections on the past, what could be my anticipations of the future? At the thought of which I was about to wish I had never been born, when the impious wish was arrested on my lips, by a bustling outside, caused by the officers, Spaniards and others, whom we had left on the street, coming to the door with the Commandant at their head, who ordered the Provost to bring out the rascals, and give them a d-mn-d good flogging. At the hearing of this I sprang to my feet overjoyed, for I well knew that without a previous trial, they could give us no more than four dozen each, which was but a trifle to hanging. We accordingly walked cheerfully out, where we found all in a train of preparation for the affair. The drummer was busy adjusting the cat-o-nine-tails, at the sight of which I was not so mortified, as to see the Spaniards who had brought us in, standing with a demonic grinning smile on their countenance, and inwardly feeling satisfaction at our degradation. The Provost, addressing Benson, said 'come, 40th, as you are the oldest man, and I am certain, the greatest rogue of the three; and above all, you had the charge of the party; you must strip, as I intend you will have the honour of being punished first,' at which the poor old fellow was tied up, and received two hearty dozen on the back, and as many on the breach. Our military gentlemen of those days, put in practice various modes of torture, which I hope, for the reputation and credit of the knights of the epaulet of the present time, has ceased to be inflicted. Not that I wish the humane and manly exercise of cutting up the back, and stripping the bones bare, should be laid aside; God forbid! I hope there is yet as mush patriotism in me left, as not to wish or even dream of such a thing. Flaying the back, and making flesh and blood fly, as it were dust, has done much for the army, especially when the victim has been lashed out of one faint into another. Such gentle treatment has been the glorious means of transforming many a young and innocent lad, to a hardened old villain; and consigned many a stout and robust young man to an untimely grave. Such is the general benefits arising from the wholesome punishment on the back, But the breach – hiss! Fie! Out upon the poltroon that ever thought of such a thing.

The other lad was next bound up, and had not got above a dozen, when the lash flew off the shaft, and the drummer having none to replace it, we were all remanded back to our confinement, until such time as another could be procured. In an hour after, the Provost and his minion – skin him alive! – returned, when I was called out to receive my quota. None being present but ourselves, I ventured to vindicate my cause with the Provost, by stating that what the Spaniard had reported concerning us, was nearly void of truth, and that the money found on me had not been received as bribes from the lousy muleteers, but that I had fought hard for it on the field of Vittoria. All, however, would not do; I was ordered to strip, the Provost declaring he was bound to do his duty. Accordingly, I was tied up, and had received nine lashes, when the drummer was ordered to take me down.

Next day, a party marching from Vittoria, to join the army, arrived in the village to which, along with my two companions in stripes, I was attached, and same day left the place. The party, which consisted of four hundred men, was but a short way on its march when several sat down by the roadside, declaring their inability to proceed farther. In a short time, old Benson did the same, and soon after I followed his example; for I conceived there was likely to be some sport on the road, and in all probability, something made of which I stood in need, as I had sold my three days' provisions before leaving quarters. About thirty yards beyond me, two other planted themselves on the wayside. The officer commanding halted the party, and caused to be gathered together all who had fallen behind, whose case he very much commiserated, and declared that if it was in his power, he would hire wagons for our conveyance; but as no vehicles of any description could be procured, he left us in charge of a non-commissioned officer, with orders to bring us on as easily as he could. This officer was a young man of a humane and feeling disposition, and newly arrived from England, consequently he knew little of what was called the 'rigs' in Spain; and had no idea that the fellows he felt so much for, were as stout and able as himself, and intended nothing but to rob and plunder. But the sergeant, to whose tender care we had been consigned, knew better; and when the party marched off, he flatly told us he was aware of our intentions, adding, 'whatever you do, I hope you will hurt no person.' Being thus admonished, we moved forward, and in a short time met two Spaniards, laden with a sack of bread apiece, which they were carrying to the village we had left, in order to sell it to the Commissary. But we soon eased them of their burdens, and gave them as much, perhaps, for their good as that gentleman would have done, save the promises given at such bargains making, for such was the currency often used in the Peninsula by that provident department, with which coin they paid thousands, and as I have heard, tens of thousands, of such cargoes as that which we had lightened the Spaniards.

Proceeding on our way, we came to a farm house, in the door of which stood a large sow, which, without any premise, was shot by one of the party, and dragged out to the road, where in a few minutes it was dissected, and secured with blood, bristles and all, in our haversacks, leaving the head and feet to the (ci devant)[8] proprietor, who inside stood peering out at a broken window, no doubt both terrified and astonished at our audacity. We soon after met a shepherd driving his flock before him, whom our sergeant ordered to bring the best sheep he had, and made the poor fellow cut the throat of his own animal, which was immediately deposited along with our pork.

Our next adventure was at an inn, situated on the road, which, without the least hesitation, we entered, and called for a quantity of wine. Here we gave the senior patron part of our meat to dress, with which a most excellent olio was made, cooked in the true Spanish mode, being highly flavoured with garlic and cayenne pepper,

8 Former.

which was an excellent stimulus, if any had been wanting, to use the liquor, which we quaffed in great style. As night approached, we were warned by the sergeant, that it was time to depart, as we had still two long leagues to walk, before we could reach our quarters, and in a knowing sort of manner, asked how the reckoning was to be paid? At which there was a kind of demur amongst us – one declared he had not a half-penny; another that he had not a rap; and one and all declared that there was not a cross amongst us. 'Well', said our hopeful sergeant, 'I think you are a pack of the veriest rascals I have ever seen; I suppose I will have the reckoning to pay myself!' With this he called our host, to whom he told a long story, for which he was well qualified, being the best speaker of the Spanish language of any Briton I ever found. Having eulogized the good qualities of the wine, and passed some encomiums on the kind usage we had received in the house, he told Boniface that we were in the guard of the commissary, whom we expected would have been up before that time; and as that officer defrayed all our expenses on the road, he would to a certainty call as he passed, and inquire what we had got. As night was approaching however, we were under the necessity of moving forward; but that he might be under no apprehension for the reckoning, he would make out a line, which he, the landlord might present to the commissary on his arrival. During this preamble, he to whom it was addressed stood at the right elbow of the speaker, timidly patting his shoulder, and muttering 'bon, bon Sergeant, monte obligate.'[9] When he received the promised document, the contents of which were very foreign to the affair in hand, he treated the sergeant to a glass of brandy. We soon after left the house, and when near midnight, arrived at the village where the party was quartered, and where, by the humanity of the officer commanding, a house was set apart for the poor men, who had been left so ill on the road.

The reader, no doubt, will think I begin to glory in my wickedness; but this night as I lay down on the clod clay floor of the hovel I was lodged in, I began to reflect on the conduct I had pursued for some time past, which to my mind now appeared hideous and glaring. It is true, my feelings had been highly excited by the loss of my money from Vittoria, yet, that was no fault of the poor peasants, whom I had since robbed and plundered, for which I now felt very sorry, and ere I fell asleep, I firmly resolved never to injure any individuals in the Peninsula. Next morning, I joined the party, which continued its march, and rested that night in Tolosa, a considerable and handsome town, with numerous and extensive orchards in the vicinity, which at this time were full of beautiful fruit, of the most delicious flavour.

On the following day, we passed the nearly sea-girt battlements of St Sebastian, closely invested by our troops, under the gallant Graham; where many British heroes were, by French intrepidity, stopped short in their career of glory, and their bodies left to fertilize the soil around this strong and memorable fortress.[10]

9 'Very good, very good, Sergeant, I am much obliged.'

10 Wellington lost nearly 2,400 men in the assaults on San Sebastian in August 1813.

Passing Lesaco, a small romantic place, deeply embosomed amongst the Pyrenees, by whose frowning and pendant 'sierras' it was nearly overhung; but which at the time was gay and animated, owing to the headquarters of our army having been established there. From this spot we commenced climbing the lofty and towering mountains, whose cliffy and rugged peaks seemed to pierce the clouds. For several days, we continued to pass these barren heights, at time enveloped in a dense fog, and again, while in the narrow defiles, almost scorched with the suns penetrating rays, and the heat reflected from the rocky sides of the mountain. When we had gained the summit of one ridge, which, while ascending, we fondly hoped was the last of those strong barriers, which nature had wisely placed between France and Spain, we invariably found it succeeded by another, more lofty and steep than the one preceding it. Sometimes a fertile valley of considerable breadth intervened, studded with villages and hamlets. In other places a deep and horrid chasm, with a rapid rolling river at the bottom, parted these giant mountains, and so narrow, that the traveller is apt to imagine he could leap from one summit to another. We at last reached the spacious and beautiful valley Arrascoon, where I found our regiment encamped with the division, in the vicinity of the village of that name.[11]

11 The 3rd Division was at Arizcun.

Chapter 19

Arrascoon Camp – Hail Shower – Advance into France – Battle of the 10th November – An Encounter – Orentes – John Duke – 'War to the knife's point' – Robbery – An Execution, – Jedburgh Law – Quarters – An outpost

> The roving Gaul, to his own bounds restrain'd,
> Learns to encamp within his native land;
> But soon as the victorious host he spies,
> From hill to hill, from stream to stream he flies.
>
> ADDISON

The ground on which the division encamped, was an elevated spot near the head of the valley, round which a lofty chain of mountains made a bold sweep, forming a semicircle, in the bosom of which lay our lines and tented fields, where floated our victorious banners, and where gleamed many a pile of burnished arms, and thousands of British hearts, ready to repel the lawless aggressions of those, who have been termed Britain's natural enemies. This delightful spot afforded and extensive prospect of the rich and fertile valley, adorned with several villages, elegant chateaus, and the humbler, but no less useful cots of the farmer; while fields of luxuriant, and gold coloured maize, waved on every side, intersected with venerable orchards, where hung in clusters the luscious pear and mellow apple, which yielding amazing quantities of excellent cider, was sold at a price, which in our free and happy country, would not nearly pay the excise duty. Indeed, apples were so plentiful that the troops almost lived on them; we had them baked, boiled and roasted; and ever after, when speaking of this spot, it was always denominated the apple camp.

I had been a few days only in this desirable situation, when the army was put in motion, by the enemy making an attempt to relieve St Sebastian. Marshal Soult, with a force from 30 to 40,000 strong, made a desperate attack on our lines, the very day on which the town was stormed and taken by our troops, but was driven back with great loss; and after repeated attempts completely routed, principally by the Spaniards, who this day stood firm and true.[1] In this affair only part of our army was engaged. During the day, our division, with several others, were drawn up on the chain of the Pyrenees next to France, from which we beheld the engagement, which was principally in the lower Bidossa.[2] There I also, and for the first time, had a most extensive view of the 'Sacred Territory'.[3] The loss of the allies in this affair was stated at 2,400 men of which only 417 were British. That of the enemy was estimated at 7,000.[4]

On the afternoon, as the troops were returning to camp, a heavy and tremendous shower of hail overtook them, which astonished all, and confounded many who had never been afraid of showers of shot and shell. It commenced with moderation, but in a few minutes descended with appalling weight and rapidity. We were at the time marching along the summit of a high ridge, without shelter of house, hall, tree or bush. It fell in hard pointed pieces of ice, near the size of a hen egg, and again bounced from the hard and benty[5] turf as high as our heads. For my own part, when I saw it get so heavy, I expected whole sheets of ice to come next; but after continuing about twenty minutes, during which the generality of the pieces that fell, weighed several ounces, the sky brightened up, and the hail ceased. Some will perhaps doubt my veracity in this relation, but several of my townsmen, who were eye witnesses of the phenomenon, and who are now at home, can vouch for the truth of what I assert.

After repeated marching and countermarching amongst these mountains, which was often very harassing, the division encamped on the chain next to France, from which we had an extensive view of that delightful country. It appeared from those lofty heights as one continual level plain, on which could be distinguished as on a map, the cities, towns and villages that chequered the surface, and the serpentine windings of the numerous rivers and mountain streams, rushing from the Pyrenees, and pouring their transparent tides to the broad Atlantic, descried on our left, which from our position appeared as a sea of molten silver.

On this elevated position, we remained until the winter was far advanced, when it became indispensable, from the inclemency of the season to find more comfortable quarters. To look for these in our rear was out of the question; therefore we had no alternative but to attack the enemy, who had of late received considerable reinforcements, and occupied a strong position in our front, which for three months they had been fortifying with great care and labour. Accordingly, long before daybreak, on the 10th of November, our troops descended from the snow-clad

1 This was the battle of San Marcial on 31 August 1813.

2 Bidasoa, in Basque territory.

3 France.

4 William is referring to the skirmishes at San Marcial, Salain, Vera, Zagarramurdi, and Urdan which took place on 31 August 1813. French losses were actually closer to 4,000.

5 An archaic form of the word bendy.

mountains, and trod the 'Sacred Territory', which from their lofty encampment, they had for nearly four months beheld with anxious impatience minds. Owing to some delay that took place the morning was well advanced ere we reached the enemy's outworks, which were a line of forts and redoubts upon a plain. Having passed these without molestation, we moved on to their main position, which was about half a mile to the rear of these works, and situated on a height, strongly entrenched along the sides, with redoubts on the summit. At the onset the enemy's centre was the principle point of attack, in which our troops encountered considerable difficulty, from the strength of the works, and the defence that was made. But British Valour ultimately overcame every difficulty; for dashing through the Sorre,[6] which by-the-by was no great cordial on a frosty morning, and surmounting the abates which the enemy had laid on the slope of the height on which they were posted, our troops drove them from their double row of entrenchments, and in a few minutes after established themselves in the redoubts. They then abandoned their strong position, after having sustained considerable loss.

While the efforts of the centre were thus crowned with success, our left attacked the enemy's right, behind Anhoa, when they were driven from all their redoubts and entrenchments on the banks of the Nivelle, which were carried in gallant style by the troops under General Clinton, and a division of Portuguese. Being driven from all their positions, the enemy commenced a retreat, and were closely pursued by our army, by whom they were sorely annoyed the whole day. About dusk in the evening, our division encamped in a wood for the night, during which the enemy abandoned all their positions and works in front of St Jean de Luz, and retired upon Bidart, destroying all the bridges on the lower Nivelle. In this affair the French loss was 3,000 killed, 1500 taken, and 51 pieces of cannon.[7]

Being for duty upon reaching the camp ground, I turned out with the piquets, and was sent several hundred yards in advance of the camp, with a sergeant and twelve men, where we were posted on a road, on which the enemy had an advance post, about three hundred yards from us. On the intervening space, which might be termed debatable ground, stood a house on the right of the road, to which, when it was dark, four of us went, in order to see what could be made, or in other words – to rob the house. On arriving at the door we found it open, and without hesitation walked into the first house I had been in since I had entered France, but found it abandoned by the inhabitants, and quite dark. In groping round we found a lamp, with a wick and some oil, which we contrived to light at a few embers which were still glowing in the hearth. Being thus enabled to see about us, we immediately set to work. With the aid of a hatchet, a large chest was soon broken open, where we found a ham and a half of bacon, a small bag containing about

6 Sare, a redoubt in the centre of the French line.

7 Wellington always considered the Battle of Nivelle, fought on 10 November 1813, one of his greatest achievements. His losses were 3,300 men to the French 5,000.

a stone weight of flour, and two large loaves, of the size they are generally made in the south of France, which is from sixty to seventy pounds' weight. This was a great prize, the like of which none of us had been in possession of for a long time, and were congratulating ourselves upon our good luck when footsteps were heard in the passage, to which our attention was immediately attracted. A man's head was seen looking in at the door of the room. On the front of his cap was an eagle; by which ensign we knew him to be a French soldier. With some hesitation, he was by one of our party addressed in Spanish, and desired to enter, when a French grenadier, full six feet high presented himself, and stepping forward, was followed by four more, as stout and robust as himself. For a short time we continued with a fixed look to eye each other, as if inquiring whether it was to be peace or war; but the good Germans, as we afterwards found them to be, having looked at us and our prize, which was still lying on the floor, civilly asked if there was any more provision in the house? We replied, that we had seen none, but that we would assist them in searching for it, and if there was no more to be got, we would willingly share what was before them. With this they seemed to be well pleased.

After a fruitless search, we fulfilled our promise, by making an equal dividend of all we had got, at which the Saxons were much elated.[8] 'Well', said they, 'we have now got abundance to eat; let us endeavour likewise to get something to drink, for we must not part thus dry!' Accordingly, with lamp in hand, we all proceeded to the outbuildings, where, in a place resembling a barn, we found thirteen un-broached pipes. These however, we did not touch, but found a sufficiency of most excellent wine in an old cask that lay in a corner, with a spigot in it. Having filled a tub to the brim, we sat sown on the floor, and soon got as hearty as bucks, and were all merry and friendly as if we had been old acquaintances met after a long and painful separation. When we had emptied the tub oftener than once, we filled our canteens, which we had providently brought with us, and after shaking hands with our boon companions, they returned to their piquet and we to ours, that we might repose a short time, and recruit our exhausted strength, and be enabled to mingle in the mortal strife and din of arms, which was again expected to commence with the dawn of morning.

At day-break our army continued the pursuit of the enemy, who retreated with precipitation in the direction of Bayonne, and were, after sustaining considerable loss, compelled to take refuge in their entrenched camp, under the walls of that fortress. In this truly formidable position, Soult, one of the most skilful of all the French Generals, with 60,000 men, held his quarters, and derided the efforts of his antagonist, but to whose superior prowess he was again destined to yield. Besides the force at Bayonne, the enemy had a considerable force at Villa

8 It is unlikely the men were Saxons, Saxony having defected to the allies in October 1813. Soult's army contained a brigade with men from Nassau, Baden and Frankfurt; the 'Germans' were likely from this brigade. It is interesting that they used Spanish as a lingua franca.

Franche and Monguerre, and also a strong division at St Jean Pied du Port.[9] But the weather proving unfavourable, from the incessant rains that fell, it was impossible to undertake and operations of consequence: our army was therefore put into quarters.

During this interval of repose, our brigade was quartered in the straggled village of Orentes,[10] where our regiment was again cooped up in a cold, damp and uncomfortable chapel. In this drear abode my comrade, John Duke, was seized with a violent colic, to which he had been for some time been occasionally subject, but was worse at this time than I had ever seen him. He was accordingly carried to the hospital, where next morning I paid him a visit, and found him in the greatest agony I ever beheld a man. He rolled on the floor and groaned most piteously. The pain he suffered must have been dreadful; his eye-balls were so protruded, that I actually thought they would have burst from their sockets. I shall never forget the look he gave when I entered the room – 'Oh William,' said he in a tone that bespoke the deepest regret, 'I shall never get over this! Oh! my dear wife you little know what I am suffering; would to god thou were here! But it is impossible; I shall never, never more behold thee or London more!' Poor fellow, he spoke with too much truth, for he was relieved from all his troubles on the afternoon of the same day. John was a native of London, and although a cockney bred and born, was a simple, honest, well-meaning man. He had a wife, as his exclamation above reports, for whom he had an ardent affection; but being one night in a tavern, he was kidnapped by a recruiting sergeant, and torn from her embraces, whom he never beheld more.[11]

The weather having somewhat cleared up, thought the roads were in a dreadful puddle, we were at the expiration of three weeks, once more called out on active operations. On the 9th of December, the right of our army, under General Hill, passed the Adour, and drove the enemy from the right bank of the river, who, after some resistance, retired towards Bayonne. Their remaining force at Villa Franche, were attacked by some Portuguese and British Regiments of light infantry, who repulsed the enemy, and gained possession of the heights and village which they occupied. At the same time, the left wing under Sir John Hope,[12] advanced from St Jean de Luz, and reconnoitred the entrenched camp below Bayonne, driving the

9 Probably Villafranque, Mouguerre, and Saint-Jean-Pied-de-Port, running south-east from Bayonne.

10 Arrauntz, immediately south of Bayonne.

11 John Duke enlisted sometime between 1806 and 1810. He deserted on 6 April 1810 and re-joined on 13 October 1812(!), later volunteered to go to Spain, and served with William Brown in Captain McDougall's No. 4 Company at Vitoria. He died on 4 December 1813. Despite the impression created by this statement, army recruits were never press-ganged as practised by the Royal Navy. Far more likely certain promises and agreements were made under the influence of alcohol.

12 Lieutenant General Sir John Hope, 4th Earl of Hopetoun, recently arrived in the Peninsula. He commanded a wing due to his seniority, without the degree of trust given by Wellington to Hill and Graham.

enemy's outposts before them. In consequence of these movements, their force at St Jean Pied de Port fell back and retired upon St Palais, where part of our troops were stationed at Haspareen to observe them.[13]

Being now aware of the danger he was in, Soult, with an intention of making a desperate effort, withdrew all his troops, with the exception of as many as were sufficient to man the works in front of our right, and on the morning of the 10th made a furious attack upon our left, but was repulsed on all points, with the loss of many killed and 500 taken prisoner. He again on the afternoon made another attempt, which proved as unsuccessful as the former. The 11th was a day of peace, but on the morning of the 12th, he again renewed his attempts on our left wing, in furtherance of his favourite object, which was to outflank our left, and interrupt our communications with the rear; but being completely foiled by the gallantry of our troops, he again retired to his entrenched camp. Finding our left invulnerable, he drew his whole force to his left, and attacked our right with great impetuosity, but met with a warm reception from the troops under General Hill, to whose assistance the Third, Fourth and Sixth divisions advanced, when the enemy were routed at all points, and compelled once more to seek shelter in their entrenched camp. In these contests, which were very sanguinary, and scarcely equalled to any in the Peninsula, the enemy's loss was very great, stated to be 10,000 men, while that of the allies did not exceed half the number.[14] During the engagement on the 10th, two German regiments came over to our lines, and were afterwards sent to their own country, to fight their enemies in that quarter.[15]

Our army, by these movements, having got command of the Nive and Adour, down which rivers the enemy received all their supplies, Soult abandoned his position in front of Bayonne, leaving a strong garrison in that city, and retired with his main body towards Dax. Owing to the incessant rains that now fell, our army was put into cantonments – our regiment being quartered in the farm houses in front of Haspareen.

About this time a robbery was committed in the regiment, upon one of our captains, who, one morning awakening from sleep, found his portmanteau, which he used as a pillow, had been carried away during the night from under his head. Amongst other things in it, were forty guineas in gold. His tent was immediately on the right of his company, some of the men of which were suspected of having a hand in the affair, the whole were put under arms in marching order, in which state they continued for two days. On the third day, an order was issued by the Colonel,[16] to level the ground on which the tents of the regiment were pitched.

13 Hasparren, south-east of Bayonne.

14 Wellington's losses were 4,900, and the French were 5,900.

15 These were the two battalions of the 2nd Nassau Regiment, many of whom later served under Wellington in the Waterloo campaign, and the Frankfurt Battalion. This occurred on 10 December 1813.

16 Lieutenant Colonel Thomas Forbes.

Accordingly, this company of unfortunates set to work with the rest, and on turning up the floor in one of their tents, five guineas were found in the earth. This was bringing things to a point – the men of that tent only were kept under arms, who, being innocent, came to bethink themselves, and recollected that two of their tent mates were absent, who being servants to the subalterns of the company, had never been thought of till then. It was suggested they ought to be sent for, which being done, they were both found drunk in the camp. They were accordingly put under arms, in which situation they had not been long ere they began to quarrel with each other; and word passing between them, conceived to be evidence of their guilt, they were both committed prisoners in the quarter-guard. Being on that guard at the time they were brought in, I had an opportunity of witnessing their conduct, which was foolish in the extreme; they loaded each other with reproaches and curses; and one accused the other of having taken the portmanteau, while the other swore he had been prompted by him to take it. Being searched, a few guineas were found on both, and when asked what they had done with the remainder, they said they did not know. A man that had been drinking with them, was asked at a venture by the Sergeant Major, what he had done with the ten guineas that Kelly had given him, when he replied, 'I did not get ten, I received only seven'. This was enough – he was likewise confined, and in a few days after tried with his companions by a General Court-Martial. One of the two robbers, and as is often the case, the greatest rascal, saved his life by giving evidence against the other, who was condemned to be hung by the neck until dead; while the other poor fellow, for having the seven guineas in his possession, was sentenced to seven hundred lashes. Both awards were carried into execution two days after. The culprits were natives of the sister kingdom.[17]

Nearly about the same time, another execution took place within the brigade. The victim was a man of the 88th regiment. One afternoon, having, after a long and harassing march, encamped in a wood, we were called out to witness this, which was by all looked upon as nothing short of cold-blooded murder. The brigade being formed into a hollow square, the prisoner was brought with his arms pinioned, and assisted by the guard to mount a car that had been brought for the purpose. The Provost Marshal, without giving the why or wherefore, without law or reason, tied the rope round his neck, and having fastened the other to the branch of a tree, the car was drawn from under the unfortunate man, who hung until next morning. As there was no trial, nor proceedings of a court, or sentence read, this man had not even got the benefit of a Court-Martial; and as there was nothing said on either side, for the Provost deigned not a word nor even a look, which was perhaps owing to his natural modesty and bashfulness, being ashamed

17 Captain James Leslie was the officer robbed; Private John Hernon received the lashes; and Private James Kelly was hanged. Kelly was the only man of the 45th to be put to death by capital punishment during the war.

to look us in the face while acting as hangman, as well he might, the scoundrel! And as the poor man was too much agitated and overcome by his feelings to speak, he was therefore launched into eternity, without us knowing what his crime was. A report however, was circulated, that he had been seized by the Provost-Marshal, when coming out of a house with a ball of worsted yarn in his hand. This was, to be sure, a horrid crime; and especially in a country whose armies had laid waste to kingdoms, and whose crimes had made desolate the whole of Europe; in which there was not a town, nor scarcely a single house, that had not experienced the fatal effects of French cupidity.[18]

It must not be supposed, though in quarters, that we were at rest, or enjoying peace and comfort; it was far otherwise. Each alternate day we were on duty, nearly the one half of our number being on piquets at the outposts, which were pushed out in advance to the very teeth of the enemy, a small stream, over which a man might leap with ease, being the only boundary between our sentinels and theirs. There we stood on the opposite banks, and conversed with as much freedom as if we had been the greatest of friends, and intimately acquainted for years. Indeed, the cordiality that subsisted between us was very surprising and pleasing, and at the time I thought it a pity that so many men, who had no umbrage at each other, should be led by the nose, and made to butcher one another, merely for the sport and aggrandizement of a few. Our situation was rendered very disagreeable by the heavy rains that fell without intermission for above a month, from which some of our piquets had no shelter. I remember of being at one of these houseless outposts for three days successively. The piquet consisted of six men and a corporal; we were posted on the brow of a hill, where we sat like so many half-drowned rats, exposed to all the winds that blew, and the deluge of the rain that continued to pour the whole time. In fact our misery was such, that we had all resolved, if we were put on the same post next day, to step over the burn, and try what kind of weather was there; but one of our party, being more adventurous, or perhaps more impatient that the rest, anticipated us, by actually going over the same night to the enemy, with some of whom we saw him next morning leave the piquet and proceed towards their quarters. We were, however, in a short time after relieved, and gave up all thoughts of following the example.

18 Wellington had ordered that the French population were not to be ill-treated, and adopted a zero-tolerance approach to the enforcement of same. He wanted the French to consider his army as liberators, not enemies, in the somewhat monarchist-leaning south of France.

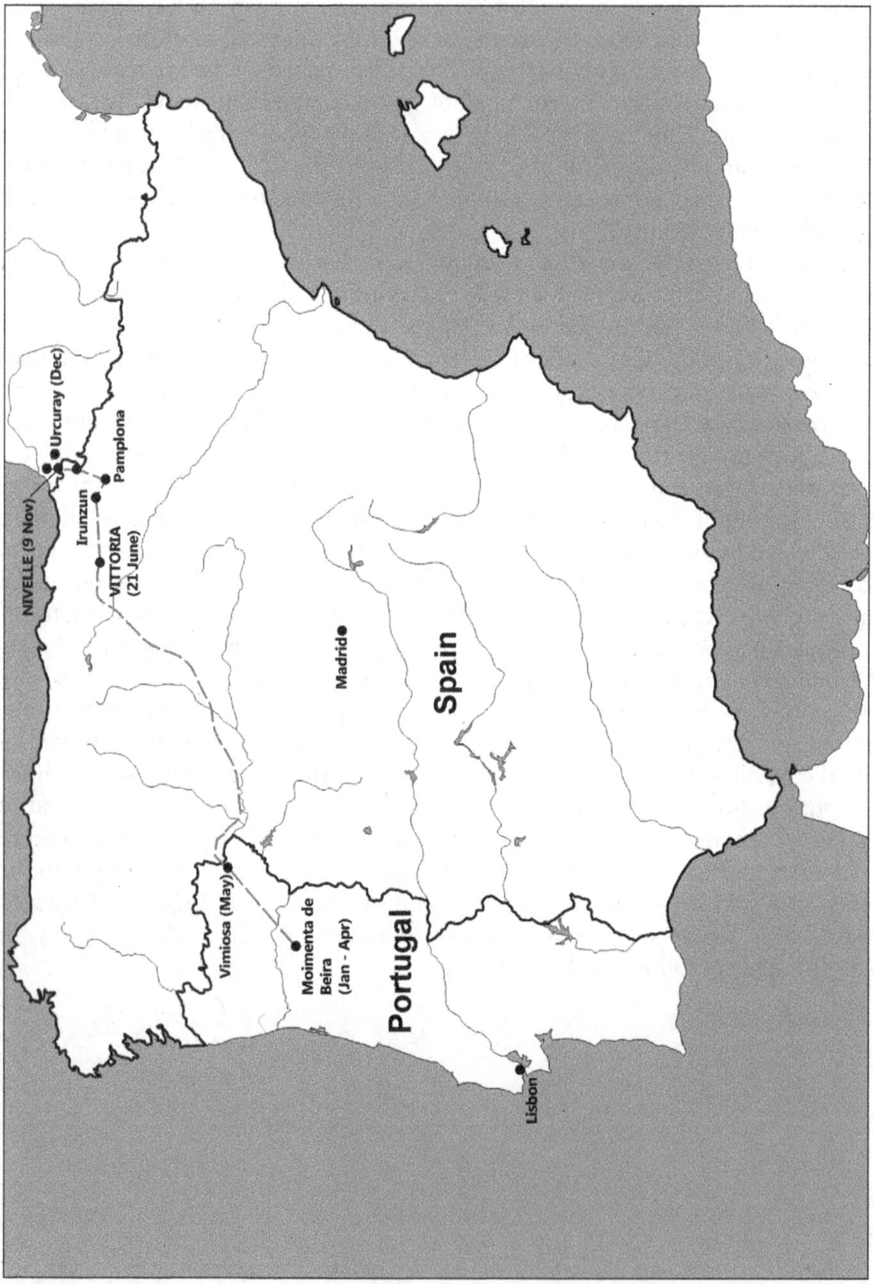

Map 5 Route of the 45th Foot in 1813.

Chapter 20

Battle of Orthes – Exhausted State of the Troops – Reflection – Dreadful Effect of a Charge by Cavalry – An Execution – Remarks – Passes the Adour – Skirmishing at Vic Bigore and Tarbes – Sacrifice to Bacchus – Pontoon Bridge – A Joke – Colonel F[orbes] – His Mania

A thousand glorious actions, that might claim
Triumphant laurels, and immortal fame
Confus'd in crowds of glorious actions lie,
And troops of heroes undistinguished die.
ADDISON

After a stay of nearly two months in front of Haspareen, the weather having become more moderate, our army prepared to advance. Leaving a strong force, under Sir John Hope, to besiege Bayonne, the remainder, early in the month of February, 1814, passed the Gave de Moulin, the enemy retiring before us, destroying the bridges, and making what obstructions they could, by cutting deep trenches across the road, in order to retard the progress of the artillery and stores, but all of which were surmounted with little difficulty. By the 24th the Gave de Oleron, and Gave de Pau rivers were passed by our army. The enemy fell back on Orthes, where they assembled their army, determined to try the fate of a general engagement, and took up a strong position in the neighbourhood of that town, on which their left rested, while their right extended to the heights on the road to Aix, and occupied the village of St Boes. Owing to the course of the heights, their centre was considerably retired, forming their line into a kind or semicircle, which, with the strength of their position, rendered them very formidable.

On the morning of the 27th, part of our light troops advanced, and commenced skirmishing with the enemy's advanced corps, while the bristling columns on both sides were drawn up in dread array, to decide the fortune of the day. In a short time orders were given to advance, when the whole like lions rushed to the combat. By a simultaneous movement of the divisions composing our army, the enemy were attacked from right to left. General Hill fell upon their right, attacked and threatened to turn their left, while their right encountered the shock of the Fourth and Seventh Divisions, supported by a strong body of cavalry. The centre and left were attacked by the Third and Sixth divisions, under General Picton, supported by Lord Edward Somerset's brigade of cavalry.[1] When advancing, our brigade passed along a narrow lane directly in front of the enemy's centre, from which they kept up a heavy cannonade, by which we were sorely annoyed, and had a number killed and wounded. We dashed forward, however, at double quick time, and soon got under cover of the heights on which the enemy were placed. Being thus secured from the destructive fire of their cannon, our General halted, and after drawing us up in close columns by regiments, he seemed to get into a kind of quandary, and appeared not to know well what to do. In the meantime the enemy advanced to the brow of the hill and continued to pour volleys of musketry upon us, until the Adjutant-general, who was a most gallant officer, came galloping from the left, exclaiming 'good God General B[risban]e, what stand you there for, like an old woman, while the brigade gets cut off? Form line and send out the 45th a-skirmishing.'[2] Two companies being left with the colours, the remaining eight ascended the hill, but were received in such a manner as I had seldom before experienced. We were but a handful of men, a skirmishing party, opposed to a dense column of infantry, supported by artillery and cavalry; the bullets flew as thick as hail, and literally tore up the ground from under our feet. Thirteen men of our company alone fell within a few yards of each other, on the brow of the hill; notwithstanding, our men continued to press on the enemy, who after a dreadful conflict and carnage, gave way, when we got possession of a ditch, which we kept until the brigade advanced in line.

Our party having been reinforced by several light companies from the division, now advanced at double quick, and giving three cheers, charged the enemy's light troops, and drove them from a ditch, in a parallel with the one we had just left. In turning round the angle of the ditch, one of our company, before he had time to front the enemy, received a shot in the hip, and fell on the bank, exclaiming, 'blast my limbs!' Having repeatedly charged and been charged in turn, our party got on a height, from which we had a complete view of the dark masses of the enemy in column, one of which was advancing to the point we were on, while their officers, with hat in hand and loud huzzas, encouraged their man to advance. By this time our party was greatly diminished in number, nearly the one half having been obliged to give way; but a staff officer came up at the critical moment and

1 The Hussar Brigade; the 7th, 10th and 15th Regiments of Light Dragoons (Hussars).

2 The Adjutant-General was Major General Sir Edward Pakenham, Wellington's brother-in-law; the brigade commander was Major General Sir Thomas Brisbane, despite the anecdote an effective and popular officer.

encouraged us to stand our ground, as we would be relieved in a few minutes by the troops that were advancing. Accordingly, two brigades of the Light Division, which had hitherto been left in reserve, formed immediately in our rear, when we retired, filing through their line, which advanced and encountered the enemy on the summit of the height, where a most desperate and sanguinary conflict ensued. Our troops, when at a distance of a very few yards, fired a volley and instantly charged, pushing with the bayonet their adversaries downhill, who fled in the greatest haste and consternation.

The enemy, being driven from their positions, commenced a retreat, which was for some time conducted in good order, but General Hill having passed the Gave de Pau, attacked and threatened to turn their left, which threw their whole army into confusion. Their retreat was soon converted into a ruinous and disorderly flight, in which they were charged by our cavalry, making dreadful havoc amongst them. Many of their soldiers threw away their arms, and thousands were taken prisoners, besides a number of cannon. The total loss in this action was estimated at 10,000 while 3,000 was said to be that of the Allies. The pursuit was continued until night, when our division encamped in a field by the wayside.[3]

This had been a day of great exertion by the greatest part of our regiment. We had since morning been running, and leaping hedges and ditches; and for my own part, I had fired two hundred and fifty rounds of ball cartridge, by which my shoulder at night was as black as coal.[4] The consequence was, the men were so fatigued, that when encamped, they either could not, or would not pitch the tents, but threw themselves on the ground exhausted. We were, however, ordered to set them up for our own welfare, which was at last, with manifest reluctance, complied with, for few entered them, but sat or lay round the fires, although it was a keen frost. Notwithstanding the toil and peril we had been exposed to during the day, there was no bread for us at night; we were therefore obliged to put up with the carrion that was served to us for beef, which we frizzled over the smoky fires, and having swallowed it, composed ourselves to sleep on the clod-frozen ground.

Next morning the bugles sounded at daylight, when I awoke, and found myself in a dreadful state with cold. I was so benumbed all over that I could scarcely move. Good God! thought I, as I sat upon the ground, how will I be able to march this day? I looked around and perceived numbers in the same condition. Poor fellows! Thought I, it would have been much better for you and I, to have been used

3 William's figures seem vastly over-inflated. According to Oman, *History of the Peninsular War*, Vol. VII, pp.551-556, Table IX, Wellington's losses were 2,100; French losses were slightly over 4,000. There were also many French desertions after the battle, symptomatic of the waning French morale, which might have influenced William's estimate. The 45th suffered severely in the battle, losing one officer and fourteen other ranks killed; nine officers, one serjeant, one drummer and 104 rank-and-file wounded, plus four men missing.

4 The average infantryman carried sixty rounds of ammunition in a leather pouch, which suggests he made at least four trips to the ammunition wagons or stores in the rear during the battle.

The Battle of Orthez in France in February 1814, a battle at which Wellington ruthlessly exposed the widening cracks in the Napoleonic French veneer. (Anne S. K. Brown Collection)

as manure for the fields of Portugal, as many of our comrades were years ago, or left with the thousands slain on Busaco's steep cliffs, than to be thus dragged on from day to day, and year to year, through distant and extensive regions, in which we have no interest, but to be at time famished with cold and hunger, at others exposed to the nearly vertical rays of a southern sun, and smothered in smoke, dust and sweat, while aiding and abetting:

> Mad ambitions gory hand;
> Sending, like blood hounds from the slip,
> Woe, Want, and Murder o'er the land![5]

At last by a straining effort, I got upon my feet, packed my knapsack, and fell into the ranks, which were then forming up. My gaiters, which to ease my ankles I had thrown off the preceding evening, I now left behind me, they being as stiff as boards with lying in the frost all night. When about to march, the animating shout of 'turn out for rum!' was heard, which soon re-echoed from all quarters. Owing

5 From *A Winter Night* by Robert Burns.

to the severity of the night, the Commander-in-Chief had been pleased to order an extra allowance of the vivifying liquor, which was accordingly received by us while standing in the ranks, and under its animating influence we marched off in pursuit of the enemy.[6]

When we got upon the road, a most horrid spectacle presented itself. Our cavalry, on the preceding evening, had at this spot charged the already routed and flying enemy, who now lay thickly strewed on the road, which was nearly blocked up with the dead and dying. Many of them had received dreadful wounds from the British sabres. Arms, accoutrements, and baggage, lay in promiscuous heaps, or were strewed on the ground. As we passed along through this havoc of blood-shed and horror, an appalling sight of another description met our eyes, which was as follows:- His excellency, the Commander in Chief of His Britannic Majesty's Forces in the Peninsula and France, Generalissimo of the Allied armies in the Peninsula, Field Marshal Arthur Wellesley, the most noble Marquis of Wellington, Duke of Ciudad Rodrigo, Lord Talavera, and Count Vimera, Knight of the most Noble Order of the Star and Garter, &c. &c, &c, in his wisdom, thought proper at this time and place, to cause a man of our division, and of the 5th Regiment, to be hanged by the neck until dead, dead, dead. The poor fellow was apparently dead enough, and hung suspended from a tree on the road side as we passed; in order, as I suppose, to greet our eyesight, and cheer our hearts, after the fatigues of the preceding day, and by was of encouragement to strain every nerve in future. What the man's crime was I never learned, but doubt not that it must have been enormous – perhaps the taking of a loaf of bread, when he was in danger of being starved to death for want of provisions, which ought to have been served him from the stores; and which, get or not get, he and all others would be charged with. Or, perhaps, he had the audacity to lift a ball of worsted yarn, an article which, my readers will recollect, his grace evinced a great respect for upon a former occasion.

Leaving this scene of horror and death at a rapid rate, we pursued our march along the road the enemy had taken, on which they had left marks indicative of their confusion and defeat. Quantities of arms and accoutrements lay on the way, which had been thrown away by the soldiers, many of whom were taken prisoners. From this time we daily met numbers, who had abandoned the standards, under which they had so long fought, now returning to their homes. This the pursuit was so eager, that we halted only once, and then but a few minutes. I do not recollect of ever being so hungry as I was at that time; the cravings of nature were so pressing, that I attempted to eat some grass I found in a ditch, but it would not go down. I was therefore obliged to push on as well as I could until dark, when we encamped in a wood, where provisions were served out about midnight.

On the 29th the division passed the Adour by a wooden bridge, which the enemy had in part destroyed by fire. In a few days we came up with them at Vic

6 Rum being as popular in the army as it was in the Royal Navy.

Bigore, from which after a smart skirmish, they fell back upon Tarbes, a handsome town, and extremely neat and clean. As we passed through this place, the inhabitants stood on the streets with pitchers of wine, and pressed us to drink, to which we were nothing loathly. From this place, every inch of ground was contested by the enemy, who destroyed all the bridges as they went along. Not a day passed without skirmishing, and some of it was very severe. But all their efforts were to no avail; Soult, with his dispirited army, was compelled to retreat across the Garonne, when, owing to heavy and incessant rains, our army was put into cantonments. Our division was quartered in a town, situated a few miles from the banks of that noble river.[7]

In quarters we remained some days, which were passed by our company, and I believe by most of the division, in a drinking bout, for every house in the place was a wine store. The whole of the company were crammed into one house, scarcely sufficient to contain the one half, which caused a deal of bustle and confusion at first. A trap-door, however, was discovered in the floor of one of the apartments, the passage of which led to the wine vault, where, though dark and damp, the greatest number took up their abode. In this subterranean temple, the sacred orgies of Bacchus were solemnized with great pomp and splendour. To illume the place, which was altogether void of light, a number of old and empty casks were broken down for fuel, and a fire kindled on the floor, which in a short time so filled the place with smoke, that it might have been deemed uninhabitable even for the lords of Pandemonium, but the lads here were proof against smoke and fire both, when wine was the prize. A fresh pipe being broached, the ruby liquor poured fourth, not into gold or silver vases, but our black tin kettles, which were filled and emptied with surprising despatch.

After a day of even more than usual jollity, while a number were still seated round the fire regaling themselves, and others, by the potency of the liquor, lay stretched on the floor, towards midnight the swelling notes of the bugle were heard to sound, 'turn out the whole,' at which great confusion and bustle ensued. Arms and accoutrements were to seek, knapsacks to pack; but numbers were incapable of doing either, being insensible to everything around them, and were in the hurry trampled upon and kicked about like so many old boots. The night was dark and dismal; the rain fell in torrents, under which we stood for two hours, being delayed all that time, owing to the men not turning promptly out. Having at last marched off, we proceeded along a road rendered most impassable by the excessive rains that had fallen, through which, however, we continued to plunge until daybreak, when we found ourselves on the left bank of the Garonne, opposite to, and within a short distance of the venerable city of Toulouse, around which we could perceive numerous and strong entrenchments, which the enemy had thrown up, who were now once more determined to try the fate of another general engagement. The

7 Samatan, south-west of Toulouse.

column having filed to the left, proceeded on a road, in a parallel line with the river, until we were about four leagues below the city, where a pontoon bridge being thrown over the river, the division immediately passed, leaving our regiment to protect the bridge.

The duty assigned us here was of a very harassing and fatiguing nature. The enemy, having command of the river above us, sent down large floats of wood, and boats stuck full of spears and sword blades, in order to destroy or damage the bridge, which required on our part the utmost activity and diligence to prevent during the day, at close of which it was taken up altogether, and replaced again in the morning. Owing to the wetness of the weather, and the numerous bodies of troops that were daily and hourly passing, the ground in the vicinity was rendered a complete puddle, in which we were generally employed the whole night, in removing the boats, boards, bolts and planks, and other materials of which the bridge was composed.

April 8th, at an early hour in the evening, orders were given to take up the bridge, which was, during the night, packed upon a number of wagons, and conveyed along the right bank of the river, until within a short league of Toulouse. Next morning before marching, I had another proof of the mild discipline, and tender regard with which we were treated by our superiors. Having been busily employed during the night, we were by daylight very fatigued, when the Provost-Marshal chancing to pass, one of our men in a jocular manner, called to his comrades to cheer up, as they would soon have done, for the 'Whipper-in' was come. This was sporting with the lion's paw, and was overheard by the man of stripes himself, who ordered the wit to be instantly seized, and tied up to the next tree, where for his joke he received four dozen ticklers.[8]

Notwithstanding the toil we had undergone, we were ordered to get our knapsacks and accompany the wagons on their route, which, when at their destination, were unloaded, and the bridge once more laid across the river, and left in charge of a party belonging to the Light Division. We then marched off and joined our brigade, which was lying in front of Toulouse, close to the enemy's lines. When we arrived at the camp, being completely exhausted, I threw myself on the green sward, but had been only a few minutes at rest, ere I was called out on fatigue. This was another bridge I was to assist in throwing over a ditch we had crossed when entering the field, in which we were encamped. I had often before seen broader ditches crossed and re-crossed, without anyone have the most distant idea of throwing anything over them, but Colonel F[orbes],[9] who had been some time our commanding officer, had got so enamoured of engineering, that he appeared

8 Lashes. A regimental court-martial could not inflict more than 300; a general court-martial not more than 1,200. Neglect of duty or threatening behavior often attracted 100, and it seems that this arbitrary punishment was felt to be some way towards those degrees of 'unsoldierlike conduct'.

9 Lieutenant Colonel Thomas Forbes, commander of the 1/45th in late 1813 and early 1814.

determined not to leave even a single cart rut without a bridge. In order that the affair might be properly done, the Colonel, although a subaltern officer superintended the party, attended in person, under whose sage directions the operations were carried on. When we had laboured hard for two hours, he was pleased to say our work was finished there, but that there was spot, a short way down the road, he wished something done at, and to which he ordered us to carry our tools. At this intimation, he was eyed with no very favourable aspect by the party, who, I believe, would rather have launched the tools at his head than carried them anywhere else; but as that might have been attended with danger, and there being no alternative, we complied with the order, by proceeding to the spot without delay – to which we were attended, or rather led, by the Aberdonian himself.[10] The place pointed out by our worthy leader, was a small narrow stream, scarcely ankle deep, over which, in his mania, he wished a bridge. As such gentlemen's wishes generally amount to positive orders, we commenced; and under his directions, by sunset, had finished a passage, which he was pleased to announce sufficient for the whole army to pass; but it was neither used by the army nor himself, as will be more fully seen in the next chapter.

10 William's footnote at this point reads: For this would-be engineer was a native of Aberdeenshire.

Chapter 21

Battle of Toulouse – An Explosion – Billy Reeves – Death of Colonel F[orbes] – A Hibernian Hero – Cordiality between the British and French soldiers

Three hoasts combine to offer sacrifice;
Three tongues proffer strange orisons on high:
Three gaudy standards float the pale blue skies;
The foe, the victim, and the fond ally
That fights for all, but ever fights in vain,
Are met – as if at home they should not die.
BYRON

After a few hours of sound repose, we were early next morning aroused by our bugles, and in a short time attacked the French outposts, who fell back upon the main body, with which we immediately came into contact. While advancing, the right flank of the division, which swept along the right bank of the Garonne, was threatened by a body of enemy, to oppose whom three companies of our regiment, together with three of the 74th and three of the 60th German Rifles, were detached.[1] A smart encounter ensued, in which the enemy were worsted, and compelled to retire to the shelter of some houses, from which they were immediately driven in gallant style by our party. From these houses we kept up a brisk fire upon the enemy, who had taken possession of some neighbouring buildings. In a small apartment, along with five others, I was busily enraged firing from the only window that faced the enemy, when an explosion took place in the room. We were immediately enveloped in smoke, and judging it to be caused by a shell, everyone made for the door; but owing to the haste of the two foremost, who stuck in the

1 The 74th were originally a highland regiment, but lost that status after 1809; nonetheless the men were principally Scots. The 5/60th Foot were officially part of the Royal American Regiment, however most of the men were German, with many other nationalities mixed in.

doorway, it was completely jammed up, detaining the others inside, who momentarily expected the bomb to burst, and blow up the house. Upon getting outside, it was discovered that instead of a shell, it was my old friend David, the glutton, of gourmandising memory, formerly mentioned, that was the sole cause and only sufferer in this affray.[2] David, wishing to be as smart as his comrades, had lodged in his cap the most of his ammunition, which coming in contact with the flash of his pan, had blown off, and reduced his headgear to a cinder, and scorched his cranium to such a degree that it resembled an old ram's when singed to cook.

Having charged repeatedly, and dislodged the enemy from house to house, they were at last driven back to the environs of the city, where they assembled in great force at a large house surrounded by a turf wall, which they strongly lined with musketry, and where I believe they thought themselves secure; but after firing some time from some buildings in the vicinity, we stormed and carried their mud fortress, which they evacuated in great haste and confusion, leaving behind them several barrels of ammunition, and a number of knapsacks. By this charge it was not only proposed to dislodge the enemy from their stronghold, but even to intercept them in their flight from it. With this in view we ran past the house, but were stopped short in our career by a canal, which was not perceived until we were on its banks. The enemy passed over on boards, which they withdrew on reaching the opposite side, and commenced firing from two houses situated on the margin. Perceiving the dilemma, we were placed in, the majority of our party returned to the house the enemy had just abandoned, when a tremendous fire commenced on both sides. A number remained in the hollow formed by a lock on the canal, that was exactly between the houses. Amongst the latter was my comrade, William Reeves, a young English boy who had lately joined the regiment, with a draft from England. This being only the second engagement he had been in, and understanding he was wounded, I was determined although at the risk of my life, to extricate him from his perilous situation. Intent on this, I went to the end of the house, by the corner of which the bullets were flying as thick as hail, and where a number of our officers were endeavouring to persuade a corporal of our regiment to go down and bring up the men from the hollow, to which the poor fellow seemed very unwilling, but at last consented to go, when he had been both cajoled and threatened. Laying off his knapsack, he sprung over the bank, on which I immediately followed, and found poor Billy stretched on the ground, extremely sick, from the loss of blood and heat of the sun. A ball had penetrated through his left arm, which was shattered and broken. Unbuckling the slings of his knapsack, I placed it upon the top of my own, and cutting his belts with my knife, 'Billy,' says I, 'we will leave these trappings here, as you will never use such harnesses again; so run for your life!' Which he manfully did, and got over the bank without further injury. I now asked the corporal, whom I had followed, if he was ready to go, but

2 David Evans, refer Chapter VII. [p. 46]

shaking his head, with a sorrowful countenance, he said he had been wounded in the heel as he came over the bank, and could not return. Poor fellow, it was worse with him than he even then anticipated, for, however remote his wound lay from the vital parts, it was the cause of his death. In a few days after he died with his jaws locked.[3]

When returned to the house, I found Billy, whose wound I bound with a bandage, which I tore from a shirt, and made a sling for his arm with the remainder. After regaling ourselves with some wine, abundance of which was in the house, I filled his canteen with the precious liquor, and putting into his haversack a loaf of bread I had found in the garden, I bade him goodbye, and God bless him. He went to the rear, where in all probability he would meet with a surgeon who would dress his wound. I have never seen him since, but I understand however, he was discharged sometime after, in England with a pension.[4]

My readers will be by this time inclined to think I have forgot the engagement, and got on the skulk; but which I assure them was by no means the case. It is true an hour had elapsed since I had fired a shot, but this will appear by no means extraordinary, when it is known that one-half of our party was never engaged at once, there not being sufficient room at the doors and windows, which were the only vomitaries for our shot. But I was induced by a stronger motive than this, to refrain from levelling the fatal tube for a time. When I heard that my comrade was wounded, I was determined to save the boy, even at the risk of my own life – an act I considered as humane to my fellow creature, and more beneficial to the world in general, and my country in particular, than if I had killed a dozen Frenchmen. But long ere the action was ended, there was ample time and opportunity for everyone to display their valour and prowess, for independent of the heavy fire that rolled on from morning till night, several attempts were made by our party to pass the canal, all of which, notwithstanding the valour and courage displayed, proved abortive. On being repulsed in one of these charges, and when all that were able had returned to the house, a German, belonging to the 60th Rifles, remained on the beam, or lever of the canal lock, from which he fired several shots. The firing ceased on both sides, and for a few seconds the attention of friend and foe was riveted on the author of this 'deed of high daring'. He however, fell a victim of his temerity; he received a shot in his breast, and fell into the canal. This action I think was more strongly tinctured with frenzy than courage.

While affairs were thus situated on the right, the division on our left, by corresponding movements, arrived in front of the canal at the same time with our party, where their progress was arrested by the enemy, who in great force occupied a fort that surmounted a bridge on the canal. Having reconnoitred the position, General Picton ordered the place to be stormed by our regiment, which accordingly formed

3 This unfortunate was Corporal Michael Hynde.
4 Billy Reeves was discharged in England on 20 November 1814.

up, and three cheers issued from the wood in which the division was posted. The assailants, under a most galling fire of round-shot and musketry, advanced with great spirit and intrepidity, and gained the outer ditch, but being deficient in ladders, it was found impracticable to take the place. The General then ordered a retreat, which was affected with great loss to the regiment. In this affair Colonel F[orbes] lost his life by a cannon ball, which struck him on the back when retiring, and literally went through his body. It was for some time a matter of speculation with the men, whether the Aberdonian would avail himself of old Charon's boat, or throw a bridge over the Styx? The only man of the regiment that entered the fort, was a gay, light-hearted Irishman, who had, in his time, received some thousands of lashes in the service. Pat Connor was what is called a tight clean soldier, generally steady when without money, but if possessed of a single ten-penny, would not withstand the allurements of women and wine, which placed him sometimes in very awkward circumstances, and for which he had often embraced the 'the three twin sisters.'[5] But though Pat loved a row in a wine shop, he was a good soldier, and on this occasion proved himself a hero. On gaining the glacis, which none did but himself, he made a fair and clean leap into the interior of the fort, plunging amongst the bristling bayonets of his enemies, and shouting as he went, 'Hurral ye b---ers, Hurrah!' But more of Pat anon.[6]

In the meantime, Marshal Beresford, on our left, with the Fourth and Sixth divisions, having crossed the Ers, carried Monblanc;[7] and moving up the river, turned the enemy's position, which upon a height was strongly fortified with redoubts, connected by lines of entrenchments. Lieutenant General Don Manuel Freyre, with the Spanish troops under his command, attacked in front supported by British cavalry.[8] His division for some time moved forward in a steady manner, but being repulsed on the right, the whole corps were compelled to retire. The Light Division which was on the right, immediately came up, when the whole rallied again, and renewed the attack. The Fourth and Sixth Divisions attacked and carried then heights on the enemy's right, and the redoubt which covered and protected that flank. The enemy, however still occupied four redoubts on the same heights, the entrenchments, and fortified houses, but from every one of these they were quickly driven. The Spanish Division, having renewed the attack, and Marshal Beresford having got up his artillery, together with the Sixth Division, and General Pack's brigade, they attacked and carried the heights, with the two redoubts, entrenchments, and fortified houses on the enemy's centre. They now made a desperate effort from the canal to regain these redoubts, but were repulsed

5 The triangle of three halberds to which soldiers were lashed when flogged.

6 Private Patrick Connor had enlisted in 1803, served in South America as well as the whole of the Peninsular War, then served in India until discharged in 1826.

7 Mont Blanc Farm, north-east of Toulouse.

8 General Don Manuel Freyre commanded the Spanish Fourth Army, the only Spanish formation Wellington considered fit to serve in France; he sent the rest home after Nivelle.

with great loss. The Sixth continuing its movement along the ridge of the height, and the Spanish Division continuing a corresponding movement in front, the enemy were also driven from the two redoubts, the entrenchments, and fortified houses on the left; and thus the whole range of heights remained in the power of the Allies. While these operations were going on on our left and centre, General Hill drove the enemy from the exterior line of their works in the suburbs, on the left bank of the Garonne. But night coming on at last put an end to the contest.

Our party having been unable to force the canal, remained until evening in the houses they had occupied the greatest part of the day, still keeping up a heavy fire upon the enemy; who; when it was dusk, sent out a flag of truce with an officer, accompanied by a trumpeter, who sounding parley, the firing immediately ceased on both sides. The object of this mission was to crave a cessation of hostilities for the night, which was no sooner granted than the French soldiers came leaping over the lock, with baskets of bread, and abundance of brandy and wine, which we willingly partook on the bank of the canal, where, with the utmost confidence and cordiality, we got seated promiscuously.

> All soldiers are,
> Or should be comrades, even though enemies;
> Our swords when drawn must cross, our engines aim
> (while levelled) at each other's hearts, but when
> A truce, a peace, or what you will, remits
> The steel into its scabbard, and lets sleep
> The spark which lights the matchlock, we are brethren![9]

But our officers thought, at least acting otherwise; for they in a short time recalled us, and prohibited all further intercourse with the enemy. Thus terminated the battle of Toulouse, fought on the 10th April, being Easter Sunday; whether it was the work of necessity or mercy, I will leave the reader to determine. It was, however, severe work for the parties concerned. The loss of the Allies was estimated at 5,000 killed and wounded; that of the French upwards of 9,000.[10]

9 From the play *Werner: or, the Inheritance* by Lord Byron, 1822.

10 In fact losses were 4,600 and 3,300 respectively, from Oman, *History of the Peninsular War*, Vol. VII, pp.556-561, Table X. But the French left many wounded and sick behind when they evacuated the city.

Chapter 22

Advance through Toulouse – Countermanded by the arrival of the News of Peace – Reflections on the Miseries of War – Table of the destruction of Mankind since the Revolution in France, together with the Amount of Contributions Levied in Europe by France during the war; also, the Total Loss of Property, and the War Expenses of the various Nations engaged – Grenade – Embarks for Ireland

> Well, that's over now, and peace
> Has turned some thousand gallant hearts adrift,
> To live as best they may; and to say truth,
> Some take the shortest.
>
> BYRON

After it was dark, our division was withdrawn, and encamped for the night at the distance of half a mile from the scene of action, and next morning got into quarters in several detached houses in the vicinity. On the evening of the same day, Soult, conceiving himself in danger of being surrounded, abandoned Toulouse, and retreated during the night, in pursuit of whom our army advanced next morning. When passing through Toulouse, Pat Connor was found drunk and happy, standing, or rather lying up against the door of a wine house. When asked how he had escaped with his life from the French – 'Wid my life!' exclaimed Pat, 'why, the Francees never offered to lay a dirty finger on me!' The truth of the matter was this – the enemy, admiring his courage and intrepidity, saved his life by taking him prisoner; and he had now eluded the vigilance of his guard during the bustle occasioned by his captors leaving Toulouse, where he remained until found by his countrymen.

When two leagues in front of Toulouse, our attention was highly excited by what appeared to be a wonderful phenomenon – a carriage, containing two French officers, came furiously past, escorted by parties of British and French Dragoons, who, as they went along, imparted to our men the news of peace having been established at Paris, and that they were then on their way to headquarters, to communicate the glad tidings to our Commander-in-Chief. This vivifying intelligence, like lightening, flew from rank to rank, but no one dared to credit the wondrous tale. We had been so long inured to the dangers and turmoil of war, and had been so often taught to believe it the noblest of all professions; that the glory of England, the freedom of Europe, and the world, was the mighty prize for which we had fought. But having no idea that such blessings were obtained, it was not until our march was countermanded, and the transactions which had taken place in Paris, were communicated to us through the medium of a General Order, that we could give implicit credence to the affair.[1]

Thus closed the dreadful drama of carnage, woe, and misery, which had desolated Europe, and distracted the world for nearly a quarter of a century, A contest, in which, by the ambition of a few lawless and unprincipled villains, millions of the human race had been butchered; and with which property, both public and private, had been destroyed, which the united industry of Europe for ages, will not, nor cannot, replace. But as no words of mine are adequate to convey the faintest idea of the enormous expenditure of blood and treasure which has been wantonly lavished in this sanguinary and ruinous struggle, I shall subjoin in abstract, as taken from official documents, an account of the destruction of mankind since the French Revolution, together with the loss of property, and the expense of the war, sustained by the different nations engaged.

Destruction of mankind since the Revolution in France (this includes killed and wounded);

Great Britain	416,667
France	4,179,506
Other Nations	2,614,167
TOTAL	7,204,340

Amount of contribution levied in Europe by France during the war (independent of plunder carried off by the troops);

Spain	150,000,000
Portugal	13,680,624
Total over Europe	980,297,708

1 The Treaty of Fontainebleau had been signed on 11 April, banishing Napoleon to exile on Elba. The War did not officially end however until the signing of the Treaty of Paris on 30 May 1814.

Property destroyed;

Spain from 1808 to 1814	30,000,000
Portugal	15,000,000
Total over Europe	1,042,330,000

War Expenses from 1793 to 1815;[2]

Great Britain	1,121,442,215
France	2,726,656,250
Total expenditure in war	5,091,864,090
Confiscations and loans over Europe	985,113,356
Destruction to Property	1,042,330,000
TOTAL	7,119,307,446

Taking, therefore, the inhabitants of Europe at 160 millions, and one-fifth of that as the number between 16 and 60 years of age, viz. 30 millions as the number whose labour may be allowed should acquire property, it follows that each individual of that number has paid £222 sterling, or about £10 sterling annually for 22 years, ending 1814. A goodly sum, indeed; and for what? Why, to support tyranny and oppression, and spread desolation and misery over the world. For all this was not done in a corner. No, every part of the habitable globe has felt and suffered by the tremendous shock.

The fertile plains of Asia; the sandy and parched deserts of Africa, and impervious woods and wilds of America, have witnessed and felt the sad and dreadful effects of ambition's train. As for Europe, she has been made shambles, her soil manured with carnage, and her rivers gorged with blood; the very ocean has, in many instances, been deeply tinged with human gore; cities have been raised, or ordered to be so; towns, villages, and hamlets destroyed and burned; the helpless and unoffending inhabitants compelled to fly their native hearths and homes, or otherwise cruelly tortured and butchered by the myrmidons of oppression. Robbery, rape and murder, have, in innumerable instances, been committed under the most glaring and aggravating circumstances; matrons have been violated, and virgins deflowered in presence of husbands and fathers, who in their turn were barbarously murdered before the weeping eyes of their families and friends. Here may well be applied the following lines of a celebrated nobleman and poet [Byron] who, when speaking of the 'fantastic tricks' played by men in authority, bids us

2 Figures quoted are in pounds sterling.

'Mark! Where his carnage and his conquests cease! He makes solitude, and calls it peace!' But it is only the past and present generation that will feel the dire and fatal effects of the French Revolution and its consequences – ages yet unborn are doomed to suffer and to toil, and curse the authors and propagators of it.[3]

Begging pardon for this digression, I will now proceed with my narrative. Having countermarched, we retraced our steps through Toulouse, and next day the brigade was put into cantonments at Grenade, where, indeed, we enjoyed the sweets of peace. Our duty was light and pleasant, and provisions abundant and cheap; bread sold at two sous per pound,[4] wine, in taverns, at half as much more the bottle, but sold in cellars a deal cheaper, There I have purchased four canteens full, which was eight quarts, for a demi franc,[5] which was the cost of a bottle of brandy. Beef and mutton were at the same rate per pound, weighing forty ounces, which reduced it to two pence per pound English. Fowls were extremely plenty, consequently cheap. A good goose sold for a franc, or ten pence British currency, and all other articles of provision equally cheap. The town was pleasantly situated near the Garonne, and of considerable extent, containing from five to six thousand inhabitants, who were kind, hospitable and friendly. It was compactly built, nearly quadrangular, with the streets running in parallel lines, and crossing at right angles, with a square in the centre. Such was Grenade, which, on account of the kind treatment I experienced from several of its inhabitants, I shall remember with the most lively gratitude and pleasure.

During our stay here, I once more became a bone polisher. Captain M-----,[6] who had, during the war, been in a bad state of health, now ventured, for the first time, to assume command of his company. Being in want of a servant, I was recommended, and accepted accordingly, in which situation I found my yoke easy, and my burden light. Having passed five weeks pleasantly in this place, the regiment received the route for the coast preparatory to embarkation. This march extended to about ninety miles, and was the most agreeable I ever had. The weather was good, the roads were excellent, and led through a most charming country, intersected with corn fields and vineyards, in which the luscious and purple grape was fast ripening to crown the joyous harvest. After the day's march, comfortable quarters awaited us at night, with a kind host, and kinder hostess, all of which tended to exhilarate our spirits, and render us cheerful and gay. Passing Beaumont and Bordeaux, and other considerable cities and towns, we at last encamped on a plain about seven miles distant from the latter, where with the greatest part of the army, we were for the last time reviewed by the Marquis of Wellington. Having

3 The 'Great War' of 1793-1815 was in many ways just as ruinous to Europe as World War One.

4 One penny sterling.

5 Five pence sterling.

6 I believe this to be Captain Alexander McDougall.

remained at this encampment fourteen days, the regiment embarked on board a transport at Poliak,[7] a small port on the Garonne.

Thus was I once more launched on the broad and dark green wave, and quitted with regret a land I had entered with almost fear and trembling – a land endeared to me by many sweet and tender recollections. Even the appalling dangers, the eminent perils, the very toils and pains I had felt and suffered, since I first trod its soil, attached me to it. But a tie more tender, affections more dear, bound me – does still, and will forever bind me to the Peninsula.

7 Pauillac.

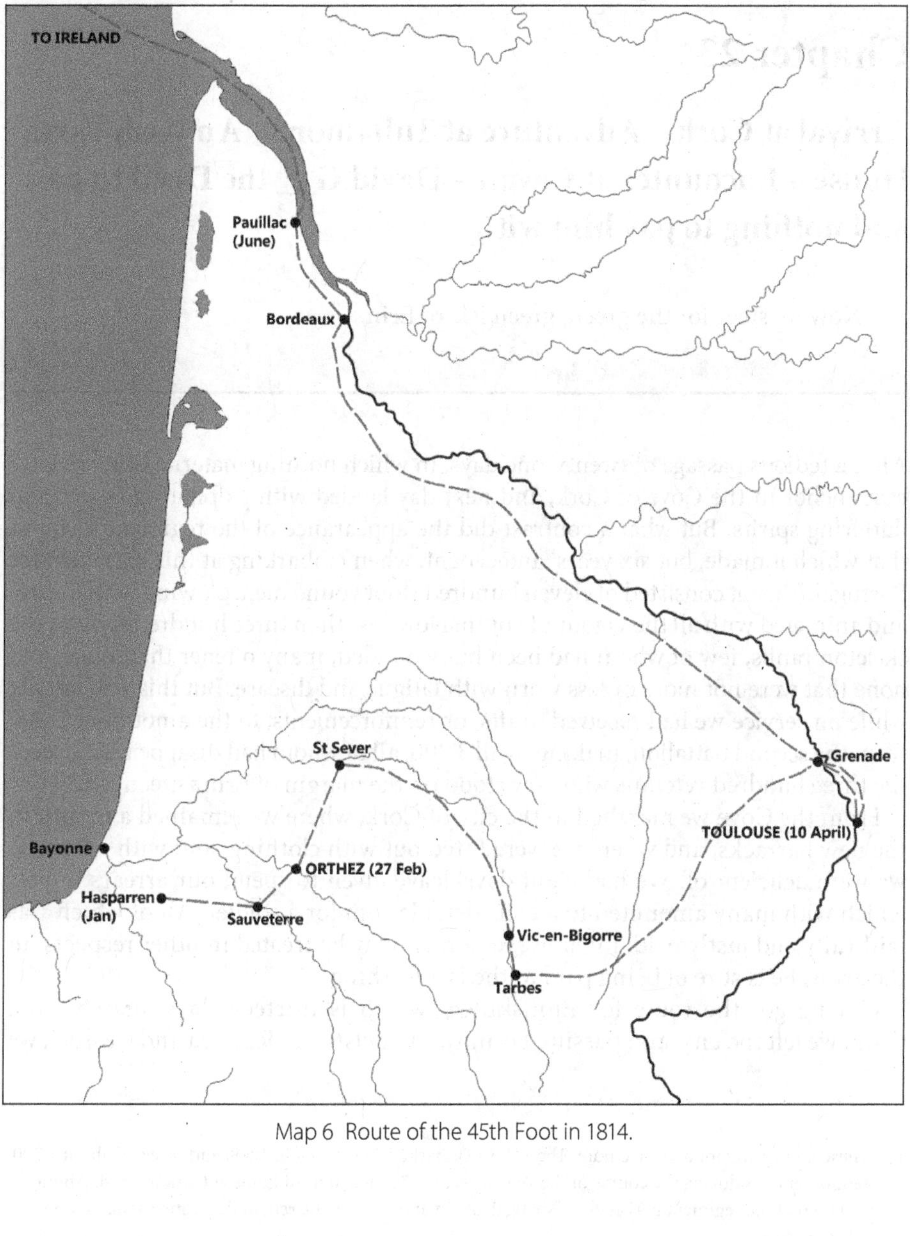

Map 6 Route of the 45th Foot in 1814.

Chapter 23

Arrival at Cork – Adventure at Tullamore – An Irish Farm-House – Encounter at Cavan – David G__ the Devil to pay, and nothing to pay him with

Now we steer for the green, green isle of Erin.

After a tedious passage of twenty-one days, in which nothing material occurred, we cast anchor in the Cove of Cork, and next day landed with palpitating hearts and fluttering spirits. But what a contrast did the appearance of the regiment form, to that which it made, but six years' antecedent, when embarking at this vary port for Portugal. Then it consisted of eleven hundred stout young men, glowing with health, and animated with all the vigour of youth. Now, less than three hundred formed the skeleton ranks, few of whom had been but wounded, many oftener than once, and none that were not more or less worn with fatigue and disease. But this was not all; while on service we had received drafts, or reinforcements, to the amount of 2,200 from the second battalion, making in all 3,300, all of whom had disappeared, except the three hundred veterans who now stood on the margin of Erin's green isle.[1]

From the Cove we marched to the city of Cork, where we remained a month in the new barracks, and where we were fitted out with clothing, and with what else we were deficient of. We had eight days' leave given to spend our arrears of pay, which with many amounted to a considerable sum for a soldier. All of which was faithfully and justly paid; for, however a man may be treated in other respects, in the army, he is sure of being paid to the last farthing.

Having got the route for Enniskillen, which is thirteen days' march from Cork, we left the city, and passing Fermoy, Michelstown, Roscrea and Cashiel, we

1 These figures are not quite accurate. The 1/45th embarked 744 strong in 1809, and received about 1,700 reinforcements during the course of the war; whereas 574 men arrived home at Cork in 1814. About 700 men of the regiment perished in Portugal, Spain and France; the remainder were discharged or taken prisoner.

arrived at Tullamore, where by the upsetting of a kettle full of boiling water, I had one of my legs sorely scalded; in consequence of which, being unable to proceed with the regiment, I was left in the hospital of the Brecknockshire Militia. After remaining there for three weeks, being perfectly recovered, I was discharged from hospital, and served with eight days pay, which was to carry me to the regiment; at the same time I received a billet for the night on a Public House, near the cavalry barrack gate. When I entered the house, two dragoons were sitting over a pot of beer at the kitchen fire, whit whom I got into conversation, and having joined them in a tankard, it was proposed that as the kitchen was crowded, we should remove to another apartment, which was accordingly done. What was said there, or done, I cannot tell, but next morning I awoke, and found myself lying under the table drenched in beer, and stiff with cold. I had, however, had the recollection to search my pockets, and was somewhat chagrined to find them empty. This is, thinks I, a fine kettle of fish I have cooked for myself. I have eight days' march before me, and not a halfpenny in my pocket; a stranger in the place, with no friends or acquaintances who might assist me, and my route is amongst the wild Irish; but I cannot, nor must not remain here. Having thus mentally given vent to my feelings, I returned to the kitchen, and meeting with the landlord, told him my story, at which he wished to appear much concerned, although I perceived, or thought I perceived, a lurking smile playing upon his countenance. This however, being no evidence of his guilt, and well knowing how acute the risible nerves of his countrymen were in general, I had nothing to say, and cared not whether he laughed or cried. He treated me, however, to a good breakfast and a dram of the real 'Inishoan', when I bid him good morning, and set out on the march, fully convinced that I had left my money in his pocket. During the whole day the rain fell fast, the roads were deep, and seventeen long Irish miles lay between me and Mullengar, proverbially famed for heavy-heeled heifers, and light armed croppies.[2] Arrived at the town, I found the billet-master, who, after perusing my route, gave me a billet upon what he called a farmer, residing a mile out of town, on the road to Granard, which was my destination next day. Leaving Mullengar I proceeded on my way in the dark, and when about a mile on the road, the distance I had been told to go, I asked a peasant whom I met, how far it might be to the house of Patrick Burns? 'Why, sure, man', said he, after some hesitation, 'it is a long and ruff road that is between us and the sheiling of Pat Burns'.

At this information I asked him how far it might be, when, in the true brogue, he replied 'Hell to my soul if I know! And myself's in the mind who'll not see it this blessed night!' I then asked his reason for thinking so. 'Hoh, man, arrh dear, you'd get lost in the bog before you'd get half way over there; then you'd have the

2 Croppy was a nickname given to Irish rebels fighting for independence in the 1798 Rising.

long fields wid the bushes to pass, and the stile – God rest her soul! Where the poor creature of a woman was found t'other blessed morning!'

Indeed sir, said I, after pointing out so many obstacles on the way, I almost despair of reaching the house I wanted tonight. In a low and inquisitive tone, he rejoined, 'Sure you're not after harassing the creature for the malt?'

The import of this interrogation I did not fully comprehend, but thought it related to what is termed still-hunting in Ireland, upon which I assured him I meant no harm to no person, but was merely passing through the country, to join my regiment at Enniskillen, and all I wanted with the people I inquired for, was a nights quarters, for which I had a billet, and in attestation of what I said, I held it out, and forgetting it was dark, desired him to read it.

'Now by the soul widin me!' said he, 'although the sun was on the hill of Houth, I could do nothing wid it; but it would be a hard time, and a poor thing, if Jemmy Shea would let a stranger be at a loss for a nights biding. If you please to come wid me, you'll have what my cabin can afford till morning'.

Without further interrogation, I followed him with implicit confidence, and striking through a gap in the hedge, in a few minutes I found myself in the clay-built dwelling of Jemmy Shea. Owing to the smoke that pervaded the place, it was some time ere I could distinguish any object around me; but the mixed and incongruous sounds, however, that issued from several quarters, announced a dense population. In one corner, an old sow, with her sucklings, kept up a concert during the night with great éclat – which was sustained in all its parts and bearings – the swelling strains were poured forth in melody, from the deep-toned bass to the squeaking treble; whilst at stated periods, a slow and solemn sound, which added sublimity to the whole, announced a cow in the opposite corner. Not only the earth, but the air seemed thickly peopled in this life-teeming region; for, if the chuck, chuck, and tuck, tuck, might be taken as a criterion to judge by, it might have been fairly estimated that a score at least of the feathered tribe were roosted there. Their chief, as if glorying in his might, now flapped his wings and crew, at which I heard (as yet I could not see) a querulous voice observe, that it was very un-chancy to hear such things over evening.

The atmosphere clearing up, or my visual organs getting used to it, I began to descry the objects around, and perceived, through the smoke, as issuing from a cloud, the lean and wrinkled visage of a female, who sat spinning at a wheel, which, making a humming noise something like a piper's drone, served as a 'chef d'ouvre' to the concert. The old lady, I learned, was the widowed mother of my host, and had been an inmate of her sons since her husband died. I now perceived Mrs Shea the younger, a plumb, jolly queen, busied preparing supper, of which I then stood much in need. In the interim, my landlord and I settled the affairs of the nation, but the burden of Jemmy's song was the tithes, by which he told me he had lost his best cow the week before. He consoled himself with the hope, however, that ere long he would have the satisfaction of carding the villainous Proctor, against whom he swore eternal vengeance. Having partaken heartily of potatoes and bacon, I retired to rest with my landlord, who, for my accommodation, parted with his better half for the night, who, with her two children, slept with her mother in law. In the morning, having breakfasted, I thanked my kind entertainers, which was all the recompense I had to give, and bidding them good morning, set out on my way for Granard.

In two days after, I reached Cavan, where I found the Ayreshire Militia in barracks, amongst whom I was sure of meeting with a number of my townsman and acquaintances. For that purpose I was making towards the barracks, when I encountered a tall gaunt figure, attired in the uniform of that Royal and Loyal corps. After fixing his eyes earnestly upon me for a moment, he accosted me with 'Blast your eyes, Telle, is this you!' This appellation I had obtained when a boy, and was by my comrades at that time seldom termed by any other, but not having heard it repeated for many a long year, I had entirely forgotten it. But now, when sounded upon my ear so abruptly, I started as if awakened from a dream – a flood of early and fond recollections rushed on my memory, I stood and gazed, and though conscious he had been a companion in my early days, I knew him not. Perceiving that I had not recollected him, 'Lord man!' said he, 'don't you know me?' I assured him I did not. 'D—n it, don't you know Davie G---?' Dear David, said I, is it you, had little thought of meeting you here. 'Aye, but,' said he, 'I have been expecting to see you every day since your regiment went through, for I was then told you would be here in a short time; so I have been on the lookout for you ever since. But come, we are not to stand here, let us go into this public house.' I told him my finances did not admit to that, and that I was then, and had been four days, without a farthing in my pocket. 'Come, come, do you think I am going to take you in and not bring you out; if you have no money, I have plenty, and that is all the same.' We accordingly stepped into a tavern, where a dram was called for, which my companion having tasted, told me he had to go out, but would return in a few minutes. In a short time he entered, bringing with him several of our townsmen, and spreading a pound on the table, swore he would not rise until it was melted. The dram, the joke, and the crack went round until a late hour, for, expecting the regiment to be broken up in a short time, discipline was greatly relaxed, of which my companions availed themselves, by not attending at Tattoo, and it was some time in the morning ere we retired to the barracks.

At daylight I proposed to proceed on my journey, but this my friend David would by no means allow. He said he had still a dirty piece of paper, for which he was determined to get rid, and if I did not remain that day and help him to spend it, he would never be friends with me after. Having consented to comply with his wish, we went to the town, where he offered to purchase stockings and hose for me, articles I then stood much in need of, but to this proposal I would by no means accede, and told him I had plenty before me with the regiment. 'That being the case,' said he, 'we must try it some other way; we will then drink it!' which was accordingly done, and that quickly. A number of his acquaintances, knowing his humour, came in and sat down, by whom poor David's dirty piece of paper, as he called it, was by mid-day reduced to one ten-penny, with which he purchased a quarter of veal, and retired to the barracks, promising to have it cooked for us by the time we might come up. From what I have seen of the squad I was with, I began to suspect that they were what is in the army denominated 'suckers'. Wishing, therefore, to have as little to do with them as possible, I wished to go up to the barracks with David; but professing great friendship, and wishing, as they said, to treat me to a dram, I was prevailed upon to remain with them, when we sat down and drank until evening. They then slunk off, one by one, leaving David's bed-fellow, (a Glasgow lad), and me to pay the reckoning.

Having waited some time, and none of them returning, we called the landlady and asked for her bill, which she told us was seven shillings. 'Well,' said my companion, when our hostess was gone, 'we have got into a mess at last, and how to get out of it I don't know. However we must try; but let us have another half mutchin, at any rate, it is as bad as it can be'. When the landlady brought it in, he told her, as we were getting cold, we wished to remove to the kitchen fire, to which he hoped she would have no objections. To this she obligingly consented. When we had been a short time in the kitchen, we both proposed to go to the door, but our landlady stopped us short, by declaring we should not stir until we had paid the reckoning. 'Well', said my companion, 'since you won't let us go to the front door, you must, as my needs are very pressing, provide me with a -----, otherwise, allow me to go to the back door.' This boon being granted, we immediately availed ourselves of it, by going to the backside of the house, and found the night both dark and wet. Groping around, for we could not see, we found the place we were in surrounded by a stone wall, of such a height as almost precluded the hope of an escape. We, however, in searching around, found some empty casks, and piling them on each other, we both gained the top of the wall. Standing with his back to the wall of the house, 'I'll jump,' said my companion, 'if I should break my neck!' and making a bound, plunged as if into a river. 'Oh Lord!' cried he, 'I am drowned!' 'Leap out, leap out,' cried I, 'I can't', said he. 'For what?' said I, 'Oh God! I will be drowned, I am in a deep draw-well; go to your left a little, drop the wall, and assist me in getting out'. Upon reaching the spot where he was, instead of a deep draw-well, I found him pent up in a barrel, apparently used for holding rain-water, of which it was then full. Having assisted in extricating him from his hold, we found ourselves still enclosed in just such another place as that we had escaped from. But here, having no reckoning to pay, we made bold to open the door, and rushing through the house, bolted into the street, and made for the barracks with what haste we could. Thus was I served by a few of my townsmen, some of whom I could point out in the streets of Kilmarnock at this day, and would here publish their names, were they not beneath my contempt. On reaching the barracks we found it so late, that all had retired to bed, with the exception of my friend David, who lay stretched on the hearth, with our promised dinner (the quarter of veal) lying in the ash-pit beside him. Having got him up on his bed, we all got to rest. Next morning at an early hour I left Cavan and poor David, whom I have ever found a warm-hearted and boon companion. But as the old women in Scotland remarked of such, 'He's just aye warst for himself.'

British infantry on campaign. Unlike the French, who lived off the land, the British were dependent upon an often-unreliable commissariat service for their supply – and so starved in the manner frequently conveyed by the author. (Anne S. K. Brown Collection)

Chapter 24

Enniskillen – A Maniac, or the Strength of Usquebagh – the Drunken Squad – A Punishment – Maguire's Bridge – Belfast – Carrickfergus – Dublin – Gets discharged – Arrives at Home – Conclusion

> I left the lines and tented field,
> Where lang I'd been a lodger;
> My humble knapsack a' my wealth,
> A poor but honest sodger.
>
> BURNS

Enniskillen, where I arrived on the second day after leaving Cavan, is a handsome well-built town, delightfully situated on an island in Loch Earn. It consists of one principal street, with by-lanes. The town stretches across the whole breadth of the island, which is about a mile at the broadest, and is joined to the mainland by a bridge at each end. It is the county town of Fermanagh, and contains the county goal, and good barracks.

On joining the regiment, I called upon my old master the captain, when it was settled that I should next day resume my wonted service; but same day I committed a blunder which nearly proved fatal to both of us, and which happened as follows: having got on the 'spree' with some of my comrades, and making to free with the liquor, I got as least, if not more than half-seas-over. When in this state, and going towards the barracks, I had to pass the captain's lodgings. Like all other fools, wise in my own conceit, I thought I might as well step in then and take charge of the baggage, and what-not, as have it to do next day. Without more ado I entered the kitchen, where I found the mistress of the house, of whom I inquired for the Captain's servant, when she informed me he had gone down to the barracks. I then asked if the Captain was in the house, to which she replied in the affirmative. Well, then, said I, since I can't find the man, I must see the master! 'Oh!' said the landlady, 'you will surely never think of appearing before the Captain in the state you are in at present!' Thinking I was in the best state imaginable to appear before any person whatever, I told her I had business with the Captain, and surely would both see and speak with him before I left the house. She continued to remonstrate, and endeavoured to represent the folly of exposing myself, and even entreated me not to go upstairs. But all would not do, I still persisted in my folly, and was about to leave the kitchen when she shut the door and told me I should not see the Captain in my present condition. This was all intended by the good woman for my benefit, but unfortunately I was not in a condition to know that. Getting into a violent rage at what I conceived her officiousness, I pushed her aside, burst from the kitchen, and drawing my bayonet, I flew up the stairs with all the rage and madness of a maniac, and rushing into the Captain's apartment, 'Now, you old B-----!' I exclaimed, 'here's at you!' So saying, I made a plunge at him with the weapon, which he luckily missed, and flying out of the room escaped to the street.

My readers, I have little doubt, will think it would have been much better had I kept this story to myself. In this opinion I perfectly coincide; but as I pledged myself at the commencement of this narrative, to let all the truth be known, and nothing but the truth, I therefore feel myself bound to relate whatever may be of interest. Whether it add or detract from my reputation.

But, to proceed, on gaining the street, the Captain found several of our men passing, whom he brought to his assistance; but before they entered the house I had fallen into a swoon, in which state, as I was afterwards informed, they found me on the top of the stairs. When animation returned, I felt myself stiff with cold, and lying in a damp dreary place, from which all light was excluded. At first I had no remembrance of what I had done, but in a short time my guilt, with all its aggravating circumstances, flashed on my memory. Oh heavens! thought I, what is this I have done! I have nearly committed a deed which the laws of my country, civil or military, would have punished by the most condign punishment, and hurried into the presence of an omniscient and immaculate judge, with the innocent blood of a fellow creature reeking on my hands! But as it is, I am still liable to the obnoxious punishment of the degrading lash, or even to death itself; for to draw, or offer to draw, or lift any weapon against a superior officer, is death. So runs the very first section of the Martial Law. But where am I? what place is this? It is not the guardhouse; here I have abundance of straw to rest on – it is not the black hole! Yet I hear no noise, no sound meets my listening ear, but a dead and deathlike stillness pervades the dreary place. I will get up and search, and endeavour to find where I am. With this intention I arose, but in crossing the floor my foot came in contact with a piece of wood, and I fell with a souse, my head coming against a stone, by which I received a severe cut on the left temple. I continued my search, however, and discovered that the place contained a quantity of potatoes, a deal of straw, lumber, and such like, which led me to suspect that I was in an outhouse belonging to some farmer. At this discovery, a new idea arose in my mind. Surely, thought I, I have not in my frenzy been endeavouring to desert, and have here in my flight secreted myself – if such be the case I am miserable indeed.

But I will to the regiment with what speed I may; better do that than taken back in chains, and bound like a felon. Upon getting to the door I found it fastened, which all the strength I was master of could not undo; and when I had exerted and fatigued myself to no purpose, I sat down on the straw, exhausted, amazed, and confounded at the dilemma into which my folly had launched me. As I thus sat ruminating and bewildered, the door slowly opened, and in walked the Captain, carrying a lantern, and two men belonging to the company following close in his rear. Without deigning a word to his old, but now disgraced servant, he desired the men to take me home to the barracks, which I no sooner heard, (being ashamed to be in his presence) than I rushed out of the house.

That night I rested little, and rose early in the morning, with the intention of presenting myself before the Captain, to supplicate for pardon. While dressing for this purpose, the sergeant of the guard entered the room, and told me I was his prisoner. Desiring to know for what, he handed me a slip of paper, which specified that I was confined by order of Captain M'D[ougall], for being drunk and riotous at his quarters. This was putting the most favourable construction on the affair that was possible, without passing it over altogether, which was more than I could reasonably expect.

It being about the 24th, the time that the army is paid the arrears of the month, (which I believe is a stirring time in all regiments, and no less in ours), when I entered the guardroom. I found in it a number of prisoners, who were soon after greatly augmented, by the Commanding Officer confining a number of men at morning parade, for being drunk. This officer had but lately joined the regiment with the second battalion from England, where he had managed to abide during the war, but now that he had joined, he seemed determined to make amends for his former remissness.[1] The Colonel being on leave of absence, this bluff Major had the temporary command of the regiment, which he ruled with a rod of iron.[2] At every parade he inspected the whole corps, and every man was confined who had even the smell of liquor. The number turned out this morning was beyond a score, which, with those already in 'durance vile', amounted to thirty-seven. Before he dismissed the parade, the 'great man', ordered all the vagabond, as he termed them, to be drawn up in front of the regiment, then calling a sergeant of each company, 'Go' said he, 'and get these blackguards immediately equipped in marching order, and bring them here directly, and I will give further orders concerning them!' Being again returned, he ordered a sergeant and corporal that had offended him, to join our squad, and Mr M-----, a gallant young officer, who had often shown

1 The second battalion of the 45th was disbanded at Exeter on 24 October 1814 and all the fit men from it joined the first battalion in Ireland. In doing so, a lot of transferring officers and NCO's who had seen out the war at home in England found themselves senior in rank to Peninsula veterans, which caused some friction within the regiment.

2 Major Hugh Stacpoole, of an ancient County Clare family.

his front where the other had never dared to show his posterior,[3] was ordered to take charge of the party, by way of punishment, on account of having been rather late for parade. 'Now, Mr M-----,' said the Major, 'you will march this party to Maguire's Bridge for three days successively, and return each evening, when you will lodge them in the guard-house. By making an example of these, I mean to deter others in future from like practice.'

For my own part I was extremely happy that I had got off so cheap. Not so the others. The Major's ears might have tingled the whole day. Even Mr M----- seemed neither easy nor pleased with himself, and halted the party at a public house only two miles from Enniskillen, where we stopped a short time in order to refresh ourselves. When about to leave the place, two men fell suddenly ill, and were left behind, upon promising not to leave the house until the party returned – to get drunk in the interim was out of the question. Being arrived at our destination, leave was given for an hour's rest, at the expiration of which we again turned for Enniskillen.

We had not got far on the way however, until it was discovered that many of the men were intoxicated, which showed they had not been idle, though resting. One fellow in particular, got so obstreperous, that he threw his firelock over the hedge, and sitting down on the road, exclaimed 'd---n my eyes! Mr M-----, if I stir another step this night!' After a deal of entreaty he was persuaded to move on, assisted by two non-commissioned officers, while the lieutenant carried his musket. In this order we carried on, until we reached the public house, where we found the two sick men who were left behind, lying drunk on the floor, and whom the party was obliged to assist in getting to the barracks, where we arrived about ten o'clock at night. About an hour after the Major called at the guard-house, when we were all relieved from confinement, with the exception of the three that had got so very drunk on the road, whom he said he would see in the morning.

Next day proved the Major a man of his word. On parade as usual, he turned out several for the old crime, whom he ordered, with the three already confined, to have their knapsacks filled with brick, and to be marched for seven days to Maguire's Bridge, a distance of fourteen Irish miles, (that is to and from) and to be lodged in the guard-room at night. One of the fellows, however, got refractory, and sitting down on a stone at the guard-house, told the Major he would be d----d if he would carry bricks in his knapsack, for him, or any other man in the service. 'And I will be d----d', said the Major, 'but you shall carry the bricks, or anything else I please to order you.' 'But,' retorted Dick, 'I will be doubly d----d if I do'. 'Well you will do worse!' said the Major, upon which he ordered the adjutant to summon a drumhead court martial, before which poor Dick was arraigned, for insolence to the Commanding Officer, and disobedience of orders. He was awarded one

3 Probably either Lieutenant Hans Stevenson Marsh or Lieutenant Charles Munro, both of whom had seen extensive service in the Peninsula.

hundred and fifty lashes, to be carried into execution at such time and place as the Commanding Officer might think fit. In the meantime the triangles were brought out, and Dick being ordered to strip, was immediately tied up. He was then asked by the Major, if he would go now? 'I will see you first d----d sir!' said Dick; at which the drummers were ordered to go on with then punishment. When he had received the first twenty-five, he was again asked if he would go, to which he indignantly replied 'No!' He received his full sentence.

In Enniskillen the regiment remained five months, which time, though it was winter, passed on very pleasantly. Provisions were cheap, and turf was served in abundance for fuel, enabling us to keep on good fires, at which we passed the long winter evenings in an agreeable and comfortable manner, very different from what we had been accustomed to for some years past. We at last got the route for Belfast, when we left Enniskillen during a keen frost. At Maguire's Bridge, which was our first stage, I was with three more quartered in a public house. In the room where we slept, we found hid in some straw, a cask of whisky, which was a temptation we were not inclined to withstand. Accordingly, the morning found us on the march, with our canteens and kettles full of the liquor, with which we treated our comrades and acquaintances, who in a short time were as deeply intoxicated as ourselves. For my part I was so much so, that I threw away my arms, and refused to march; indeed, in a short time I was quite unable, and got so stupid that I could not stand on my feet. I was therefore left lying insensible on the road. On recovering my senses I found myself sitting in a small cabin, eating, or rather worrying, a pot-full of potatoes which stood on the hearth before me. Three of my comrades lay asleep on the floor, while a non-commissioned officer, who had been left to take charge of us, sat by the fire. In a short time the snorers were roused, and we set forward; but we had many a sore and clumsy fall before reaching Cloher, out quarters for the night, where we were ordered on extra guard, by way of expiation of our sins.

On reaching Belfast we were put into barracks, and in a short time our company was sent on detachment to Carrickfergus, where I remained four months. The regiment was then ordered to Dublin, in which city I was but three weeks when I received my discharge, my time of service being expired.[4] Same day I engaged for my passage in a vessel bound for Irvine, but being detained in port by contrary winds, after three days' delay, I left Dublin for Donaghadee, with only four and six-pence in my pocket, having previously purchased clothes with what money I had. Arriving at Donaghadee my funds were reduced to a three-ten penny-piece, which I paid for my passage to Port-Patrick, where, after all my toils and dangers, I landed in my own dear country, seventy-two miles from home without a halfpenny. At Girvan I was under the necessity of selling a pair of stockings to procure a supper, and next day reached home with a palpitating heart.

4 William's seven years were up. This was on 7 April 1816.

Thus have I noted down the most prominent occurrences of my early life, and fought by battles o'er again. Not that I think them any way peculiar, for I am well aware that numbers of my countrymen, and even many of my townsmen, have felt and suffered more in the service of their country, and gone through a greater variety of surprising adventures than has been here related. Neither is it from vanity, but from pure vexation of spirit that I have gone over my old ground, for I feel grieved, deeply grieved, for my former folly, and inconsiderate thoughtlessness.

My youthful imprudence has launched me into a sea of trouble – an ocean of misery has engulfed me, from which I will never be able to emerge on this side of time. When I received my discharge I fondly hoped that all my hardships were at an end, but for some time prior to that event, a disease, an enervating and an incurable disease had seized me, which has since, and ever will prey upon, and unman me. This malign disorder was but in its infancy when I left the service, and having no idea of what was the matter, I came away without my ailment being known, else I make no doubt but I would have been provided for in my infirmity. I therefore can blame none but myself. It is this that galls and confounds me. After suffering such hardships and fatigues, to live in poverty and pain, and die in misery, perhaps 'un-pitied and unknown', is to my imagination dreadful. But there is no alternative – no hope – 'want and incurable disease, fell pair', approaching old age, and all the misery and woe that can assail human nature, has surrounded me. Yet how often does the following lines of the unfortunate Otway intrude upon my memory.

> How many men have spent their blood in their dear country's service,
> Yet now pine under want, whilst selfish slaves,
> The e'en would cut their throats whom they now fawn on,
> Like deadly locusts eat the honey up,
> Which these industrious bees so hardly toil'd for.[5]

It is now at this period (1829) thirteen long years since I left the service, which time has been filled up with a series of losses, crosses, and disappointments. Yet for these eleven years past, I have had great and infinite consolation, which springs from an alliance with a most deserving and amiable woman, who is indeed my better half. But as it has in these times become quite unfashionable to speak well of wives – even to mention them at all, is deemed by some a sort of egotism, (of which crime I already stand convicted), I will therefore refrain from speaking any more of her or myself, but will close my 'Narrative', by wishing, and even hoping, that the four little daughters she has made me father of, may inherit the virtues of their mother.

The End.

5 Quote from Thomas Otway's tragedy, *The Orphan; or The Unhappy Marriage*, from 1680.

For the following lines I am indebted to a friend. They so vividly portray my present situation and circumstances that I have been induced to insert here without apology, and in the hope that they will prove acceptable to the reader. – AUTHOR.

Oh! Why should the soldier, return from afar,
Escape from the dangers of famine and War,
See the Demon of Poverty frowning appear,
And moisten his morsel with many a tear?

Survey the poor shed where his little ones lie,
And mark for a moment that heart-rending sigh –
Tis the Mothers! Who mourns o'er her infants so dear,
And moistens their morsel with many a tear,

But who can the father's sensations define?
He feels all their sorrows, yet scorns to repine!
But when the bright beams of the day disappear,
His pillow is moistened with many a tear!

Oh! Do not, my country, thus leave him forlorn,
Who for thee, in all climates, has misery borne;
Place hope in the van, and disappear in the rear,
And near let his morsel be moist with a tear.

Select Bibliography

War Office. *Army Lists 1791 to 1818*. London: various years.

Brown, Steve. *Wellington's Redjackets – the 45th (Nottinghamshire) Regiment on Campaign in South America and the Peninsula, 1805-1814* (Barnsley: Frontline Books, 2015).

Dalbiac, Colonel P.H. *History of the 45th First Nottinghamshire Regiment* (London: Swann Sonnenschein And Co., 1902).

MacQueen, James. *General Statistics of the British Empire* (London: B. Fellowes, 1836).

MacQueen, James. *The campaigns of 1812, 1813, and 1814: also the Causes and Consequences of the French Revolution, to which is added the French Confiscations, Contributions, Requisitions, &c., from 1793, til 1814* (Glasgow: W. Summerville, A. Fullarton, J. Blackie, 1815).

Napier, William Francis Patrick. *History of the War in The Peninsular and in the South of France from The Year 1807 to the Year 1814*. 6 volumes. (London: J. Murray, 1828-1840).

Philippart, John. *The Royal Military Calendar, or Army Service and Commission Book* (London: A.J. Valpy, 1820).

Wylly, H.C. *History of the 1st and 2nd Battalions the Sherwood Foresters (Nottinghamshire and Derbyshire Regiment)* (Two volumes. London: Privately Published for the Regiment, 1929).

National Archives

WO 12/5726 to WO12/5730 – Pay-lists and Muster Rolls for 1/45th Foot 1807 to 1814

WO 17/157 – Monthly Returns for 45th Foot

WO 25/1275 – Muster-master General's Index of Casualties &c.

WO 25/1-88 – Commission Books

WO 25/744-748 – Field Officer Service Returns 1809

WO 25/749-779 – Half-pay Officer's Records 1829

WO 25/808-821 – Retired Officers Records

WO 25/3896-3909 – Surgeon's Records

WO 42/1-51 – Officer's Wills

WO 65/1-119 – Army Lists
WO 100/1-10 – Medals and Awards
WO 116/1-102 – Chelsea Pensioner Records
WO 117/1-4 – Long Service Pensions
WO 119 – Kilmainham Pensioner Records.

Index

From Reason to Revolution series – Warfare 1721-1815

http://www.helion.co.uk/published-by-helion/reason-to-revolution-1721-1815.html

The 'From Reason to Revolution' series covers the period of military history c. 1721–1815, an era in which fortress-based strategy and linear battles gave way to the nation-in-arms and the beginnings of total war.

This era saw the evolution and growth of light troops of all arms, and of increasingly flexible command systems to cope with the growing armies fielded by nations able to mobilise far greater proportions of their manpower than ever before. Many of these developments were fired by the great political upheavals of the era, with revolutions in America and France bringing about social change which in turn fed back into the military sphere as whole nations readied themselves for war. Only in the closing years of the period, as the reactionary powers began to regain the upper hand, did a military synthesis of the best of the old and the new become possible.

The series will examine the military and naval history of the period in a greater degree of detail than has hitherto been attempted, and has a very wide brief, with the intention of covering all aspects from the battles, campaigns, logistics, and tactics, to the personalities, armies, uniforms, and equipment.

Submissions

The publishers would be pleased to receive submissions for this series. Please contact series editor Andrew Bamford via email (andrewbamford18@gmail.com), or in writing to Helion & Company Limited, 26 Willow Road, Solihull, West Midlands, B91 1UE.

Titles

No.1 *Lobositz to Leuthen. Horace St Paul and the Campaigns of the Austrian Army in the Seven Years War 1756-57* Translated with additional materials by Neil Cogswell (IBN 978-1-911096-67-2)

No 2 *Glories to Useless Heroism. The Seven Years War in North America from the French journals of Comte Maurés de Malartic, 1755-1760* William Raffle (ISBN 978-1-1911512-19-6) (paperback)

No 3 *Reminiscences 1808-1815 Under Wellington. The Peninsular and Waterloo Memoirs of William Hay* William Hay, with notes and commentary by Andrew Bamford (ISBN 978-1-1911512-32-5)

No 4 *Far Distant Ships. The Royal Navy and the Blockade of Brest 1793-1815* Quintin Barry (ISBN 978-1-1911512-14-1)

No 5 *Godoy's Army. Spanish Regiments and Uniforms from the Estado Militar of 1800* Charles Esdaile and Alan Perry (ISBN 978-1-911512-65-3) (paperback)

No 6 *On Gladsmuir Shall the Battle Be! The Battle of Prestonpans 1745* Arran Johnston (ISBN 978-1-911512-83-7)

No 7 *The French Army of the Orient 1798-1801. Napoleon's Beloved 'Egyptians'* Yves Martin (ISBN 978-1-911512-71-4)*

No 8 *The Autobiography, or Narrative of a Soldier. The Peninsular War Memoirs of William Brown of the 45th Foot* William Brown, with notes and commentary by Steve Brown (ISBN 978-1-911512-94-3)

Books within this series are published in two major formats. 'Falconets' are paperbacks, page size 248mm × 180 mm, with high visual content including colour plates; 'Culverins' are hardback monographs, page size 234mm × 156mm. Books marked * in the list above are Falconets, all others are Culverins unless otherwise noted.